Bicycling Tennessee

Bicycling Tennessee

Road Adventures from the Mississippi Delta to the Great Smoky Mountains

Owen Proctor

Writers Club Press
San Jose New York Lincoln Shanghai

Bicycling Tennessee
Road Adventures from the Mississippi Delta to the Great Smoky Mountains

Writers Club Press
an imprint of iUniverse, Inc.

For information address:
iUniverse, Inc.
5220 S. 16th St., Suite 200
Lincoln, NE 68512
www.iuniverse.com

Edited by Susan Schulman
Front cover photo by Bob Peden
Back cover photo by Susan Schulman
Interior photos by Owen Proctor unless otherwise indicated
Maps by Associates By Creative Design, LLC

Always be aware of your surroundings, know your limitations and practice safe cycling. Neither the author nor publisher can be responsible for any mishaps you experience.

ISBN: 0-595-21811-3

To my wife, Susan Schulman, for her love and support.

ACKNOWLEDGEMENTS

The author could not have written this book without the advice, support and assistance of his family, friends and fellow cyclists. He would like to thank his parents, Gary and Hope, who first introduced him to the joys of being outdoors, as well as other family members and friends with whom he lost time with while riding and writing.

A very special thanks goes to Tracey Jacoby, Susan Schulman and Vickie Spickard for their extensive and tireless assistance in researching the routes. Thanks to Susan Schulman for editing the book, and thanks to Becky Babineaux and Jenny Engler for their assistance with the maps. The author also appreciates the contributions of Jon Anderson, Dee Blake, Laverne Daley, Ken Garland, Bill Jacobs, Dr. Kent Jones, Susan Jones, Doreen Kunz, the Memphis Hightailers Bicycle Club and Dan Smithhisler.

INTRODUCTION

Rich in beauty and history, Tennessee offers a wide range of discovery for bicyclists. The state covers a variety of terrains that includes the plains of West Tennessee, the rolling hills of Middle Tennessee and the mountains of East Tennessee. You'll discover natural beauty along the Mississippi River, the Natchez Trace and the Great Smoky Mountains. You'll follow the paths once traveled by Native Americans, frontiersmen and Civil War heroes.

Once a part of the Southwest Territory, Tennessee became the 16th state in the Union on June 1, 1796. Gov. John Sevier, U.S. Senators William Blount and William Cocke, and U.S. Representative Andrew Jackson were its first leaders. The Chickasaw Treaty of 1818 expanded Tennessee's boundary to the Mississippi River. Nashville became its permanent capital in 1826. Fertile land and natural resources led to fast settlements.

Tennessee contributed tremendously to the nation's growth during the 19th century. Legions of its citizens fought in the War of 1812, the Texas Revolution, the Seminole Wars and the Mexican War, coining the nickname, "The Volunteer State." Andrew Jackson, Davy Crockett, Sam Houston and William Lauderdale became national heroes. Jackson and James Polk served terms as U.S. presidents during the first half of the 1800s.

During the Civil War, Tennessee fought for the Confederacy, more to preserve slavery than secede from the Union. Although the anti-slavery movement had roots in East Tennessee, the economic benefits of slave labor in West and Middle Tennessee prevailed. Tennessee was the last state to withdraw from the Union. Its citizens joined both sides of the war, truly pitting brother against brother. As a border state, Tennessee was a major strategic and bloody battleground during the war. At the war's end, President Lincoln's successor, Tennessean Andrew Johnson, oversaw the beginning of Reconstruction.

In the 20th century, Tennesseans continued to make an impact on American society. In the first part of the century, W.C. Handy became the father of the blues in Memphis. Radio station WSM began broadcasting a program from Nashville in 1925 that would evolve into the Grand Ole Opry. The Grand Ole Opry and the Carter family's recordings in Bristol established Tennessee's country music foundation, now a billion-dollar state industry. In 1952, Sam Phillips' creation of Sun Records in Memphis changed the face of popular music forever, particularly with his discovery of Elvis Presley in 1954.

You'll learn more about Tennessee history as you ride these routes during the new millenium. These tours total close to 2,000 miles, covering 47 of Tennessee's 95 counties.

RIDE PREPARATION

This book is written for experienced cyclists. If you are new to the sport, I'd recommend you first learn the basics of cycling. Numerous books offer cycling information on nutrition, training, equipment and riding techniques. I recommend *Greg LeMond's Complete Book of Bicycling*, a well-rounded introduction for beginners as well as a continual resource for seasoned cyclists. Your local bike shop can also assist you. After learning the basics, start cycling slow, short rides with a buddy, building up mileage and frequency as you physically progress. Always eat before you are hungry, and drink before you are thirsty. To avoid traffic, ride early in the morning on weekends.

Wear bright clothing. Shorts and tops made specifically for cycling reduce chafing and wind resistance. During cooler seasons, always dress in layers. Generally, Tennessee weather is good for year-round cycling. The lowest average maximum temperature is 48.4 degrees Fahrenheit in January. The highest average maximum temperature is 89.0 in July. There are usually a few weeks of freezing temperatures in the winter and a few weeks of blistering heat in the summer. On the other hand, sometimes fall-like weather extends into early December and spring-like weather arrives in late February. The climate also depends whether you are cycling in a mountainous or plains region.

Bicycles, of course, are legal street vehicles in Tennessee. The following are state laws pertaining to bicycles ridden on state-maintained roads. Efforts to make laws consistent for all public roads in Tennessee have failed, and local laws may vary. According to state law, you must obey all traffic laws. Under normal conditions, you must ride as close as practical to the right-hand curb or edge of the road except when passing another vehicle, preparing to make a left turn, avoiding an object or hazard, and riding in a lane too narrow for a bike and another vehicle. You can ride two abreast as long as it doesn't impede normal traffic movement.

It is against the law to cling to other vehicles, carry more people for whom your bike was designed, and carry any package or article that prevents you from keeping both hands on the handlebar.

When riding at night, your bike must have a white light visible from at least 500 feet to the front, and a red reflector or light visible from 50 to 300 feet to the rear. You must have a brake that stops your bike within 25 feet from 10 miles per hour on a dry, level, clean pavement.

Last, but not least, children under 16 years old must wear a protective bicycle helmet, fastened securely. It is against the law for a parent or guardian to permit a child under 16 to ride a bike without a helmet. I recommend all cyclists, regardless of age, wear a helmet.

In another state law pertinent for cyclists, dogs are not allowed off their owners' properties without a leash. This law is vastly ignored in rural areas, but owners are responsible if their dog injures a person or damages property. Usually, the dog is just protecting his owner's property. A verbal threat or a squirt from your water bottle usually keeps a dog at bay. The primary danger is a dog forcing you to wreck or fall off your bike. If you fall off your bike and the dog attacks, use your bike as a shield and tire pump as a weapon.

That's my summary on cycling basics. Once again, numerous books on the market provide more details on the basics as well as tour planning.

TOUR SELECTION

My criteria for selecting these rides included scenery, low-volume traffic, paved roads, points of interest, conveniences and accommodations. Some of the trips are official state bicycle routes, developed and maintained by governmental agencies. The Tennessee Department of Transportation introduced its Cycling Tennessee's Highways program in 1995. These routes feature official "Bike Route" and "Share the Road" signs, helping you follow the tour and alerting motorists of cyclists on the road. Other route selections are popular rides for local bicycle clubs.

In this book, each chapter/route begins with a map, history of the area, and a ranking and description of the terrain. Cue sheets follow with mile markers, landmarks and points of interest. Each chapter/route ends with a listing of places to stay and area bike shops. The index includes state tourism and bicycling contacts, as well as information on local bicycle clubs.

Select a tour that meets your terrain, mileage and points of interest specifications. My general terrain descriptions are easy for flatland, moderate for rolling hills and difficult for very hilly or mountainous. If the route is part of an organized tour or a club's favorite ride, you may want to contact the organizers or club about joining them for the ride. Organized rides typically offer support and several mileage options. Most of the tours in this book are loop rides; however, some of the tours (official state routes) are not and extend across an entire region. If you do not want to follow these tours exactly as they are written here, you can ride out and back on any section of the routes. Also, using county maps provided by the Tennessee Department of Transportation, you can create your own variation of the routes. I'd recommend carrying county maps anyway, in case you get lost or need to find routes to accommodations or a bike shop.

This book includes cozy or quaint lodging accommodations unique to the area, except where only chain hotels are available. I also include camping facilities, where available. Bicycle shops listed are the ones closest to the route, but some of these routes are in the middle of nowhere. If that is the case, the bicycle shops could be far away, even by car. Always carry spare tubes and a few repair tools.

DISCLAIMER

Keep in mind, when following these routes, things change. Street names change, people knock down signs, business names change, businesses close or move, bridges go out, road construction begins and traffic is detoured. Everything in this book was accurate at the time it was written, but things along the routes will eventually change.

Different levels of traffic intimidate different cyclists. While I considered low-volume traffic in route selection, certain roads may still be busy at certain times of the day. Sometimes, traveling busy roads is necessary to link less-busy roads on the tour. Also, keep in mind that the state bike route program is called Cycling Tennessee's *Highways*. All roads are not country back roads. I alert you to possible traffic problems when I state, "watch for traffic," in the directions, but traffic problems in other areas may develop.

This book provides a guide for cycling in Tennessee, but always be aware of your surroundings, know your limitations and practice safe cycling. Neither the author nor publisher can be responsible for any mishaps you experience. Be safe and enjoy the rides.

BICYCLING TENNESSEE
Tour Overview

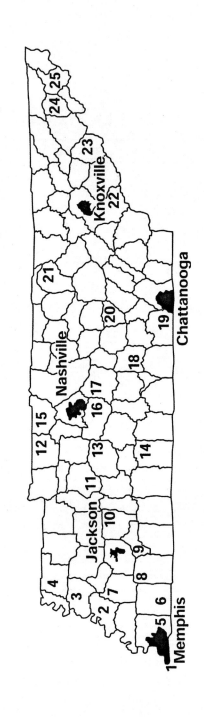

CONTENTS

East Tennessee

BICYCLING TENNESSEE
Tour 1: Memphis-Tunica

N

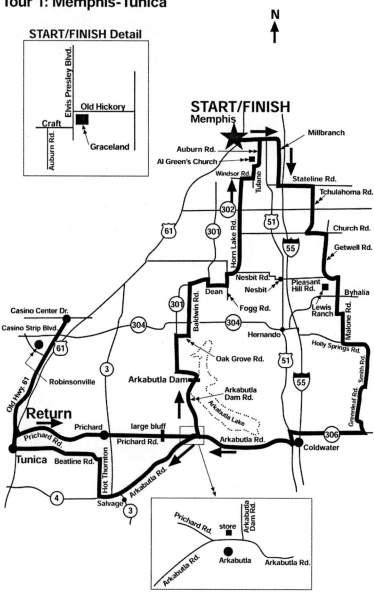

START/FINISH Detail

Elvis Presley Blvd.

Old Hickory

Craft

Auburn Rd.

Graceland

START/FINISH
Memphis

Millbranch

Auburn Rd.

Al Green's Church

Windsor Rd.

Tulane

Stateline Rd.

Tchulahoma Rd.

302

61

301

Horn Lake Rd.

51

55

Church Rd.

Getwell Rd.

Nesbit Rd.

Nesbit

Pleasant
Hill Rd.

Byhalia

Casino Center Dr.

Casino Strip Blvd.

61

301

Dean

Baldwin Rd.

304

304

Fogg Rd.

Lewis
Ranch

Malone Rd.

Old Hwy. 61

Robinsonville

3

Hernando

Holly Springs Rd.

Oak Grove Rd.

51

Greenleaf Rd.

Smith Rd.

Return

Arkabutla Dam

Arkabutla
Dam Rd.

55

Prichard

Prichard Rd.

large bluff

Arkabutla Lake

Tunica

Beatline Rd.

Prichard Rd.

Arkabutla Rd.

Coldwater

306

Hot Thornton

Arkabutla Rd.

4

Salvage

3

Prichard Rd.

store

Arkabutla
Dam Rd.

Arkabutla Rd.

Arkabutla

Arkabutla Rd.

1. MEMPHIS—TUNICA: A TWO-DAY TOUR

Easy to moderate terrain; 145.0 miles

Slavery no longer ruled the Mississippi Delta in the early part of the 20th Century, but segregation was alive and well. African-Americans didn't have many choices in life. They worked the cotton and soybean fields as sharecroppers. Their social life was built around the church. But the spirituals in the fields and gospel in the churches spurred another musical style and emotional outlet—the blues.

"As a little kid, blues meant hope, excitement, pure emotion," B.B. King, a native of Indianola, Miss., writes in his autobiography, *Blues All Around Me*. Just as city folks went to the movies to escape hard times during the Depression, rural people in the Mississippi Delta turned to music for healing. The early bluesmen made their instruments by hand, performing on street corners, juke joints or anywhere anyone would listen. Eventually, the opportunities were calling from the northern urban centers, and the migration began. Memphis was the first stop.

Blues legends such as B.B. King, Howlin' Wolf, Sonny Boy Williamson, John Lee Hooker and Elmore James landed on Beale Street in the middle of a thriving African-American community. Some laid down their guitars, found non-musical work and raised families in Memphis. Others moved further north, up U.S. Highway 61 toward Chicago. A few became international superstars.

The Multiple Sclerosis Society's Mid-South Chapter developed this route in 1996 for the MS 150 Rock 'n' Roll Tour. The ride starts at Graceland, the home of Elvis Presley, rolls through the hills of northern

3

Mississippi, and pours into the Mississippi Delta. Once bleak and deso-
late, the delta is now a thriving community, boosted by Mississippi's gambling industry. To get to Graceland, take Interstate 55 south from
downtown Memphis to the Elvis Presley Boulevard (or U.S. Highway 51)
exit. Head south on Elvis Presley Boulevard. Graceland is a couple of miles
on your left.

Day 1
**Easy to moderate terrain, once you ride the rolling hills through north-
ern Mississippi, the last 22 miles cover the Mississippi Delta flatlands;
81.8 miles**

Miles

0.0   **Begin ride at the pavilion across from Graceland. Turn left out of
the pavilion parking lot and head north on Elvis Presley
Boulevard. Watch for traffic.**

When Elvis Presley was a child growing up in Tupelo, Miss., he
asked his parents for a bicycle. They gave him a guitar. Imagine
who your bicycling partner may have been if it wasn't for that little
twist of fate.

According to *The Rolling Stone Illustrated History of Rock & Roll*,
Presley joined the working class after high school, driving a truck
for a living, playing music on the side. Shortly, after recording the
Ink Spots' "My Happiness" and "That's When Your Heartaches
Begin" at Sun Studio, that all changed. "You had to be blind not to
know the guy had something," owner Sam Phillips says in the documentary "Elvis Presley's Graceland." "Something nobody could
describe, but he had it. And he had it in abundance."

The regional success with the Sun recordings and rigorous tour-
ing throughout the South landed Presley a lucrative contract with
RCA. With the help of new manager Col. Tom Parker, "Heartbreak
Hotel" became Presley's first gold record. In 1957, he bought the

14-acre Graceland estate on U.S. Highway 51 for $100,000—a far cry from his family's 30- by 15-foot shack in Tupelo.

Graceland is the second most visited residence in the United States, only behind the White House in annual attendance. Elvis Presley Enterprises opened it to the public in 1982, five years after the singer's death.

Graceland's decorum varies as much as Presley's music. Each room has a distinct personality. The living room and dining room are very traditional and elegant. Some of the other rooms show a more creative side of the legend. The poolroom is covered in 700 yards of fabric, including the ceiling and walls. The television room in the basement has appropriately three televisions lined in row, an idea inspired by President Lyndon B. Johnson.

Then, there is the legendary 1965 addition of the Jungle Room. Presley went to a local furniture store and picked all the room's furnishings within 30 minutes. He added an artificial waterfall. Some people describe the room as gaudy. Presley said it reminded him of Hawaii. He recorded *From Elvis Presley Boulevard Memphis, Tennessee* and his last album, *Moody Blue*, in this room.

Other sites on the Graceland tour include the racquetball court, horse stables, trophy room and hall of gold, and the gravesites of Presley, his father, mother and grandmother. At this writing, a wedding chapel was planned. The bicycle ride actually begins next to the Lisa Marie, the luxurious airplane that Presley bought for $250,000 in 1975.

0.4   **Turn right onto Old Hickory into Presley's old neighborhood.**
1.7   **Turn right onto Millbranch at the stop sign. Watch for traffic.**
5.3   **Turn left onto Stateline Road at the traffic light. Watch for traffic.**
8.4   **Turn right onto Tchulahoma Road.**
       Soon, you will enter DeSoto County, Miss., named for Hernando DeSoto. The Spanish explorer's expedition through this area in 1541 led to his discovery of the Mississippi River.

Carey Whitehead was the first developer in Southaven in 1959. The community on the Tennessee-Mississippi border grew into a major suburb of Memphis and was incorporated in 1980.

Southaven's most famous resident was best-selling author John Grisham. He moved to Southaven with his family in 1967, graduated from Southaven High School in 1973 and opened a law firm here in 1981. Grisham was elected to the Mississippi state legislature in 1983. He published his first book, *A Time to Kill*, in 1989.

10.4 You'll see an Exxon Tigermart on your left. Cross Goodman Road (also called Highway 302) at the traffic light. Watch for traffic.

12.7 Turn left onto Church Road.

14.3 You'll see Wildwood Baptist Church on the left. Turn right onto Getwell Road at the traffic light.

17.8 Turn left onto Pleasant Hill Road.

18.9 Turn right onto Malone Road.

19.2 You'll see Jerry Lee Lewis' Ranch on your right.

Lewis grew up in Ferriday, La., not far from Natchez, Miss., playing boogie-woogie piano since he was 15 years old. According to *The Rolling Stone Illustrated History of Rock & Roll*, shortly after Presley's success at Sun Records, Lewis packed his bags and headed for Memphis, cornering Sam Phillip's assistant, Jack Clement, for an audition.

With "Whole Lot of Shakin' Going On," he burst onto the new rock and roll scene in 1957. "Great Balls of Fire," "Breathless" and "High School Confidential" followed. Demanding top billing on the package tours, he didn't disappoint with his fiery performances. Lewis has two famous cousins, evangelist Jimmy Swaggert and country pianoman Mickey Gilley, but when he married his third cousin, Myra Lewis, in 1958, his career came to a screeching halt. His rebellious spirit made and broke him.

Nevertheless, Lewis continued to record occasionally and toured prolifically, performing in any honky tonk that would have him. His persistence paid off when he signed a contract with Mercury/Smash in 1967. The deal revitalized his career with a string of country hits, including "What's Made Milwaukee Famous."

Now in his 60s, Lewis still records and performs. When he isn't touring, he enjoys living at this ranch in Nesbit, Miss., with his wife, Kerrie, their two sons and 25 stray dogs (don't worry, they're kept behind a long white wall). The 33-acre ranch includes a piano-shaped swimming pool and small lake, where the Killer often jet skis. Occasionally, Lewis offers tours of his home to the public.

Shortly after the Lewis ranch, you'll find a Citgo station on the left at the intersection of Byhalia Road.

Cyclists ride by the entrance to Jerry Lee Lewis' ranch in Nesbit, Miss. Photo by Tina Lovett.

25.6 Turn left onto Holly Springs.
27.9 You'll see Smart's Grocery on left. Turn right onto Smith Road.
30.7 Turn right onto Greenleaf at the T-intersection.
35.7 Turn right onto Highway 306. Watch for traffic.

You are now entering the small community of Coldwater, Miss., named after the nearby Coldwater River. Located in the northwestern corner of Tate County, the town was once literally rolled down the hills on logs to make way for the construction of nearby Arkabutla Lake.

42.0 Turn left onto U.S. Highway 51. Watch for traffic.

42.2 Veer right onto the access road.

42.6 Turn right onto Scenic Highway 304.

50.7 Continue straight ahead on Arkabutla Road.

50.9 You'll see a convenience store on the right.

59.1 Continue straight ahead. You are about to ride down a bluff with a sharp curve.

59.9 Soon after crossing the railroad tracks, turn right onto Highway 3. Watch for traffic.

60.2 Turn left onto Highway 4. Watch for traffic

61.3 Turn right onto Hot Thornton Road.

This begins a long stretch through the Mississippi Delta. Although it is as flat as you can get, there are also no trees to protect you against the elements. I once rode this on a very windy day. I might as well have been on a stationery bike. You have to constantly pedal.

64.3 Turn left onto Beat Line Road.

If you ride this route in the heat of the summertime, you may be hot and beat after riding Hot Thornton and Beat Line roads.

72.1 Cross U.S. Highway 61. Watch for traffic.

72.1 Turn right onto Edwards at the city park.

You are now riding through downtown Tunica, Miss., an old delta town near the Mississippi River. This town has changed tremendously since the gambling industry opened in the county.

An interesting chain of events happened here in 1908. On March 30, two prominent citizens and old friends, J.T. Lowe and P.M. Houston got into argument. The reason for the argument was unclear, but it resulted in Lowe shooting Houston to death. Lowe was free on bond, awaiting trial, when Houston's daughter, Una Mai Weinstein, shot Lowe. Lowe survived and left town. Neither party was prosecuted, and their descendents continue to be friends to this day.

72.5 Edwards turns into Old Hwy 61 Highway.

81.8 End ride at the intersection with Casino Strip Resort Boulevard. Watch for traffic.

Once called the poorest county in the country, Tunica County got a much-needed boost when Mississippi legalized riverboat casino gambling in 1990. The first casino, Splash, was just that.

Today, there are 10 casinos, which generate more than $1 billion in revenue each year. Tunica stands only behind Las Vegas and Atlantic City in America's gambling destinations. In addition to the gambling halls, every casino has luxurious accommodations and nightly entertainment. Several outlet shops are also popping up in the area. Tunica has become a serious competitor for tourism dollars in the Mid-South.

Turn left on Casino Strip Resort Boulevard to go to Fitzgeralds Casino & Hotel, Harrah's Tunica Casino & Hotel, Hollywood Casino & Hotel, Isle of Capri Casino or Sam's Town Hotel & Gambling Hall. Go straight ahead about two miles and turn left at the Exxon station at Casino Center Drive to go to Bally's Saloon & Gambling Hall Hotel, Gold Strike Casino Resort, Horseshoe Casino & Hotel and Sheraton Casino Tunica. Or continue straight and turn left on Grand Casino Parkway to go to Grand Casino Tunica.

Day 2

Easy to moderate terrain, you'll have a nice 20-mile flat workout before climbing the bluff and hitting the rolling hills of northern Mississippi; 63.2 miles

Miles

0.0 Begin ride at the intersection of Old 61 Highway and Casino Strip Resort Boulevard. Head south on Old 61 Highway.

If you want to taste a little bit of local fare without the Vegas influence, drop by the Blue & White Restaurant, featuring home-cooked specialties. It originally opened on Old Highway 61 in 1934, but moved in 1937 to its current location, 1355 Highway 61 N.

3.3 **You'll see St. Peter's Church. Turn left onto Prichard Road at stop sign.**

9.9 **Cross U.S. Highway 61. Watch for traffic.**

Ready for another long stretch of Delta flatlands? This part of the route climaxes with a large bluff to climb, followed by rolling hills.

24.3 **Turn left onto Arkabutla Road.**

24.5 **You'll see a convenience store on the left.**

24.8 **Turn left onto Arkabutla Dam Road.**

You'll soon be rolling along Arkabutla Dam. Built in the early 1940s, the dam is 11,500 feet long and rises up to 67 feet high. The U.S. Corps of Engineers' Mississippi Valley Division operates the dam, lake and accompanying 37,700 acres of land. The area offers hunting, fishing, sailing and water skiing. There are also three public beaches.

Arkabutla Dam is on the Coldwater River and one of four flood control dams in the Yazoo River Basin. The other dams are located in Enid on the Yocona River, Sardis on the Little Tallahatchie River and Grenada on the Yalobusha River.

30.1 **Turn left onto Scenic Highway 304. Watch for mountain bikes.**

Arkabutla Lake offers great mountain bike trails. Two paths cross this road.

32.0 **Turn right onto Scenic Highway 304.**

35.0 **Turn right onto Oak Grove.**

36.0 **Turn left onto Baldwin.**

41.1 **Turn right onto Highway 301.**

42.7 **Veer right onto Mabry.**

43.3 **Turn left onto Dean.**

44.8 Turn left onto Fogg. There is no street sign. Up ahead, you'll see Pounders Grocery on the left.

45.9 Turn right onto Nesbit Road.

46.6 Turn left onto Horn Lake Road.

54.5 Turn right onto Windsor Drive at the T-intersection.

59.8 Turn left onto Tulane Road at the stop sign.

60.1 Turn right onto Wilson Road.

60.4 Turn left onto Amy Road.

60.4 Make an immediate right onto Whitehaven Lane, crossing the railroad tracks.

60.6 Turn left onto Auburn Road.

61.2 Cross Hale Road.

If you turn left on Hale Road, you'll soon see Al Green's Full Gospel Tabernacle Church. When not touring, the Rock and Roll Hall of Famer, having been successful in both the soul and gospel fields, can be found Sundays at the pulpit here. He lives on a small farm near Shelby Forest, north of Memphis.

According to his web site, Green was raised in a large sharecropping family just south of Forrest City, Ark. His family attended two churches in the Dansby community, Taylor Chapel and the Church of the Living God. After moving to nearby Jacknash, the Green Brothers began singing gospel at the Old Jerusalem M.B. Baptist Church. Soon, they toured the gospel circuit in the South and Midwest.

In the late 1950s, the eldest son, Walter, convinced the family to follow him to better opportunities in Grand Rapids, Mich. Al graduated from South High School in 1966, and his musical tastes soon turned secular. He found regional success with the Creations and had a No. 5 rhythm and blues hit with Al Green and the Soulmates. Later, as a struggling solo artist, he met producer Willie Mitchell at a club in Midland, Texas.

Mitchell invited Green to his studio in Memphis. Royal Recording Studios was the home base of Hi Records. Between his first Hi recording, *Green is Blues*, and the 1978 album, *Truth 'n' Time*, Green established himself as a soul legend, cranking out such hits as "I Can't Get Next to You," "Let's Stay Together," "I'm Still in Love with You" and "Love and Happiness." Then, in 1979, he abandoned his soul repertoire. Being "born again" in 1973, becoming an ordained minister and purchasing the Full Gospel Tabernacle in 1976, Green received the calling to only record and perform gospel.

Such a change, while spiritually satisfying, could have been a bad career move, but not for Green. He became as renowned for his gospel recordings as his secular work. In the course of 15 years devoted strictly to gospel, Green won eight Grammy awards, including his first all-gospel album, *The Lord Will Make a Way*, recorded at his own American Music studio. He returned to secular recording in 1994, singing "Funny How Time Slips Away" with Lyle Lovett on *Rhythm Country and Blues*.

62.8   Turn right onto Craft.

63.2   Turn left into the employee parking lot at Graceland and follow the storage areas back to the pavilion, where the tour began.

If the gate is closed, turn left on Elvis Presley Boulevard to go to the main entrance, but watch for traffic. Graceland is open daily from 8 a.m. to 6 p.m. Memorial Day through Labor Day. It is open daily from 9 a.m. to 5 p.m. the remainder of the year, and closed New Years Day, Thanksgiving Day and Christmas Day.

For general information on lodging and attractions, contact the Memphis Convention & Visitors Bureau, 47 Union Ave., Memphis, TN 38103 (901-543-5300), or Tunica Convention & Visitors Bureau, P.O. Box 2739, Tunica, MS 38676 (888-488-6422).

Places to Stay

Bonne Terre Country Inn and Cafe, 4715 Church Road W., Nesbit, MS 38651 (662-781-5100), is a 100-acre estate just 25 minutes south of Memphis. French and English country antiques adorn a Greek Revival style mansion which features 10 lovely guest rooms offering fireplaces, Jacuzzis and balconies with sweeping views of lake and pool. It is not far off day one's route.

Elvis Presley's Heartbreak Hotel, 3677 Elvis Presley Blvd., Memphis, TN 38116 (901-332-1000 or 877-777-0606), opened in 1999. The 128-room hotel features four themed suites offering 1950 and 1960 interior designs. The outdoor swimming pool is heart-shaped. Other amenities include a continental breakfast, exercise room and airport shuttle service. Across the street from the Graceland Mansion, the hotel is literally as close to Elvis as you can get.

Graceland KOA Campground (camping), 3691 Elvis Presley Blvd., Memphis, TN 38116 (901-396-7125 or 800-562-9386), features 72 grassy full hook-up sites, four rustic cabins, and large tenting area and tent sites located across the street from Graceland. Services include a laundromat, showers, pool and store on the grounds.

Hollywood Bed & Breakfast, Perry-Cox Road, Tunica, MS 38676 (662-363-4115 or 800-353-5796), also provides a quiet, country atmosphere just minutes from the casinos. Perry-Cox Road is located off Old 61 Highway, along both days' routes.

Hollywood Casino RV Park (camping), 1150 Casino Strip Blvd., Robinsonville, MS 38664 (800-871-0711), puts you within walking distance of the gambling action.

Levee Plantation Guest House, Perry-Cox Road, Tunica, MS 38676 (662-363-1309 or 800-353-5796), built around 1900, offers a quiet, country atmosphere just minutes from the casinos. Perry-Cox Road is located off Old 61 Highway, along both days' routes.

Bicycle Shops
The Peddler Bike Shop, 525 S Highland Street, Memphis, TN 38111 (901-327-4833).

Southland Bicycle Shop, 3187 Winchester Road, Memphis, TN 38118 (901-365-6892).

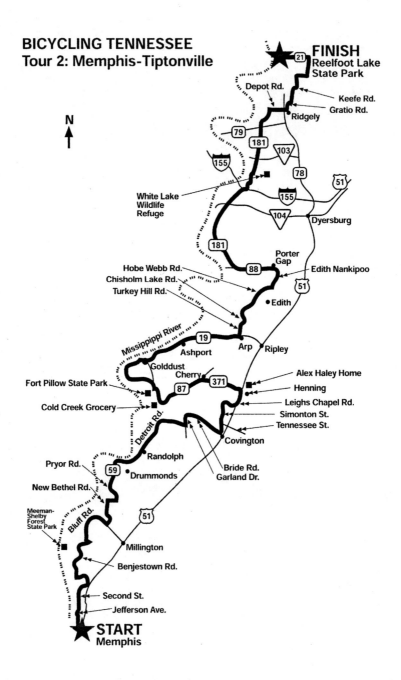

BICYCLING TENNESSEE
Tour 2: Memphis-Tiptonville

N

FINISH
Reelfoot Lake
State Park

21

Depot Rd.
Keefe Rd.
Gratio Rd.
Ridgely

79
181
103
155
78
51

White Lake
Wildlife
Refuge

155
104
Dyersburg

181

Porter
Gap
88
Edith Nankipoo
Hobe Webb Rd.
Chisholm Lake Rd.
Turkey Hill Rd.
51
• Edith

Missippippi River
19
Ashport
Arp
Ripley

Golddust
Cherry
Alex Haley Home
Fort Pillow State Park
87
371
Henning
Cold Creek Grocery
Leighs Chapel Rd.
Simonton St.
Tennessee St.
Covington

Detroit Rd.

Pryor Rd.
Randolph
Bride Rd.
Garland Dr.
59
• Drummonds
New Bethel Rd.
Meeman-
Shelby
Forest
State Park
Bluff Rd.
51
Millington
Benjestown Rd.
Second St.
Jefferson Ave.

START
Memphis

2. MEMPHIS—TIPTONVILLE: A THREE-DAY TOUR

Easy to moderate terrain, 177.1 miles

The Civil War was over. Union soldiers had faced the senselessness of war and the deplorable treatment of Southern prison camps. But their troubles were just beginning when they boarded the Sultana in Vicksburg, Miss., for their journey home.

The steamer traveled up the Mississippi River with more than six times the Sultana's legal capacity of 376 passengers. A boiler leak discovered in Vicksburg was hastily patched up, despite a boilermaker's demand for more thorough repairs. At 2 a.m. on April 27, 1865, about seven miles north of downtown Memphis, three of the steamer's four boilers exploded, blowing out the steamer's center section. The blast sent debris and passengers flying into the sky, and then plunging down into the cold Mississippi waters. Those still onboard suffered burns from the boilers' scalding steam and water, followed by the inferno that engulfed the boat.

Approximately 1,800 of the more than 2,400 passengers, mostly Civil War prisoners of war returning home, died on the 260-foot wooden hull steamboat or in Memphis hospitals. By comparison, on the famed Titanic voyage, 1,522 of its 2,227 passengers perished. News of Civil War treaties, President Lincoln's assassination and the capture of John Wilkes Booth during the same week overshadowed the Sultana disaster, making it but a footnote in American history.

The story is finally detailed in Jerry O. Potter's *The Sultana Tragedy: America's Greatest Maritime Disaster*. It is one of the many fascinating stories about the Mississippi River. Another great source is *Historic Names and Places on the Lower Mississippi River* by Marion Bragg.

The Lower Mississippi Delta Development Commission inaugurated the Mississippi River Trail (MRT) on April 20, 1996. The Tennessee segment was the first of a multi-state Mississippi River bicycle route, which now runs from St. Louis to New Orleans. Tennessee and Arkansas agencies plan to link their segments by converting an old automobile section of the Harahan Bridge over the Mississippi River into a bike lane. The U.S. Department of Transportation recently selected the route as one of 16 National Millennium Trails for hiking or biking.

The Tennessee MRT runs along scenic backroads and features a variety of landscapes from winding, shaded roads in Shelby Forest to flat, bottomland farms in the Mississippi flyways. It is a favorite of the Memphis Hightailers bicycle club, which usually holds its annual Charles Finney and Fall Century rides along the route. Finney founded the club in 1963.

Day 1
Moderate terrain, 64.4 miles.

Miles
0.0   Begin ride at Interstate-40 Welcome Center in downtown Memphis. Ride south out of the parking lot.

Memphis is known as America's Distribution Center. That name also holds true for its musical heritage. The sounds of blues, jazz, gospel and country migrated to this city, forming and spreading a sort of musical melting pot and making Memphis one of the premier cities in forming what is today known as American music.

It all began in the rural settings—the cotton fields and juke joints of the Mid-South—working its way to the crossroads of U.S.

Highway 61 and a placed called Beale Street, which meets the river about a mile south of the Welcome Center.

By the early 1900s, Beale was a street bustling with activities. Places on the east side of Fourth Street were social centers for African Americans. Beale Street to the west of Fourth Street had its own social activity, especially after dark when the street included a dangerous mix of seedy characters, easy money and liquor. But out of the seedy nightlife arose a man named W.C. Handy. His "Memphis Blues," written in 1909, is considered by many to be the first blues song.

Other legends followed in the 1930s, 1940s and 1950s. These included Muddy Waters, John Lee Hooker, Junior Wells, Albert King, Howlin' Wolf, James Cotton and B.B. King, to name a few. For some, Memphis was just a pit stop on the way to Chicago, but Memphis had an influence, and these artists left their footprints here as well. Rock and roll and soul didn't have their beginnings in Memphis by accident. As Muddy Waters is often quoted, "Blues had a baby, and they called it rock and roll."

According to *Elvis: The Sun Years*, by Howard A. DeWitt, Sam Phillips leased 706 Union Ave. in downtown Memphis in October 1949, and opened Memphis Recording Service in January 1950. The one-story building featured a 30-by-18 foot recording studio and a make-shift control room. Eight mikes were set in various positions, but not scientific by any means. The famous Sun sound was produced by one mike bleeding into the next. His initial plan was to sign and record the best local artists and sell the master tapes to independent labels. He recorded the likes of Howlin' Wolf, Little Walter, B.B. King, Rufus Thomas and Ike Turner.

In 1952, Phillips started his own label, Sun Records, getting his first taste of commercial success with bluesman Little Junior Walker. Then a young man named Elvis Presley walked in Memphis Recording Service to cut the Ink Spots' "My Happiness" and "That's When Your Heartaches Begin." Phillips didn't express much interest at that time, but a few demos later, in July 1954, he called Presley in for an audition. The July 5th and 6th session with Scotty Moore on guitar and Bill Black on bass resulted in "That's All Right" and "Blue Moon of Kentucky." Almost immediately, a dub was delivered to Dewey Phillips (no relation), who hosted the popular Red, Hot and Blue radio program. The record was an overnight regional success. Soon, Carl Perkins, Johnny Cash, Jerry Lee Lewis, Roy Orbison and Charlie Rich were knocking on Sun's door.

Other places to visit in downtown Memphis are the Memphis Rock 'n' Soul Museum, National Civil Rights Museum, the historic Peabody Hotel and Memphis Fire Museum. Popular restaurants include the Hard Rock Café, Elvis Presley's Memphis, Huey's and the Rendevous.

0.1   **Turn left onto Jefferson Avenue, across Riverside Drive, over the railroad and up the steep hill.**

0.2   **Confederate Park is on the bluff to your right. Turn left on Front Street. Watch for traffic.**

Confederate Park, overlooking the Mississippi River, features an odd assortment of veteran memorials, artifacts and World War I cannons. A United Confederate Veterans reunion took place on the grounds in 1901. The site stayed dormant until 1908 when Memphis opened the park as "A Memorial to the Old South." A recent attempt to transform it into one of growing number of cancer survivor parks failed.

On the northwest corner of Front Street and Adams Avenue, you'll see the entrance to Mud Island River Park. Once an airstrip, this island has been developed into a tourist attraction on the south end and a residential community on the north end. You enter the park via a monorail, featured in the Tom Cruise movie, "The Firm."

The three attractions include the Mississippi River Museum, the River Walk and the Memphis Belle.

The Memphis Belle was the first B-17 to complete the 25-mission quota over Nazi-occupied territory during World War II. The plane was immortalized in the 1943 documentary, "The Memphis Belle," directed by William Wyler. It was named for Memphian Margaret Polk, wartime sweetheart of pilot Robert Morgan. The citizens of Memphis rescued the Belle from an airplane graveyard. It was moved from place to place for 40 years, before moving to its current location in 1987.

On the northeast corner of Front Street and Poplar, the Cook Convention Center is undergoing expansion. This is the former site of the Ellis Auditorium, built in 1924. Before its demise, the auditorium hosted performances by such artists as Elvis, John Phillip Sousa, Leontyne Price and Bruce Springsteen.

On the northwest corner of Front Street and Jackson Avenue, you'll see The Pyramid. This unique 20,000-seat arena was built by the city in 1991. Although plans for a Hard Rock Café, a College Football Hall of Fame, American Music Award museum and Grammy Hall of Fame all failed, the 32-story building features many high-profile concerts and is the home of the University of Memphis men's basketball team. It also hosts Wonders, a rotating series of exhibits. Past exhibits have included "Ramesses the Great," "Napolean" and "Titanic." Plans are underway for an inclinator, an outside elevator that will take visitors to the 10,000-square foot observation deck at the pinnacle.

0.8   **Turn left onto Auction Avenue. You'll have a steep climb to the top of the A.W. Willis Jr. Bridge over the Wolf River.**

1.3   **Turn right onto Mud Island at the stop sign at the T-intersection.** You are now on the north end of Mud Island. The greenbelt to the left offers another spectacular view of the Mississippi River. The homes and apartments to your right, which began appearing in the late 1980s, represented the first new residential development downtown in more than 100 years. Turn right on Harbor Town Circle and go east a couple of blocks to visit Miss Cordelia's grocery.

3.4   **Turn left onto Second Street.**

5.2   **Second Street becomes Whitney Avenue.**

5.3   **You'll see an Amoco station on your left. Turn left onto Benjestown.**

6.6   **Turn right onto Carrolton.**

7.2   **Turn left onto Old Millington Road. Road is subject to flooding.**

8.3   **Turn left onto North Watkins. Watch for traffic.**

9.9   **Turn left onto Northaven Drive.**

10.3   **Turn left onto Circle at the four-way stop. Road is subject to flooding.**

12.0   **Turn right onto Benjestown at the stop sign at the T-intersection.**

13.2   **You'll see a sign for the Riverbluff Lodge. Turn left onto Ramsey.** You'll soon curve to the right, climb a steep hill and wind through a dense forest. You'll encounter about three steep hills.

16.2   **Turn right onto Island 40.**

16.6   **Turn left onto Benjestown at the intersection.**

19.9   **You'll see Shelby Forest General Store on your left. Turn left onto Bluff Road at the four-way stop.**

21.1   **You'll pass the entrance of Shelby Forest State Park.** Shelby Forest State Park is believed to be the site of Fort Prudhomme. French explorer Rene-Robert Cavelier de la Salle constructed the fort while searching for one of his men, Pierre Prudhomme, who was lost in the woods for nine days. La Salle's journey down the Mississippi River in 1662 confirmed his theory that the river emptied into the Gulf of Mexico.

The park's nature center is open from April 1 to October 1. Exhibits include live snakes, a fish aquarium, stuffed animals and a Native American exhibit. Special programs include bird feeder construction, nature videos and pontoon boat rides. At this writing, the park, in conjunction with the Memphis Zoo, is starting a program to make a caged home for injured birds, and reintroducing them to the wild if possible.

22.1 **Keep right on Riverbluff Road.**

23.0 **Continue straight ahead. You are in for a quite winding, downhill ride.**

25.1 **Continue straight on Herring Hill.**

26.1 **After a nice downhill and uphill straightway, turn right onto Herring Hill.**

26.7 **Turn left onto West Union.**
You'll see the Shake Rag, Tennessee, Store and Bar, at the intersection of Rankin Branch. Yes, they do serve sports drinks.

27.5 **Keep left.**

28.0 **Turn left onto New Bethel.**

28.4 **Turn left onto Bass.**

28.7 **Keep right onto New Bethel.**

29.3 **Keep left.**

30.4 **New Bethel becomes Ray Bluff Road.**
You are entering Tipton County and will be winding through a residential area.

33.1 **Keep left.**

33.7 **Keep left onto Quito Drummonds. You'll see Produce and More store on your left.**

34.3 **Turn left onto Bluff Road for a steep downhill ride.**
If you continue straight on Quito Drummonds, you can bypass the steep uphill and downhill, and visit a store. Take Quito Drummonds until you see Warren Grocery and B & M Grocery (no public restrooms) on your left. Turn left onto Richardson's Landing.

36.1 **Turn right onto Pryor for a steep uphill ride.**

38.9 **Turn left onto Richardson's Landing. You'll see a tan brick church on your left.**

After passing St. Paul Road to the right, there is another steep downhill ride.

41.2   Turn right onto State Highway 59 East.

If you turn right onto State Highway 59, the road ends about a half a mile at the Mississippi River. One of the deepest points of the river, this treacherous bend is under controversy because of the erosion of the Tennessee banks that threatens bluff homes and a nearby U.S. Corps of Engineers facility.

Touring bikers overlook the Mississippi River's Devil's Racecourse, literally at the end of State Highway 59.

44.0   Left onto Needham. There is no street sign.

45.1   Pass Ballard Slough Road. Turn left onto Randolph Road.

Turn left on Ballard Slough to visit the town of Randolph.

The small community of Randolph was once a major river town. Established in 1828, it competed successfully with Memphis, becoming the state's biggest western shipping port. Eventually, the town faded from glory due to increased stagecoach stops in Memphis, a military road constructed from Little Rock to

Memphis and the government's refusal to built a harbor at Randolph. Federal soldiers burned the town in 1862.

Three miles south of Randolph lies the Devil's Racecourse, considered to be one of the most dangerous channels in the Mississippi River. The tall Chickasaw Bluffs are to the north of Randolph, on the Tennessee side of the river.

46.1 **Keep left.**

47.7 **You'll see Buntyn's Grocery on the right. Keep left at Jamestown.**
If you turn right on Jamestown, the town of Gilt Edge and the Gilt Edge Café are 1.6 miles to the east. From there, you link back up to the MRT by taking State Highway 59 east and making a left onto Candy Lane, then a right onto Waits Road.

48.1 **Keep right.**

50.2 **Keep left at Detroit.**

51.2 **Cross the bridge.**

56.6 **After a steep uphill ride, you'll see the Garland Fire Department on your right. Turn left onto Garland Drive.**

58.1 **Turn right onto Bride Road.**

64.0 **Turn left onto Simonton Street at the four-way stop.**

64.4 **End ride at the four-way stop at Tennessee Street.**
Turn right on Tennessee Street and travel a half a mile to U.S. Highway 51 North, where you'll find several motels and eateries. Watch for traffic.

You are in the town of Covington, located near the center of Tipton County. The area was part of the Chickasaw nation until the Native Americans and the federal government signed a treaty in 1818, opening the land for settlement. The county, formed in 1823, was named for Captain Jacob Tipton, who was killed fighting Native Americans near Fort Wayne in 1791. Covington became the county seat in 1826.

Area attractions include the South Main Historic District, home of the annual Heritage Festival, David and Patricia Busby's Seldom

Rest Ostrich Farm on Gilt Edge Road, the only surviving Confederate powder magazine in Tennessee, and the Tennessee Gin, where you can watch raw cotton being processed and baled. Tipton County ranks fourth in the state in cotton production. Local events include the annual SummerFest in Covington.

Day 2
Moderate terrain, 52.4 miles.

Miles

0.0 **Begin ride at the intersection of Simonton Street and Tennessee Street. Head north on Tennessee Street.**

3.7 **Turn right onto Leighs Chapel. There is no street sign.**
Former Memphians Jerry and Claire Norman have created a bird sanctuary around their home on Leighs Chapel. For 30 autumns, the Normans have greeted a 90-nest colony of purple martins migrating south to Central and South America. They also provide six feeders for humming birds heading south.

5.3 **Turn left onto U.S. Highway 51 North. Watch for traffic.**
You'll cross the Hatchie River, a 100-mile waterway that stretches through the bottomlands of West Tennessee and into North Mississippi. According to the Nature Conservancy of Tennessee, it is one of the largest unchanneled and undammed rivers in the Lower Mississippi Valley, and one of the world's 75 "last great places" that need protection. The group is exploring ways to protect the diverse biology of the river's entire drainage basin.

7.5 **You'll see the Alex Haley Roadside Park on the right.**

7.9 **Pass State Highway 209 to the right.**
To visit the boyhood home of author Alex Haley, turn right onto State Highway 209. After about one mile, you'll enter the small town of Henning. Turn left on Haley Avenue. Ride three blocks, and you'll see the home on the left. The entrance is in the back.

Haley lived here with his grandfather, Will Palmer, from 1921 to 1929. Stories told on the front porch by his grandmother and aunts inspired Haley's *Roots: The Saga of an American Family*.

After serving in the U.S. Coast Guard and writing for distinguished magazines, Haley wrote the critically acclaimed *Malcolm X* biography, published in 1965. He then began 12 years of research on his family history. *Roots* chronicled the life of his ancestors, beginning with Kunta Kinte, who was brought to America as a slave. *Roots* won the Pulitzer Prize in 1976 and became one of the most watched television miniseries of all time. Haley, along with David Stevens, also wrote the best-selling novel *Queen*, published in 1993.

Haley died of cardiac arrest in Seattle, Wash., on Feb. 10, 1992. He is buried in the front yard of his boyhood home. A tour of the home not only provides a tribute to Haley but also an interesting look at life during the 1920s.

There is a grocery in downtown Henning that you can visit before joining back up with the MRT.

8.2   **Turn left onto Cooper Creek Road.**

11.4   **After a steep uphill and downhill, turn left onto State Highway 371.**

You'll ride through the community Pleasant Hill, then go over some rolling hills in farm country.

15.7   **You'll see the blue Fort Pillow Grocery and Bait Shop on your right. Turn left onto State Highway 87. You'll pass between two prisons—the Cold Creek Correctional Facility and the West Tennessee State Penitentiary.**

Cold Creek was founded as the Fort Pillow Penal Farm in 1938, a medium security farming facility in Lauderdale County. It still operates as a medium security prison that includes a 6,000-acre farming operation. Wheat, soybean, timber and corn are grown, as well as vegetables for the staff and inmates.

The West Tennessee State Penitentiary is a high security facility. It features Tricor plants, which provide state and local government, and non-profit agencies, with products and services produced by inmates. Products and services include office and institutional furniture, signs, paint, uniforms, milk, eggs, printing, data entry, refurbishing and vehicle repair.

22.8 After passing Cold Creek Grocery and Bait Shop on your left, turn right onto Crutcher Lake.

You'll immediately climb a steep hill and wind through a forest.

24.1 Fort Pillow State Park is to your left.

The Confederate army built Fort Pillow in 1861 to defend Memphis. It quickly succumbed to Union forces in 1862. The fort would have been just a footnote in history if not for a visit from Nathan Bedford Forrest, a major general in the Confederacy. Forrest and his men sealed off the fort on April 12, 1864. Historians still debate whether or not Major William Bradford, the Union commander, offered to surrender before Forrest stormed the fort, killing 700 soldiers, many former slaves, and their families.

The *New York Herald* printed the story under the headline, "The Fort Pillow Massacre," bringing outrage in the North. A congressional inquiry followed immediately at Cairo, Ill., but Forrest was never tried for war crimes. Some dismiss the incident as a federal government propaganda campaign. Others view Forrest's actions as a lesson to President Abraham Lincoln not to arm former slaves to fight against their former masters.

After leaving Fort Pillow State Park and crossing the Sullivan Bridge, the route covers the flat delta. The road becomes narrow, bumpy and rough in places. You'll pass near Plum Point Bend, another dangerous point on the river. Captain Henry Shreve successfully demonstrated his snagboat here in 1829, according to Corps of Engineers records.

36.6 **Crutcher Lake becomes State Highway 19. This road is subject to flooding.**

Continuing in the flatlands, on State Highway 19, you'll pass Golddust on the left. Golddust exists on map only. It is named for a sidewheel steamer, ridden by Mark Twain while researching his *Life on the Mississippi*. The Golddust sank after a boiler explosion three months after Twain's ride.

For conveniences, you'll pass both Fullen's Grocery and Pop's Place on your right on State Highway 19. You may need the refreshment before climbing the huge bluff, just before you reach the community of Ashport. The overlook is incredible.

52.4 **You'll see Arp One grocery on the right as you enter the community of Arp. End ride at the intersection of Arp Central.**

If you continue for four miles on State Highway 19, you'll enter the town of Ripley. (Ignore the MRT sign at Luckett-Lightfoot. It is an alternate route.) Turn left on U.S. Highway 51. Watch for traffic. You'll find a Days Inn a half a mile to your left, along with a few eateries.

Ripley is home of the annual Tomato Festival, sponsored by the Lauderdale County Chamber of Commerce. Since the summer of 1984, Ripley has offered entertainment in its city park as a tribute to local tomato farmers. The festival offers food with the red tomato as the main ingredient, as well as Southern favorites, green tomato pie and fried green tomatoes.

Day 3
Moderate terrain, 61.2 miles

Miles

0.0 **Begin ride at the intersection of State Highway 19 and Arp Central. Head north on Arp Central at the cemetery.**

0.1 Turn left immediately on Turkey Hill Road at Mt. Pleasant Methodist Church.

This road is fairly rugged.

2.0 You'll pass Walnut Grove on your left. Continue straight ahead.

3.0 Turn left on Chisholm Lake Road.

4.5 Turn right on Hobe Webb.

You'll have a couple of steep climbs along this road. You'll also get some nice overlooks.

8.8 Turn left on Edith Nankipoo

10.4 Continue straight ahead.

12.0 Turn left on Porter Gap.

The road is a little bumpy and narrow, but it is a quiet ride offering spectacular views of the Mississippi River delta.

13.6 Turn left on State Highway 88 for a fast downhill ride into the delta.

20.7 Keep left onto State Highway 181.

32.1 Cross State Highway 104.

You are now on the Great River Road, which also connects to a bike route developed by the Tennessee Department of Transportation. In addition to the MRT signs, you'll see the Bike Route signs, clearly marking the way.

If you turn left on State Highway 104, you'll enter Dyersburg in about 13 miles. You can read more about the Great River Road and the town of Dyersburg in the chapter on the Dyersburg-Tiptonville route.

35.7 Cross over Interstate 55. You are now entering the White Lake Wildlife Refuge.

40.7 Cross State Route 103, to the right and left.

42.6 Leave Dyer County and enter Lake County. Continue north on State Route 181.

45.2 Riding northbound on State Route 181 (Great River Road), turn left onto State Route 79.

45.4 State Route 79 turns left, but follow the Great River Road north.

48.3 Make a sharp right turn. Robinson Bayou Road is on the left.

49.8 Enter Ridgely city limits. The route changes to Depot Street.

49.9 Cross the railroad tracks.

50.2 At the three-way intersection, Alicia's Apparel and Gifts will be in front of you. Turn right onto South Main Street.

50.25 Make an immediate left turn onto Poplar Street.

50.8 Cross State Route 78, to the left and right. Watch for traffic. Conveniences at this intersection include Shell Hiway Gas and Grocery, Dorothy's Restaurant, Country Sisters Restaurant, an Exxon station and a BP station.

50.9 Leave Ridgely city limits; route becomes Gratio Road. Road is subject to flooding.

51.2 Turn left onto Madie Thompson Road.

52.9 Turn right onto Madie Church.

54.3 You'll see the white Willingham Baptist Church on the left. Turn left turn onto Keefe Road.

57.3 Turn right onto Wynnburg-Keefe Road. Watch for traffic.

58.0 Turn left onto Bluebank Road.

59.2 At the three-way intersection, you'll see Cypress Point Resort in front of you. Turn left onto State Route 21. Watch for traffic.

61.2 Turn right into the Reelfoot Lake Visitor Center. End of Day 3 route.

The Airpark Inn resort is located on State Highway 78, ten miles north of Tiptonville. Other motels and camping areas are located along State Highways 21 and 22.

Reelfoot Lake is a 15,000-acre lake near Tiptonville. A series of earthquakes in 1811 created the lake—a winter home for thousands of ducks and geese, as well as a growing number of American bald eagles. You can read more about Reelfoot Lake in the chapters on the Dyersburg-Tiptonville and Tiptonville-Martin routes.

For general information on lodging and attractions, contact the Memphis Convention & Visitors Bureau, 47 Union Ave., Memphis, TN 38103 (901-543-5300); Covington/Tipton County Chamber of Commerce, P.O. Box 683, Covington, TN 38019 (901-476-9727); Ripley/Lauderdale County Chamber of Commerce, 1103 East Jackson Ave., Ripley, TN (731-635-9541); Dyersburg/Dyer County Chamber of Commerce, P.O. Box 747, 2455 Lake Road, Dyersburg, TN 38025-0747 (731-285-3433), or Reelfoot Lake Area Chamber of Commerce, Route 1, Box 1205, Tiptonville, TN 38079 (731-253-8144).

Places to Stay

Airpark Inn and Restaurant, Reelfoot Lake State Park, Route 1, Tiptonville, TN 38079 (731-253-7756 or 1-800-250-8617), extends out over Reelfoot Lake amid the towering cypress trees. There are 12 rooms with double occupancy. The other eight are suites accommodating up to six persons each. Two meeting rooms accommodate from 25 to 60 persons. The inn is closed October, November and December.

Backyard Birds Lodge Bed & Breakfast, Route 1, Box 2300, Air Park Road, Tiptonville, TN 38079 (731-253-9064), features two rooms with private baths. Located on Reelfoot Lake, the lodge also offers pontoon eagle and nature tours.

Best Western Inn, 873 U.S. Hwy. 51 N., Covington, TN 38019 (901-476-8561), has 72 rooms that feature coffee makers, hair dryers and cable television with HBO and ESPN. Suites are available. Small pets are allowed.

Comfort Inn, 891 U.S. Hwy. 51 N., Covington, TN 38019 (901-475-0380), features a pool and cable television. Some rooms have a whirlpool in bath.

Days Inn, 555 U.S. Hwy. 51 N., Ripley, TN (731-635-7378) underwent a renovation in 1999. Amenities include a pool, cable television, and microwaves and refrigerators upon request. Pets are allowed for a charge.

Fort Pillow State Historic Park (camping), 838 Park Road, Henning, TN (731-738-5581), has a 40-site rustic campground, designed for tents although pop-up trailers, pick-up trucks and recreational vehicles are accommodated. The park provides two bathhouses with hot showers, restrooms and a laundry. Water faucets are available, but there are no electrical hookups.

The Peabody Hotel, 149 Union Ave., Memphis, TN 38103 (800-PEABODY), is the city's best-known hotel. The 450-room, luxury hotel was built in 1927 in downtown Memphis. Tourists from around the world gather in the lobby for the famous duck walk. The Peabody ducks have their own suite on the roof. At 11 a.m., they are escorted from their suite to the fountain in the lobby. At 5 p.m., they return to their quarters.

Reelfoot Lake State Park (camping), Route 1, Tiptonville, TN 38079 (731-253-7756 or 1-800-250-8617), has two campgrounds with a total of 102 campsites. The main campground is on the south side of the lake and is open seasonally. The other campground is located at the airfield and open year-round. Only the main campground offers a playground and laundromat. Both have centrally located bathhouses and dumping stations.

Shelby Forest State Park (camping), 910 Riddick Road, Millington, TN 38053 (901-876-5215), features a campground, swimming pool and six two-bedroom cabins. The cabins, located along Poplar Tree Lake, accommodate up to six people. They feature a television, fully equipped kitchen and fireplace.

Talbot Heirs Guesthouse, 99 South Second St., Memphis, TN 38103 (901-527-9772), is located in the heart of downtown, within walking distance of The Peabody, Beale Street and famous Memphis eateries, such as the Rendevous, Huey's and Automatic Slim's. Jamie and Phil Baker are the hosts at the nine-room guesthouse. Breakfast is brought directly to your room, or visitors can prepare their own meals in a kitchen with all the modern conveniences of home. Celebrity guests have included David Copperfield, Claudia Schiffer and Francis Ford Coppola.

Bicycle Shops

Midtown Bike Co., 1830 Poplar Ave., Memphis, TN 38104-2657 (901-726-4511).

Outdoors Inc., 1710 Union Ave., Memphis, TN 38104-6141 (901-722-8988).

BTR Cycle & Hobbies, 207 N. Second Street, Union City, TN 38261 (901-885-0707).

Bicycle City, 29 North Star Drive, Jackson, TN 38305 (901-668-0368 or 800-244-5834).

BICYCLING TENNESSEE
Tour 3: Dyersburg-Tiptonville

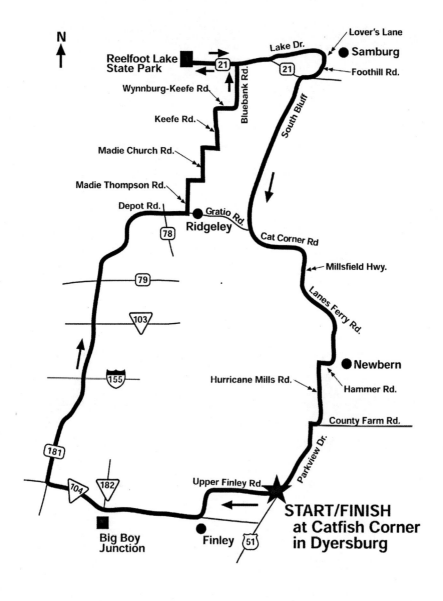

N

Lover's Lane

Lake Dr.

Reelfoot Lake State Park

21

21

● Samburg

Foothill Rd.

Bluebank Rd.

South Bluff

Wynnburg-Keefe Rd.

Keefe Rd.

Madie Church Rd.

Madie Thompson Rd.

Depot Rd.

Gratio Rd.

78

● Ridgeley

Cat Corner Rd

Millsfield Hwy.

79

Lanes Ferry Rd.

103

155

● Newbern

Hurricane Mills Rd.

Hammer Rd.

County Farm Rd.

181

Parkview Dr.

104

182

Upper Finley Rd.

★ **START/FINISH**
at Catfish Corner
in Dyersburg

Big Boy Junction

● Finley

51

3. DYERSBURG—TIPTONVILLE: A TWO-DAY TOUR

Easy terrain; 81 miles

Only a few settlers had moved to Northwest Tennessee, when they had a rude awakening at 2 a.m. on Dec. 16, 1811. In one of the strongest earthquakes recorded in the United States, residents saw their dense forest crash to the ground and the ground sink. The Mississippi River reportedly ran upstream and flooded the sunken lands, forming what is today Reelfoot Lake.

"From this time until February, the earth was in continual agitation, visibly waving as a gentle sea," wrote Eliza Bryan, who lived in nearby New Madrid, Mo. On Feb. 7, 1812, another earthquake as powerful as the first struck. Aftershocks continued throughout the year.

Reelfoot Lake was virtually untouched for nearly 50 years, before settlers began to realize the abundance of fish and game available. Struggles to control ownership of the lake were notorious before the state took control of the lake in 1914. Tennessee bought additional land around the 15,000-acre lake in 1925 for fish and game management.

There are a few legends about the earthquakes and how the lake was formed. Most popular is the story of Chief Reelfoot, the clubbed-foot Chickasaw Indian, who sought to marry Laughing Eyes, a Choctaw Indian. Her father, Chief Copiah, opposed the marriage, as did the Great Spirit of all Indians.

The Great Spirit warned if Reelfoot stole a wife from a neighboring tribe, the earth would rock and the waters would swallow up his village. Lonely and desperate, Reelfoot eventually ignored the warning and kidnapped Laughing Eyes. In the midst of the Chickasaws' celebration, the earth rocked and the waters rose. Reelfoot and his tribe were buried in a watery grave under the newly formed lake.

The U.S. Corps of Engineers recently announced a multimillion-dollar plan to rehabilitate Reelfoot Lake. The corps will temporarily lower the water level, consolidating the sediments at the lake's bottom. This will improve water quality and wildlife's habitat. Water levels will be better managed with the construction of a larger spillway. Silt heading into the lake will be reduced with the development of a sediment-retention basin.

This loop ride is a combination of two one-way bicycle routes, between Dyersburg and Reelfoot Lake, as developed by the Tennessee Department of Transportation.

Day 1
Easy terrain, after a few hills from the start to the Finley community, it's practically all Delta flatlands; 42.9 miles

Miles

0.0 **Start ride at U.S. Highway 51 and Upper Finley Road in Dyersburg at the Catfish Corner restaurant, a log house. Follow Upper Finley Road to the west.**

Andrew Jackson, who would later become U.S. president, and Gov. Isaac Shelby of Kentucky negotiated this region from the Chickasaw Indians. Tennessee created Dyer County on Oct. 6, 1823. A 60-acre community soon developed on McIvers Bluff and became the town of Dyersburg, incorporated on Jan. 10, 1850.

The county courthouse in Dyersburg, built in 1912, is a National Historic Landmark. Asa Biggs of Dyer County designed the classical-revival structure. Rows of columns topped by Ionic capitals mark the north and south entrances. The building's white round dome features clocks facing the north and south. The court-house is located in Veteran Square. Plaques commemorating veter-ans of the Civil War and World War I are on the north wall of the courthouse. Statues in the square also commemorate those that died in the Civil War and Vietnam War.

Another place of interest in town is the Dr. Walter E. David Wildlife Museum, located at Dyersburg State Community College. The museum contains a species of every kind of duck on the Mississippi Flyway. The admission is free, and it is open daily.

4.7   Cross railroad tracks in Finley.

5.0   You'll see the red-brick Finley United Methodist Church on the right. Turn right onto State Route 104. Follow State Route 104 to the west. Watch for traffic.

If you need to visit a convenience store, there is a BP station about a block on the right if you turn left on State Route 104.

6.1   Pass State Route 182 on the right.

The Phillips 66 Big Boy Junction and a BP station are at the left of this intersection. Traffic is not as busy from here. There are also no conveniences for 20.7 miles. You are now entering the Mississippi Delta. The good news is that it is flat. Your only challenge perhaps will be the wind. You are surrounded by farmland; there are no trees to protect you from the elements.

9.4   Cross over the Obion River.

This overpass will be your last significant hill for the day.

13.8   Turn right onto State Route 181. Follow this route north.

You are now travelling on the Great River Road, along the Mississippi River levee. The Mississippi River Parkway Commission, a multi-state organization, developed this 3,000-mile network of roads, extending from Canada to the Gulf of Mexico. The commission works with its affiliates in Arkansas, Illinois, Iowa, Kentucky, Louisiana, Minnesota, Mississippi, Tennessee,

Wisconsin and the Canadian province of Ontario, to preserve, promote and enhance economic growth on the Mississippi River corridor. It also coordinates efforts on federal, state, and local levels to leverage dollars for highway improvements, recreation trails, bikeways, scenic overlooks and historic preservation.

This road is also a part of the Mississippi River Trail, developed by the Lower Mississippi Delta Development Commission. In addition to the Bike Route signs, you will see the MRT signs, clearly marking the way. These come in handy when there are no road signs.

17.4 **Cross over Interstate 55. You are now entering the White Lake Wildlife Refuge.**

22.4 **Cross State Route 103, to the right and left.**

24.3 **Leave Dyer County and enter Lake County. Continue north on State Route 181.**

26.9 **Riding northbound on State Route 181 (Great River Road), turn left onto State Route 79.**

27.1 **State Route 79 turns left, but follow the Great River Road north.**

30.0 **Make a sharp right turn. Robinson Bayou Road is on the left.**

31.5 **Enter Ridgely city limits. The route changes to Depot Street.**

31.6 **Cross railroad tracks.**

31.8 **At the three way intersection, Alicia's Apparel and Gifts will be in front of you. Turn right onto South Main Street.**

31.85 **Make an immediate left turn onto Poplar Street.**

32.4 **Cross State Route 78, to the left and right. Watch for traffic.**
Conveniences at this intersection include Shell Hiway Gas and Grocery, Dorothy's Restaurant, Country Sisters Restaurant, an Exxon station and a BP station.

32.5 **Leave Ridgely city limits, route becomes Gratio Road. Road is subject to flooding.**

32.8 **Turn left onto Madie Thompson Road.**

34.6 **Turn right onto Madie Church.**

36.0 You'll see the white Willingham Baptist Church on the left. Turn left onto Keefe Road.

39.0 Turn right onto Wynnburg-Keefe Road. Watch for traffic.

39.7 Turn left onto Bluebank Road.

40.9 At the three-way intersection, you'll see Cypress Point Resort in front of you. Turn left onto State Route 21. Watch for traffic.

42.9 Turn right into the Reelfoot Lake Visitor Center. End of Day 1 route.

Reelfoot Lake State Park, located in Lake and Obion counties, takes up 280 acres along 22 miles of the shoreline. The park's Airpark Inn resort is located on State Highway 78, ten miles north of Tiptonville. The visitor center, auditorium, picnic and camping areas are located along State Highways 21 and 22.

Day 2
Easy terrain; 38.1 miles

Miles

0.0 Start ride at the Reelfoot Lake Visitor's Center on State Route 21, where the Day 1 route ended. Follow State Route 21 to the east. Watch for traffic.

The visitor center features exhibits pertaining to Reelfoot's natural and cultural history. Admission is free. Behind the center, take a stroll on the cypress boardwalk nature trail and see the bald eagle and bird of prey flight cages. The adjacent auditorium offers seating for 400 people for banquets and conventions.

The Reelfoot Lake Visitor Center marks the halfway point on this tour.

3.1   You'll see the Reelfoot Lake spillway to the left and right. You are leaving Lake County and entering Obion County.

3.7   Turn left onto Lake Drive.
This road takes you off sometimes-busy State Route 21, onto a lakeside road populated with retiree homes and summer getaways.

6.2   Turn left onto State Route 22. Watch for traffic.

6.4   Turn right onto Lovers Lane.
No services are available for approximately 30 miles.

6.9   Turn right onto Foothill Road.

8.1   Turn right onto State Route 21.

8.15   Turn left onto South Bluff Road.

10.5   Cross Webb Stone Road, to the right and left.

14.85 Pass Minnick-Elbridge Road on the left. Continue south on South Bluff Road.

19.4   Turn left onto Cat Corner Road.

21.4   Leave Obion County, enter Dyer County. Street name changes to Dew Drop Road.

22.4   Turn right onto Millsfield Highway.

23.6   Cross over the Obion River.

24.3   Turn a sharp left onto Lanes Ferry Road.

27.3   Turn a sharp right. Hartsfield Road is on the left.

29.8   Turn right onto Hammer Road.

      If you turn left on Hammer Road, you'll enter the town of Newbern within a couple of miles. Owen Philyou of New Bern, N.C., staked a claim in this area in 1850. Newbern was incorporated in 1857. The historic depot, a downtown Amtrak stop, is open daily.

33.6   Hammer Road changes into Hurricane Hill Road. Continue riding south.

35.9   Cross over Interstate 155.

36.1   Turn right. County Farm Road is on the left.

36.4   Turn left Parkview Drive.

37.1   Turn left onto U.S. Highway 51.

38.1   Turn right onto Upper Finley Road. You'll see the Catfish Corner restaurant on your right. End of Day 2 route, where the tour began.

For general information on lodging and attractions, contact the Dyersburg/Dyer County Chamber of Commerce, P.O. Box 747, 2455 Lake Road, Dyersburg, TN 38025-0747 (731-285-3433), or Reelfoot Lake Area Chamber of Commerce, Route 1, Box 1205, Tiptonville, TN 38079 (731-253-8144).

Places to Stay

Airpark Inn and Restaurant, Reelfoot Lake State Park, Route 1, Tiptonville, TN 38079 (731-253-7756 or 1-800-250-8617), extends out over Reelfoot Lake amid the towering cypress trees. There are 12 rooms with double occupancy. The other eight are suites accommodating up to six persons each. Two meeting rooms accommodate from 25 to 60 persons. The inn is closed October, November and December.

Aunt Ginny's Bed & Breakfast, 520 Sampson Ave., Dyersburg, TN 38024 (731-285-2028), features three rooms with private baths, a Victorian porch, garden with a hot tub and a licensed massage therapist.

Backyard Birds Lodge Bed & Breakfast, Route 1, Box 2300, Air Park Road, Tiptonville, TN 38079 (731-253-9064), features two rooms with private baths. Located on Reelfoot Lake, the lodge also offers pontoon eagle and nature tours.

Hampton Inn, 2750 Mall Loop Road, Dyersburg, TN 38024 (731-285-4778 or 800-426-7866), is located at Interstate 155 and U.S. Highway 78. It offers a pool and laundry/valet services. Cribs and connecting rooms are available.

Reelfoot Lake State Park (camping), Route 1, Tiptonville, TN 38079 (731-253-7756 or 1-800-250-8617), has two campgrounds with a total of 102 campsites. The main campground is on the south side of the lake and is open seasonally. The other campground is located at the airfield and open year-round. Only the main campground offers a playground and laundromat. Both have centrally located bathhouses and dumping stations.

Bicycle Shops
BTR Cycle & Hobbies, 207 N. Second Street, Union City, TN 38261 (731-885-0707).

Bicycle City, 29 North Star Drive, Jackson, TN 38305 (731-668-0368 or 800-244-5834).

BICYCLING TENNESSEE
Tour 4: Tiptonville–Martin

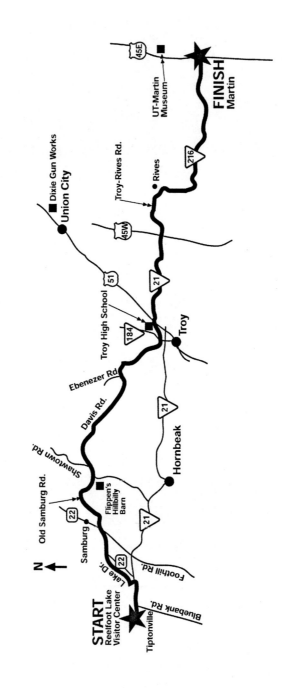

4. TIPTONVILLE—MARTIN

Moderate terrain, after cycling on level ground around the southern edge of Reelfoot Lake, you'll experience the rolling hills of Tennessee's western uplands; 44.9 miles

Look on the back of a dollar bill and you'll find the United States symbol of beauty, strength and courage—the American bald eagle. Although native to North America, its existence in the lower 48 U.S. states was in danger as recently as the 1980s.

Through much of this century, Western ranchers routinely killed the eagles to "protect" their livestock, and the construction of locks and dams destroyed fisheries, where eagles hunted for food. By the 1960s, the National Audubon Society discovered a link between the pesticide DDT and eagle sterilization. In 1963, the society calculated less than 500 nesting pairs of bald eagles in the lower 48 states.

The American bald eagle was one of the first species to join the endangered species list, started in 1973. Further government action banned DDT in 1974. Almost immediate efforts and results followed, and the eagle's miraculous climb from near extinction began. Wildlife officials began transporting eaglets and eggs to areas with extremely low eagle populations. They also began an aggressive effort to treat injured birds and release them back to the wild. Conservation groups began buying private lands to protect nesting areas from development.

By the early 1990s, wildlife organizations estimated more than 4,000 nesting pairs of eagles in the lower 48 states, and the U.S. Fish and Wildlife Service took the bald eagle off its endangered species list in 1994.

"This is America's greatest wildlife success story," nature photographer Frank Oberle says in Return of the Eagle. Our national symbol reflects our nation's soul, and the fight to save the eagle in a sense was a fight to save our country's soul, he says.

Between 150 to 200 American bald eagles migrate to Reelfoot Lake in the winter. Park naturalists conduct daily tours from December to March. Special weekend programs include slide shows, guest lectures and bus tours. In recent years, the park has begun setting up a webcam at nesting sites. The nesting site can be viewed during the winter months at www.eaglewatch.com, set up by St. George's Day School in Germantown, Tenn.

Reelfoot Lake is a natural wonder. Almost every kind of shore and wading bird can be found on the 15,000-acre lake and surrounding area. As a natural fish hatchery, the lake supports crappie, bream, largemouth bass and 53 other types of fish. It has the state's only commercial crappie fishing program. Many fisherman take to the lake in "stump jumpers," flat-bottomed boats that handle the lake's unusual shallow waters. Water rarely gets more than six to eight feet deep. The Calhoun family in nearby Tiptonville have been making stump jumpers for decades.

This bike ride is an out-and-back state bicycle route through Tennessee's western uplands. I'd recommend doing an overnight to Martin and back, or split the ride up between Tiptonville and Union City, or Union City and Martin.

Miles

0.0 **Start ride at the Reelfoot Lake Visitor Center on State Route 21. Follow State Route 21 to the east. Watch for traffic.**

Just behind the visitor center, cruise boats offer scenic rides on Reelfoot Lake. Daily tours run from May to September (weather permitting). Shorter tours are available on Saturday and Sunday afternoons, and occasional cookout, sunset and moonlight cruises are offered. A guide is available on each trip to answer questions and to interpret the natural and cultural interests of the lake.

Up to 200 American bald eagles migrate to Reelfoot Lake each winter. Park naturalists conduct daily tours from December to March.

3.0 **You'll see the Reelfoot Lake spillway to the left and right.**
You are leaving Lake County and entering Obion County. You'll see Spillway Bait & Grocery on your right.

3.7 **Turn left onto Lake Drive.**
You'll see Blue Bank Resort on the left. This road takes you off sometimes-busy State Route 21, onto a lakeside road populated with retiree homes and summer getaways.

6.2 **Turn left onto State Route 22. Watch for traffic.**

6.4 **Go straight at Lovers Lane.**
Lovers Lane is the road that takes you back to Dyersburg on Day 2 of the Dyersburg-Tiptonville tour. Continue straight ahead. You'll see the Walton Quik Mart (Phillips 66) on your right and the Amoco Mart on the left.

7.6 **You'll see a sign on the right for Flippen's Hillbilly Barn. Follow the arrow, making a sharp right turn onto Old Samburg Road; continue east on this route up the steep hill.**

Just before the next turn, you'll see Flippen's Hillbilly Barn on your right. Jack Flippen started his orchard in 1953. Since then, the enterprise has expanded into several businesses, owned and operated by his family.

The market, opened in the 1980s, sells 27 varieties of apples and peaches, fried fruit pies and apple cider. The pies are now mass-produced and sold wholesale. The Flippen family also runs a country-cooking restaurant onsite that seats 150 people. The market and restaurant are open daily except Sunday mornings.

11.1   **Riding east on Old Samburg Road, turn left onto Shawtown Road.**

13.9   **Turn right onto Davis Road.**

16.4   **You'll see the white-wooden Ebenezer Cumberland Presbyterian Church on the left. Turn left onto Ebenezer Road.**

20.15 **Enter Troy city limits; street name changes to Church Street.**

20.8   **Street name changes to Bright Street.**

21.0   **Cross State Route 184, to the right and left.**

21.6   **Turn left onto U.S. Highway 51. Watch for traffic. You'll see Troy High School Stadium on the left.**

21.7   **Turn right onto State Route 21.**

If you continue straight on U.S. Highway 51, you'll soon enter Union City. A couple of points of interest there include the Dixie Gun Works and Old Car Museum, and the Obion County Museum.

Dixie Gun Works is located at 1412 W. Reelfoot Ave., just off U.S. Highway 51, about seven miles north of the bicycle route. The company, founded by the late Turner Kirkland in 1948, specializes in muzzle-loading and rare antique gun supplies. In 1954, it became the first company to mass produce muzzle-loading replica firearms. The company is still family owned and operated.

Adjacent to Dixie Gun Works is the Old Car Museum. The museum sports 36 antique automobiles as well as a collection of farm engines, steam engines and whistles, and even three antique bicycles. The Old Car Museum is open daily except Sunday. There is a small admission fee.

In addition to rotating exhibits, the Obion County Museum, located at 1004 Edwards Street, provides a permanent exhibit tracing the history of Obion County. A model shows the railroad intersection on Church Street that gave the city its name in 1854. The museum also features a reproduction of a country general store, a 1917 Ford and an elaborate collection of old photographs. An 1870 log cabin stands next door. The museum is open seasonally from 1 to 4 p.m. Saturday and Sunday. Donations are accepted.

26.6 Cross U.S. Highway 45W; State Route 21 ends. Continue biking east on Troy-Rives Road.

26.8 Cross the railroad tracks and continue cycling east.
    This is a flat stretch with a tree farm on your right.

28.2 You'll see the old Rives Union Church on your right. Turn left onto Church Street, and enter Rives city limits.

28.6 You'll see the white-brick Chamber of Commerce on the left. Turn right onto State Route 216.

35.8 Continuing east on State Route 216, you'll leave Obion County and enter Weakley County at this point. Street name is also Mt. Pelia Road. Watch for traffic.

39.0 Cross Cane Creek Bridge and enter Martin city limits. You'll see Foley's Three-Point Grocery on the right. Street name is also Baker Road.

40.7 You'll see K & K Wholesale Inc. on the left. Turn right onto State Route 216 (also called U.S. Highway 43S).

44.9 You'll come to the intersection with U.S. Highway 45E. End of route.
    While in Martin, visit the University of Tennessee Martin Museum, located in the Holland McCombs Center on University Street. The museum features rotating exhibits, lectures and field trips in northwest Tennessee. It is open Monday-Friday from 1 to 4

p.m. during school sessions and is free to the public. The building is named for the former Time-Life correspondent, whose family owned the land where UT Martin is located today.

For general information on lodging and attractions, contact the Reelfoot Lake Area Chamber of Commerce, Route 1, Box 1205, Tiptonville, TN 38079 (731-253-8144), Obion County Chamber of Commerce, P.O. Box 70, Union City, TN 38261 (731-885-0211), or Weakley County Chamber of Commerce, P.O. Box 67, Dresden, TN 38225 (731-364-3787).

Places to Stay

Airpark Inn and Restaurant, Reelfoot Lake State Park, Route 1, Tiptonville, TN 38079 (731-253-7756 or 1-800-250-8617), extends out over Reelfoot Lake amid the towering cypress trees. There are 12 rooms with double occupancy. The other eight are suites accommodating up to six persons each. Two meeting rooms accommodate from 25 to 60 persons. The inn is closed October, November and December.

Backyard Birds Lodge Bed & Breakfast, Route 1, Box 2300, Air Park Road, Tiptonville, TN 38079 (731-253-9064), features two rooms with private baths. Located on Reelfoot Lake, the lodge also offers pontoon eagle and nature tours.

Econo Lodge, 853 University Street, Martin, TN 38237 (731-587-4241 or 800-553-2666, offers 43 rooms and a swimming pool.

Reelfoot Lake State Park (camping), Route 1, Tiptonville, TN 38079 (731-253-7756 or 1-800-250-8617), has two campgrounds with a total of 102 campsites. The main campground is on the south side of the lake and is open seasonally. The other campground is located at the airfield and open year-round. Only the main campground offers a playground and laundromat. Both have centrally located bathhouses and dumping stations.

Super 8 Motel, 1400 Vaden Ave., Union City, TN 38261 (731-885-4444 or 800-800-8000), offers 62 rooms and meeting facilities.

Bicycle Shops
BTR Cycle & Hobbies, 207 N. Second Street, Union City, TN 38261 (731-885-0707).

Bicycle City, 29 North Star Drive, Jackson, TN 38305 (731-668-0368 or 800-244-5834).

BICYCLING TENNESSEE
Tour 5: Germantown-Rossville

N

Shelby Farms

Walnut Grove Rd.

Germantown Pkwy.

Wolf River

START/FINISH
Seessel's Grocery

Germantown

Farmington Rd.

Dogwood Rd.

Houston Levee Rd.

Canale's

Raleigh LaGrange Rd.

Wolf River

Elba Grocery

Collierville-Arlington Rd.

Collierville

Chulahoma Rd.

RETURN

Wolf River

57

72

Rossville Rd.

Wolf River Cafe

Rossville

57

72

5. GERMANTOWN—ROSSVILLE

Easy terrain, only a few hills throughout the ride; 43.4 miles

For centuries, the 14-mile stretch of the Wolf River from LaGrange to Moscow, Tenn., was thought to be impassable. It was called the Ghost River because about halfway through this section the main channel disappears into a dense, water bald cypress and tupelo gum swamp.

According to Keith Kirkland, a manager at Outdoors Inc. in Memphis, only one corridor of many takes canoeists through the swamp. The rest take you on a disorienting trip through floating itea and button bush islands, eventually coming to a dead end.

That predicament changed in 1990, when the Wolf River Conservancy marked a canoe trail through the Ghost River between LaGrange and the Bateman Road Bridge, just south of Moscow. Now outdoor enthusiasts, botanists and biologists can enjoy one of the most beautiful and diverse wetland canoe trails in the Southeast. The trip begins at LaGrange in a bottomland hardwood forest. The flora changes every three to four miles from hardwood to sawgrass, bald cypress to tupelo gum and itea bush. Maple and birch trees provide a canopy for the trail. Otters, minks and muskrats feed on open mussel shells along the shore. The trip ends at the Bateman Road Bridge, just south of Moscow.

A developer/timber company briefly threatened the area in 1994, buying 4,000 acres along the Ghost River's banks. Citizens and businesses quickly raised $4 million to save the section, convincing the state of Tennessee to buy the property and create the Ghost River State Natural

Area in early 1995. The Moscow-LaGrange bicycle route featured in this book includes a ride through this area.

The 90-mile Wolf River begins in Holly Springs National Forest in Mississippi, winding through Fayette and Shelby counties in Tennessee, and emptying into the Mississippi River at Mud Island in downtown Memphis. This out-and-back bike ride, a favorite annual trek for the Memphis Hightailers Bicycle Club, parallels much of the river's course through eastern Shelby County and western Fayette County.

Also note, Shelby Farms, about two miles north of this ride's start, offers two mountain bike trails along the river. Just north of those trails is the site of the Tour de Wolf, one of the largest mountain bike races in the Southeast. Sponsored by Outdoors Inc., the fall event draws up to 1,000 cyclists competing for a $20,000 purse. Past participants have included legends Tinker Jaurez and Gary Fisher.

Miles

0.0   Start ride at Seessel's Grocery at the corner of Germantown Parkway and Farmington Road. Leave out of the south end of the parking lot, turning right onto Farmington Road.

Take advantage of the bike lanes; they are the only ones you'll find in the Memphis area. Germantown also recently opened a two-mile greenbelt system along the Wolf River.

Once called Pea Ridge, Germantown was chartered by the state of Tennessee in 1841. A plank road built in 1849 and railroad stop established in 1852 brought prosperity to the city. The growth, however, was curtailed during the Civil War and yellow fever epidemic of the 1860s, much like that of its neighbor Memphis. Today, the primarily residential community boasts a population of 40,000 people.

Cycling east of Germantown, you'll see quite a few horse ranches and stables. The town hosts numerous horse shows throughout the year, with the crème de la crème being the Germantown Charity

Horse Show held each June. Founded in 1948, this five-day event is one of the largest multi-breed horse shows in the United States, drawing 700 to 1,000 horses. Up to 350 classes compete for a piece of the $100,000 in prize money. The benefiting charity changes each year.

Another world-class charity event in Germantown is the annual FedEx-St. Jude Classic golf tournament, a PGA tour stop at the Tournament Players Club at Southwind. The summer classic benefits the St. Jude Children's Research Hospital, founded in Memphis by the late television actor, Danny Thomas.

Recently, the city built the Germantown Performing Arts Centre, featuring 800 seats in European rows—500 in the orchestra section and 300 in the balcony.

Shelby Farms, about two miles north of this ride's start, hosts the annual Tour de Wolf, one of the largest mountain bike races in the Southeast.

3.4 **Farmington Road becomes Dogwood Road.**

4.3 **Turn left onto Old Houston Levee Road.**

5.2 **Turn left onto Houston Levee Road. You'll cross the Wolf River, and ride around a winding curve. Watch for traffic.**

6.2 You'll see Canale's Grocery straight ahead. Turn right onto Raleigh LaGrange Road.

10.2 Turn right onto Collierville-Arlington Road (also called State Route 205). Watch for traffic.

10.4 Turn left onto Raleigh LaGrange Road. The road turns into a country road with no marked lanes.

14.5 You'll see Elba Grocery on your left.

15.6 Bear right to continue on Raleigh LaGrange Road.

18.3 Turn right onto Rossville Road (also called State Route 194). You'll cross the Wolf River and enter the town of Rossville.

The primary reason that the Memphis Hightailers make this trip each year is to stop at the Wolf River Café, to your left as you enter Rossville. The cyclists enjoy a late breakfast or early lunch, and the blackberry cobbler dessert is to die for. The café serves all-you-can-eat catfish on Mondays, Fridays and Saturdays.

Rossville is home to Tom's Pumpkin Patch. In recent years, Tom Johnson tired of growing row crops and began raising 13 varieties of pumpkins on his farm. He soon plans to expand his operation to include hayrides and other family activities. Also in Rossville, Kellogg's Eggo plant employs 275 people, and the Longreen Foxhounds Hunt Club opens its season each year at Fairfield Farms.

21.7 Turn around at the Wolf River Café. Head north on Rossville Road (also called State Route 194).

25.1 Turn left onto Raleigh LaGrange Road.

27.8 Bear left to continue on Raleigh LaGrange Road.

28.9 You'll see Elba Grocery on your right.

33.0 Turn right onto Collierville-Arlington Road (also called State Route 205). Watch for traffic.

33.1 Turn left onto Raleigh LaGrange Road.

37.2 You'll see Canale's Grocery on the right. Turn left onto Houston Levee Road. You'll ride around a winding curve, and cross the Wolf River. Watch for traffic.

38.1 Turn right onto Old Houston Levee Road.

39.1 Turn right onto Dogwood Road.

40.0 Dogwood Road becomes Farmington Road.

43.4 Turn left into Seessel's parking lot. End of route, where the tour began.

For general information about lodging and attractions, contact the Wolf River Conservancy, P.O. Box 11031, Memphis, TN 38111-0031, (901-526-9653) Fayette County Chamber of Commerce, P.O. Box 411, Somerville, TN 38068, (901-465-8690) and City of Germantown, 1930 Germantown Road South, Germantown, TN 38138 (901-757-7200).

Places to Stay

Courtyard by Marriott, 7750 Wolf River Parkway, Germantown, TN 38139 (901) 751-0230, has 93 rooms featuring a work desk, voice mail, data ports and cable/satellite television. Other hotel features include a restaurant for breakfast, exercise room, indoor pool and whirlpool.

The Bridgewater House, 7015 Raleigh-LaGrange Road, Cordova, TN 38018 (901-384-0080), is located in a restored schoolhouse, more than 100 years old. There are two spacious guestrooms and private baths. Steve and Katherine Mistilis are the innkeepers.

Bicycle Shops

BikeLane, 3096 Village Shops Dr., Germantown, TN 38138 (901-755-7233).

Bike World, 758 W. Poplar Ave., Collierville, TN 38017 (901-853-5569).

The Germantown Bicycle Shop, 5910 Mount Moriah Road, Memphis, TN 38115 (901-375-0777).

Mt. Moriah Bicycle Company, 5715 Mount Moriah Road, Memphis, TN 38115 (901-795-4343).

Outdoors Inc., 5245 Poplar Ave, Memphis, TN 38119 (901-767-6790).

The Peddler Bicycle Shop, 2095 Exeter Road, Germantown, TN 38138 (901-757-8485).

BICYCLING TENNESSEE
Tour 6: Moscow-LaGrange

N

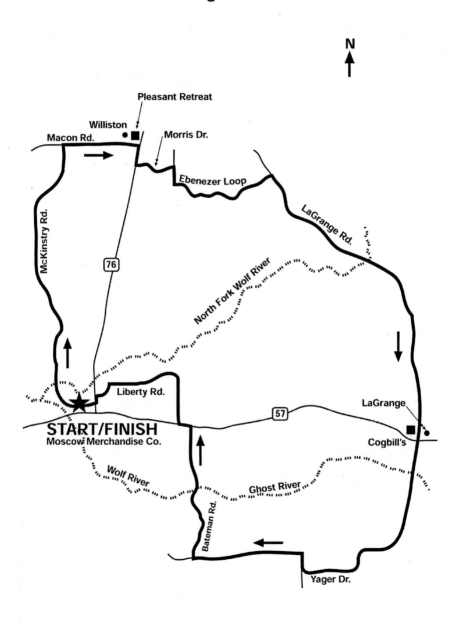

Pleasant Retreat

Williston

Macon Rd.

Morris Dr.

Ebenezer Loop

LaGrange Rd.

McKinstry Rd.

76

North Fork Wolf River

Liberty Rd.

57

LaGrange

START/FINISH
Moscow Merchandise Co.

Cogbill's

Wolf River

Ghost River

Bateman Rd.

Yager Dr.

6. Moscow—LaGrange

Easy to moderate terrain, many flat stretches with occasional rolling hills or river bluffs; 41.0 miles

Ames Plantation is a throwback to the era when cotton was king in the South, but it eventually became better known for its dogs than cotton.

John T. Pattern built a homestead on the North Fork of the Wolf River in the 1820s. The settlement grew quickly during the boon of the cotton era in the 1830s and 1840s. In addition to Pattern's homestead, notable structures included the Ames Manor House built by John W. Jones in 1847, Robert G. Thornton's homestead built in 1824, Mount Comfort (Morgan) Store and Andrews Chapel Methodist Episcopal Church in the town of Pattersonville.

Southern cotton plantations, many worked by slaves, ruled the roost until after the Civil War when sharecropper arrangements became more commonplace. But the area later to be called Ames Plantation still played a significant part in Fayette County's history, particularly when the National Bird Dog Championship moved its event there.

The national championship started in West Point, Miss. in 1896, later moving to field trial grounds south of Grand Junction, Tenn. Hobort Ames, president of the championship, moved the competition to 6,000 acres on the Ames Plantation in 1915. Each February, more than 30 English Pointers and/or English Setters, which have won or placed at 69 previous qualifying trials, participate in the event, hunting for native bob-white quail.

The National Bird Dog Museum is located in nearby Grand Junction. Created by the Bird Dog Foundation Inc., the museum highlights the talents of 36 bird dog breeds, including pointing dogs, spaniels and retrievers. A special section is devoted to the Field Trial Hall of Fame for pointing dogs. Each year for 35 years, American Field magazine readers elect two dogs and two people into the Hall of Fame. A Wildlife Heritage Center is under development.

This is a very rural route, relatively flat with a few hills and river bluffs. Moscow is located about 40 miles east of downtown Memphis. From Memphis, take Poplar Avenue through Germantown to Collierville. Take State Route 57 to Moscow, making a left on Memphis Street.

Miles

0.0 **Begin ride at the Moscow Merchandise Co. in the town square. From the east side of the square, head north on Memphis Street.**

No one is sure how Moscow received its name, but not many believe it was named after the Russian city. One speculation is that it was derived from an Indian word meaning "between two rivers." This is according to Dorothy Rich Morton in the Tennessee County History Series' *Fayette County*. The town does sit between the Wolf River and North Fork Wolf River, and at one time, Indians followed the similar-sounding Mossac Trail through the village.

The town was reportedly established around 1851, but records prior to the Civil War are lost. On Dec. 3, 1863, Federal troops fought the Battle of Moscow to keep the Memphis and Charleston Railroad open for Union supplies. The troops burned the town at the end of the war. Moscow received another charter in 1870.

0.1 **After crossing the railroad tracks, the street veers to the left and becomes Watermill Road.**

Watermill Road shortly becomes McKinstry Road before crossing the bridge over the North Fork Wolf River. McKinstry Road is a nice, scenic backroad, bumpy in places with some rolling hills.

7.7 Turn right onto Macon Road (or State Route 193) at the stop sign at the T-intersection. There is no road sign.

9.7 Turn right onto State Route 76 at the stop sign at the T-intersection. Watch for traffic.

10.2 You'll see a concrete building on your left. Turn left onto Morris Drive.

11.3 Turn right onto Ebenezer Loop at the stop sign at the T-intersection.

Morris Drive and Ebenezer Loop are both winding backroads with a few hills. Nearby, a not-for-profit organization maintains the historic Ebenezer Baptist Church, restored in 1990. The church cemetery dates back to 1838.

14.9 Turn right onto LaGrange Road at the stop sign at the T-intersection.

The next eight miles, for the most part, will take you on a steady downhill before you get to the North Fork Wolf River and a gradual uphill ride after you cross the river. You'll soon enter the town of LaGrange.

23.5 At the stop sign, cross State Route 57.

Incorporated in 1829, LaGrange sits on a high bluff overlooking the Wolf River. It took its name from the French ancestral home of Marquis de la Fayette. The entire town is on the National Register of Historic Places. Many antebellum homes still line the streets, including the birthplace of Lucy Holcombe Pickens.

The "queen" of the Confederacy was born in LaGrange in 1832 but later moved to Texas with her family, according to historian Morton. She married Francis Wilkinson Pickens in 1858. Francis became the U.S. Ambassador to Russia, but they returned to the states during the Civil War. He was elected governor of South Carolina. It was during this time that Lucy was the only woman whose image appeared on at least three series of Confederate bills.

Cogbill's Store & Museum is located at the corner of LaGrange Road and State Route 57. Owned by her family since the 19th century, Lucy Cogbill, the mayor of LaGrange, reopened the historic structure in 1991. In addition to food and drink, the store showcased the work of more than 100 craftsmen as well as artifacts and documents detailing the history of LaGrange. The store burned down in 1998. Cogbill, however, with a little help from her friends, rebuilt and opened the store in October 2000. The town hosts the Celebrate LaGrange festival each year, as well as an annual Christmas concert.

Back on the route, after leaving LaGrange, you'll take a steep descent to the Wolf River. Be careful, the downhill is winding and bumpy. This is the part of the Wolf River called Ghost River, described in the Germantown-Rossville chapter. LaGrange Road basically follows a loop around the south side of the Wolf River, turning into Yager Drive as it heads back north. This loop, while scenic, is primarily bottomlands. The road is bumpy, and there are not many trees to protect you from the elements.

32.6   Turn right onto Bateman Road.

Once again, in a couple miles, you'll cross the Ghost River, with a spectacular view to the right.

Riders trek across the Bateman Road Bridge,
where canoeists launch into the Ghost River.

36.2 Turn left onto State Route 57 at the stop sign at the T-intersection. Watch for traffic.

36.5 Turn right onto Liberty Road.

37.8 Continue straight. Liberty Road becomes Montague Drive.

40.2 Turn left onto State Route 76 at the stop sign at the T-intersection. Watch for traffic.

40.3 Just before the railroad tracks, turn right onto Old Sommerville Avenue. There is no sign.

40.7 Turn left onto Sommerville Street and cross the railroad tracks.

40.8 Turn right onto Fourth Street.

41.0 You are back at the Moscow Merchandise Co. in the town square, where you started. End of ride.

For general information about lodging and attractions, contact the Fayette County Chamber of Commerce, Fayette County Chamber of Commerce, 107 West Court Square, Somerville, TN 38068 (901) 465-8690.

Places to Stay

Hampton Inn, 1280 W. Poplar Ave., Collierville, TN 38017 (901-854-9400), features laundry services, exercise gym, cable television and outdoor pool. Pets are allowed.

Pleasant Retreat Bed & Breakfast, 420 Hotel Street, Williston, TN 38076 (901-465-4599), is located near the northern part of the bicycle route. Pleasant Retreat is an antebellum home listed on the National Register of Historic Places. Owned by Judith and James Freeland, the inn also offers a variety of tours for its visitors, including the Ames Plantation, National Bird Dog Museum, historic LaGrange, the Longreen Hunt Club and a sheep farm/wool museum.

Bicycle Shops

Bike World, 758 W. Poplar Ave, Collierville, TN 38017-2544 (901-853-5569).

BICYCLING TENNESSEE
Tour 7: Henning-Nutbush

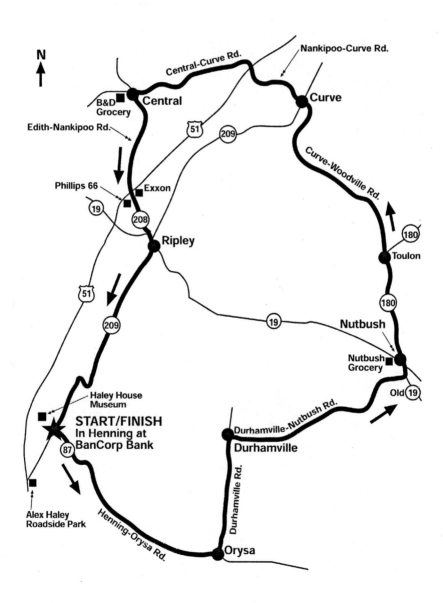

7. Henning—Nutbush

Easy to moderate terrain, 39.0 miles

Anna Mae Bullock was born Nov. 26, 1939. Growing up in the small community of Nutbush, she dreamed of a better life. Her parents constantly fought. When she was 10 years old, her mother moved to St. Louis. Her father soon remarried and moved to Detroit, leaving Anna and her sister, Alline, with a cousin.

"I couldn't believe it," Anna says today on her web site. "There I was, 13 years old, with no mother. And now my father was gone too." She found happiness singing in church on Sundays. She was fascinated with the fast organ music.

At 16, she pursued her musical interests further when she followed Alline to St. Louis. "I always wanted to leave the fields," she says. "Tennessee was fine. I loved sitting under a tree at the end of the day, but I knew there was more. That's why I joined my mother in St Louis. To me, that was the big city."

In St. Louis, Anna discovered the Club Manhattan. The Kings of Rhythm were playing the first night that she visited the nightclub. Her meeting with the band's leader, Ike Turner, evolved into a new name and a new life for Anna Mae Bullock. Tina Turner was born.

The Ike and Tina Turner Revue became one of America's hottest acts during the late 1960s and early 1970s. The band's hits included "River Deep Mountain High," "Proud Mary" and "Nutbush City Limits." The marriage fell apart, and Tina left the band in 1976. She finally regained stardom in 1984 when her "Private Dancer" album rocked the international charts. The single, "What's Love Got to Do It," won the Grammy for best record.

Today, Tina continues to record and tour successfully. She and her boyfriend, record executive Erwin Bach, have homes in Switzerland and France.

This ride to Tina Turner's hometown is a favorite of the Memphis Hightailers. The terrain is more easy than moderate. To get to the starting point, take U.S. Highway 51 about 45 miles north of Memphis. A few miles north of Covington, turn right on State Route 209. In about one mile, State Route 209 becomes Main Street in downtown Henning.

Miles

0.0 **Start ride at Bancorp Bank at Main Street and Thum Avenue. Head south on Main Street (also called State Route 209).**

Dr. D.M. Henning founded this community in 1873. Its first merchant was C.L. Strickland in 1874. Henning was first incorporated in 1883, but soon after surrendered its charter for a time to prohibit the sale of whiskey next to a chartered school, according to the series *The Goodspeed History of Tennessee*. Fire destroyed the community in 1886, but the town was rebuilt.

Henning is now best known as the childhood home of author Alex Haley. You can read more about Haley in the Memphis—Tiptonville chapter. The town elected Haley's childhood friend, Fred Montgomery, as mayor in 1987. He was 71 years old at the time. He still serves as mayor today.

Henning is the boyhood home and final resting place of author Alex Haley, author of
Roots: The Saga of an American Family.

0.1   Turn left onto McFarlin Avenue (also called State Route 87) at
      the traffic light. Road becomes Henning-Orysa Road.

6.2   You'll see an old white church on your left. Turn left onto
      Durhamville Road.

      You are in the community of Orysa.

9.4   You'll see St. Paul Methodist Church on your right. Shortly there-
      after, turn right onto Durhamville-Nutbush Road.

      Durhamville, founded around 1930, is the second oldest town in
      the county. (Fulton is the oldest.) The town is named for Col.
      Thomas Durham, who operated a store there in 1826.
      Durhamville-Nutbush Road is a quiet back-country road. The road
      becomes better after you cross the county line.

11.0 Enter Haywood County.

      If you turn left on Willette Beard Road, you'll find the Wild Onion
      Ridge Music Heritage Park, new home of the Nutbush/Tina Turner
      Resource Center. Nutbush Heritage Productions of Brownsville
      plans to develop the site for special events, family picnics and Tina
      Turner tours.

15.0 You'll see the red Trinity Baptist Church and Joe Stevens Road on your right. Continue around the curve on State Route 19.

15.3 Turn left onto State Route 19 at the stop sign, then right onto State Route 180 (also called Woodsville Road).

You are in the heart of Nutbush. If you continue straight on State Route 19, you'll see the Nutbush Grocery and Deli on your left.

18.3 You'll see the red Maranatha Baptist Church straight ahead. Cross Forked Deer Road and continue straight on Woodsville Road.

Just before crossing the county line, you'll enter the community of Woodsville, founded in 1836 by its first merchants, Eubank and Bowers.

21.0 Enter Lauderdale County. Road becomes Curve-Woodville Road.

The next community you'll enter will be Curve.

24.3 Turn right onto Food Store Road, which curves back into Curve-Woodville Road.

24.4 Cross State Route 209 at the stop sign. Road becomes Nankipoo-Curve Road.

26.3 Cross U.S. Highway 51.

There is usually a fruit stand set up here during the summer months.

26.4 Turn left onto Central-Curve Road.

29.9 You'll see B & D Grocery straight ahead and Central Grocery on your left. Turn left onto Edith-Nankipoo Road (also called State Route 208).

You are in the community of Central. This turn intersects with the Mississippi River Trail, going in the other directions. See the Memphis—Tiptonville chapter.

32.7 Cross U.S. Highway 51. An Exxon station is on the left. A Phillips 66 station is on the right. Road becomes Cleveland Street.

You are entering Ripley city limits. The seat of Lauderdale County was founded in 1836 on 50 acres donated by John Brown, according to *The Goodspeed History of Tennessee*. It was incorporated in 1849.

You can read more about Ripley in the Memphis—Tiptonville chapter.

33.3 Turn right onto Washington Street (also called State Route 209).
39.0 Turn right into the Bancorp parking lot. End of ride.

For general information on lodging and attractions, contact the Haywood County Chamber of Commerce, 121 W. Main St., Brownsville, TN 38012 (731-772-2193); Nutbush Heritage Productions Inc., 255 Cottondale Dr., Brownsville, TN 38012 (731-772-4265); or Ripley/Lauderdale County Chamber of Commerce, 103 East Jackson Ave., Ripley, TN 38063 (731-635-9541).

Places to Stay
Best Western Inn, 873 U.S. Hwy. 51 N., Covington, TN 38019 (901-476-8561), has 72 rooms that feature coffee makers, hair dryers and cable television with HBO and ESPN. Suites are available. Small pets are allowed.

Days Inn, 555 U.S. Hwy. 51 N., Ripley, TN 38063 (731-635-7378), underwent a renovation in 1999. Amenities include a pool, cable television, and microwaves and refrigerators upon request. Pets are allowed for a charge.

Fort Pillow State Historic Park (camping), 838 Park Road, Henning, TN (731-738-5581), has a 40-site rustic campground, designed for tents although pop-up trailers, pick-up trucks and recreational vehicles are accommodated. The park provides two bathhouses with hot showers, restrooms and a laundry. Water faucets are available, but there are no electrical hookups.

Bicycle Shops

Midtown Bike Co., 1830 Poplar Ave., Memphis, TN 38104-2657 (901-726-4511).

Outdoors Inc., 1710 Union Ave., Memphis, TN 38104-6141 (901-722-8988).

Bicycle City, 29 North Star Drive, Jackson, TN 38305 (731-668-0368 or 800-244-5834).

BICYCLING TENNESSEE
Tour 8: Lakeland-Jackson

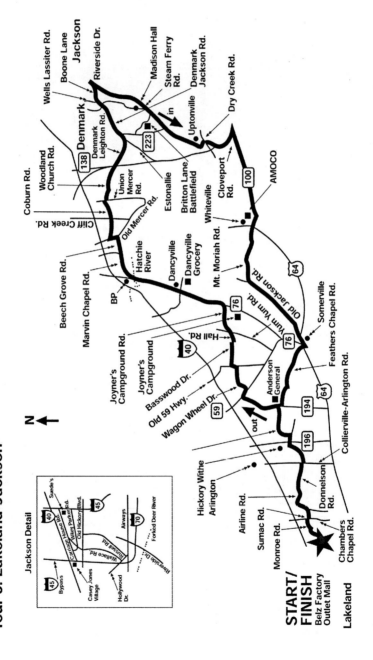

N

Jackson Detail

Jackson

Wells Lassiter Rd.
Boone Lane
Riverside Dr.
Madison Hall
Steam Ferry Rd.
Denmark Jackson Rd.
Dry Creek Rd.
Uptonville
in
Denmark
Woodland Church Rd.
Coburn Rd.
Denmark Leighton Rd.
138
223
Union Mercer Rd.
Estonallie
Britton Lane Battlefield
Cloveport Rd.
Whiteville
100
AMOCO
Cliff Creek Rd.
Old Mercer Rd.
Hatchie River
Dancyville
Dancyville Grocery
Mt. Moriah Rd.
Beech Grove Rd.
BP
Marvin Chapel Rd.
Old Jackson Rd.
64
Somerville
Feathers Chapel Rd.
76
Yum Yum Rd.
76
Joyner's Campground Rd.
Joyner's Campground
Hall Rd.
40
Basswood Dr.
Old 59 Hwy.
Anderson General
64
Wagon Wheel Dr.
59
194
out
196
Collierville-Arlington Rd.
Hickory Withe
Arlington
Donnelson Rd.
Airline Rd.
Sumac Rd.
Monroe Rd.
Chambers Chapel Rd.

START/FINISH
Belz Factory Outlet Mall

Lakeland

Suede's
45
40
Old Hickory Blvd.
Carriage House Rd.
Valley Park Rd.
45
Bypass
Casey Jones Village
Wallace Rd.
Russell Rd.
Hollywood Dr.
Riverside Dr.
Airways
70
Forked Deer River

8. LAKELAND—JACKSON: A TWO-DAY TOUR

Moderate terrain; 157.0 miles

In "Mystery Train," a film by Jim Jarmusch, a Japanese tourist sits in awe of the Elvis Presley statue on Beale Street, since replaced and relocated to Memphis' downtown Welcome Center. Her companion remarks, "Carl Perkins was better."

I call this the Rockabilly tour, in memory of Perkins. His life is chronicled in *Got, Cat, Go!*, by Perkins and David McGee.

Perkins was born a sharecropper's son in Tiptonville, Tenn. His childhood home still stands near Reelfoot Lake. Moving to Madison County in 1946, the Perkins Brothers Band made a name for itself playing the honky-tonks around Jackson. With Carl on lead guitar, Jay on rhythm guitar and Clayton on upright bass, their music was an up-tempo country sound, later termed rockabilly. Perkins was amazed when he heard Presley's rocking version of "Blue Moon of Kentucky" in 1954.

"There's a man in Memphis who understands what we're doing," Perkins tells his wife in *Go, Cat, Go!* "I need to go see him."

His meeting with Sam Phillips at Memphis Recording Service led to several regional hits and Southern tours with Presley and newcomer, Johnny Cash. At Cash's suggestion, Perkins wrote a song about an ever-growing fashion. "Blues Suede Shoes" became the Sun label's first record to sell one million copies.

Some argue that Perkins would have been bigger than Presley if he wasn't involved in a serious automobile accident in March 1956. His band was driving to New York City to make its first national television appearance on the Perry Como Show. Presley performed his version of "Blue Suede Shoes" the following month on Milton Berle's show.

Perkins continued to record and tour. The Beatles invited him to Abbey Road in the early 1960s. They later recorded their versions of his "Everybody's Trying to Be My Baby," "Honey Don't" and "Matchbox." Perkins toured with Cash for most of the late 1960s and early 1970s. He wrote Cash's hit "Daddy Sang Bass." In 1975, two of his sons, Greg and Stan, began recording and touring with him.

On Jan. 19, 1998, Perkins died of a stroke. Whether or not he was better than Presley, his contributions live on through his music and the Exchange Club—Carl Perkins Center for the Prevention of Child Abuse in Jackson.

The Multiple Sclerosis Society's Mid-South Chapter developed this ride for its MS 150, which now goes from Memphis to Tunica, Miss., and back. The trip begins at the Belz Factory Outlet Mall in Lakeland, a suburb east of Memphis. The Factory Outlet Mall is just off Canada Road, just south of exit 20 on Interstate 40. The halfway point is Suede's, Carl Perkins' restaurant in Jackson operated by his daughter, Debbie Swift, and her husband, Bart. Suede's is located on Highland Avenue (or Highway 45), just a block south of Interstate 40.

Day 1
Moderate terrain; 78.8 miles

Miles

0.0   Belz Factory Outlet Mall. Exit out the back (southeast) of the parking lot. Turn left onto Monroe Road.

The Belz Factory Outlet Mall's 45 stores allow you to buy direct from the manufacturer. It offers 320,000 square feet of shopping space, plus a 60,000-square-foot annex, which was recently added. The Memphis-based firm also owns outlet malls in Pigeon Forge, Tenn., Orlando, Fla., and Las Vegas, Nev. Unfortunately, the mall recently banned cyclists from parking and riding from its property, so you'll need to find another location to leave your vehicle.

Lakeland hosts its annual Funfest each summer, featuring a barbecue contest, key tosses and outhouse races. Nearby attractions include Davies Manor Plantation and Cordova Cellars. Davies Manor Plantation, 9336 Davies Plantation Road in Brunswick, was built in 1807, making it the oldest log home in Shelby County. Special tours are offered by calling (901) 386-0715. Cordova Cellars, 9050 Macon Road in Cordova, is a full-production winery. Tours and wine tastings are offered year-round, Tuesdays through Sundays.

0.1 **Turn right onto Monroe Road.**

0.7 **Turn left onto Monroe Road again.**

2.2 **Turn right onto Chambers Chapel at the stop sign at the T-intersection.**

2.4 **Turn left onto Sumac Road.**
You are entering Arlington city limits, which celebrated its centennial in 2000. To commemorate its past, the town recently built a replica of a blacksmith shop that originally stood in the square. At this writing, the town officials were discussing establishing an historic district around the Depot Square. Officials were also proposing to build a Shelby County Welcome Center near Interstate 40 and Airline Road.

3.3 **Turn left onto Airline Road at the stop sign at the T-intersection.**

5.0 **Turn right onto Donnelson Road.**

6.2 **Cross Collierville-Arlington Road.**

6.4 **Continue right on Donnelson Road.**

7.1 **Road turns into a country road, a little bumpy with some hills.**

9.9 **Cross State Route 196 at the community of Hickory Withe.**

10.3 **Turn left onto Ivy Road. Terrain features fewer trees and a few flat stretches.**

14.2 **Turn right onto Feathers Chapel Drive.**

16.4 Murrell's Grocery is on the right.

17.1 Turn left onto State Route 194 (or Oakland Road) at the stop sign at the T-intersection. Anderson General Merchandise is a block on the left in the other direction.

20.8 Turn right onto State Highway 59 at the stop sign at the T-intersection. Watch for traffic.

21.9 Turn left onto Brewer.

22.1 Turn right onto Wagon Wheel Drive. Mike's Grocery is on the left just before the next turn.

25.1 Turn left onto Old Highway 59 Drive.

26.0 Turn right onto Basswood Drive.

27.1 Jog right onto Stanton for a few hundred feet; then turn left on Hall.

29.8 Turn left onto Yum Yum at the stop sign at the T-intersection.

30.7 You'll see Lumus System cotton gin on the right. Turn right onto Joyner's Campground Drive.

You'll soon pass Joyner's Campground on the right. Each summer, about 150 people from all around the Mid-South gather at the rustic setting for a 10-day retreat. During "camp," participants reaffirm their Christian beliefs. The tradition has taken place at Joyner's since 1893.

A rural view seen along the ride to Jackson.

32.7 **Turn left onto State Highway 76. Watch for traffic.**

You'll be on this highway for awhile. About four miles on Highway 76, you'll intersect with State Route 179 in Dancyville. If you turn right on Route 179, the Dancyville Grocery is about one block on your right. About eight miles, the Koko Community Grocery is on your left at the junction of (another) State Route 179. About 10 miles, you'll pass the Oneal Lake Wildlife Refuge on your right. About 12 miles, you'll cross the Hatchie Scenic River.

45.2 **Turn right onto Marvin Chapel at National W.L. Preserve office. There is no street sign here.**

If you go straight here, exit 56 on Interstate 40 is about 1/4 mile ahead. There is a BP and Exxon station, several fast food restaurants, a Best Western, Days Inn, Comfort Inn and Holiday Inn Express.

47.2 **Turn right onto Beech Grove Road.**

49.3 **Turn right onto Old Mercer Road at the stop sign at the T-intersection.**

51.2 **Turn left onto Cliff Creek Road. Rosson's Grocery is on the right.**

52.1 **Turn right onto Coburn. There is no street sign here.**

54.3 **Turn left onto Union Mercer Road.**

54.5 **You'll see a pinkish old Gulf station on your right. Turn right onto Woodland Church Road at the stop sign at the T-intersection.**

57.9 **Keep ahead onto Denmark Leighton Road.**

61.0 **Turn left onto Estonallie (turns into Denmark Jackson Road). You are now entering the community of Denmark.**

If you are interested in Civil War history, turn right on State Route 223 and follow the signs to Britton Lane Battlefield, about five miles off the route. James D. Brewer, a Jackson native and U.S. Army Major at West Point, has studied the Battle of Britton Lane since 1977.

According to Brewer, in the summer of 1862, Confederate Colonel Frank Armstrong left Guntown, Miss., with his cavalry brigade, stopping in Holly Springs, Miss., to pick up three more regiments. He crossed the Tennessee border with 3,300 troops. Scholars debate whether his mission was to take Jackson, Tenn., away from Federal control, or to simply engage in a series of skirmishes in West Tennessee to disrupt enemy supply lines.

After small skirmishes near Bolivar and Medon, Tenn., Federal forces began preparing against an attack on Jackson. Federal Colonel Elias Dennis and his 1,500 troops, camped at Denmark, were ordered to Medon to head off trouble. They took a dusty, country lane named for farmer Thomas Britton. But Dennis and Armstrong's troops surprised each other on Sept. 1, 1862, meeting where today Steam Mill Ferry Road intersects with Collins Road and Britton Lane. A four-hour battle ensued.

It is still arguable which side won the Battle of Britton Lane. If Armstrong's mission was to disrupt enemy supply lines, the mission was a success, but at a cost of at least 100 Confederate lives. Otherwise, the Federal troops successfully defended Jackson, sending Armstrong's brigade back to Mississippi and reportedly only losing eight Union soldiers.

Back on the route, you'll see the Denmark Presbyterian Church, built in 1854. Dennis' troops camped near here the night before the Battle of Britton Lane. Once an Indian settlement, Denmark was incorporated in 1830. The town grew steadily, becoming prosperous during the 1850s, writes Emma Inman Williams in her book, *Historic Madison*. Railroads, however, played a role in the community's demise. New railroads would soon route through Jackson and Mercer, bypassing Denmark.

Denmark Jackson Road becomes State Route 223. Watch for traffic.

66.5   Turn right, continuing on Denmark Jackson Road.

70.7 Turn left onto Wells Lassiter Road at the stop sign at the T-intersection.

71.2 Turn right onto Boone Lane at the stop sign at the T-intersection.

72.1 Turn left onto Riverside Drive at the stop sign at the T-intersection. Watch for traffic.

73.7 Turn left onto Airways. (If you turn right, you will be on Jackson's Main Street.)

74.2 You'll see an Exxon station on the right. Turn right onto Hollywood Drive.

75.2 Turn right onto Russell Road.

77.1 Turn left onto Old Hickory Boulevard.

77.5 Turn right onto Wallace Road.

78.6 Turn right onto Carriage House Drive.

Turn left here and ride a couple of miles to visit Casey Jones Village. Watch for traffic at the intersection of U.S. Highway 45 Bypass, just south of Interstate 40.

John Luther "Casey" Jones is America's most famous train engineer, made famous in story and song. During a trip through Mississippi on April 29, 1900, Jones was running two hours behind schedule and decided to open the throttle wide on his Cannonball Express, an Illinois Central locomotive. Crews were rushing to switch a freight train onto a side track, when the Cannonball came barreling through the fog at 100 miles an hour into Vaughn, Miss.

By the time Jones saw the stalled train, he knew it was too late. He hollered for the crew to jump and put his skills to work, immediately throwing his train in reverse. The Cannonball smashed into the stalled train all the way through its last car. His heroics saved the crew and passengers. Casey was the only person killed in the collision.

Casey Jones Home and Museum offers a view of Jones' home at the time of his death and a glimpse into the railroad industry's past. Nearby, Brooks Shaw's Old Country Store recaptures a turn-of-the-century general store with 15,000 antiques on display, a confectionery shop and a Southern home-cooking restaurant. Casey Jones Village also features miniature golf and a miniature train ride (seasonal).

78.8 Turn right onto Highland Avenue. Watch for traffic.

78.85 Turn into Suede's restaurant. End Day 1 ride.

Suede's contains memorabilia of Carl Perkins, as well as related materials of Elvis Presley, the Beatles and other recording artists that Carl knew. The food is excellent, the atmosphere is nostalgic, and the service is great.

Day 2
Moderate terrain; 78.2 miles

Miles

0.0 Start ride at Suede's restaurant. Head south on Highland Avenue.
Jackson was incorporated on August 17, 1821. Part of the city's growth in the 1800s was the creation of its waterworks plant in 1885. By 1888, 27 wells furnished the city's water from two powerful pumps, according to historian Williams. Chicago chemists deemed the water "remarkably pure."

Another advancement for the city was its road system in the early 1900s. Sam Lancaster was the city's engineer in the late 19th Century. Building on ideas previously proposed by J.J. Williams, Lancaster and others coordinated a Good Roads convention in Jackson in June 1901. The hub-and-spoke road development that followed became a national model. Lancaster later became a consulting engineer for the Columbian Highway through the Cascade Mountains to the Pacific Ocean.

0.3 Turn right onto Wiley Parker Road.

1.2 Turn left onto Wallace Road.

1.5 Turn left onto Old Hickory Boulevard.

1.9   **Turn right onto Russell Road.**

3.8   **Turn left onto Hollywood Drive.**

4.8   **Turn left onto Airways.**

5.3   **Turn right onto Riverside Drive. Watch for traffic.**

If you continue straight, you'll enter downtown Jackson. The Exchange Club-Carl Perkins Center for the Prevention of Child Abuse is located at 217 East College Street. Moved by a newspaper account of a child's death, Perkins helped organize the first benefit concert for the center.

The proceeds from the benefit and funds from a National Exchange Club grant led to the center's opening in October 1981. The Blue Suede Dinner and Auction remains a successful annual fundraiser. Today, the center has more than 50 staff members and hundreds of volunteers that serve children and their families. Its goal is to prevent and deal with child abuse in West Tennessee.

7.7   **You'll see Sadie Lou's gas station on the left and a Texaco station on the right. Turn right onto Steam Mill Ferry. There is no street sign.**

Enjoy this long, scenic backroad. About 10 miles on Steam Mill Ferry, you'll pass Britton Lane, and Lela Robinson's Grocery will be on the right. If you turn right on Britton Lane, Britton Lane Battlefield (described above) is only about two miles on your left.

23.8   **Turn right onto Dry Creek Road at the stop sign at the T-intersection.**

24.6   **Turn left onto State Route 138 at the stop sign at the T-intersection. There is no street sign. After you turn, you'll see white wooden Cloverport Baptist Church on the right. Watch for traffic. Cloverport Grocery is about a mile ahead.**

26.0   **Turn right onto Cloverport Road just after crossing the creek.**

28.6   **Turn right onto State Highway 100. Watch for traffic.**

36.8 Turn right onto U.S. Highway 64. Watch for traffic. You'll see an Amoco station on the right. Morris Grocery and Phillips Grocery are on the left further down.

38.1 Turn right onto State Route 179.

You are now entering Whiteville city limits. Shoppers line up and down Main Street every Wednesday morning to get first dibs at the A & L Bargain House. The clothing store offers used clothing by big-name designers for as low as a dollar. Other area points of interest include the Boxwood Manor, Bass Home, Anderson Fruit Farm, and Backermann's Mennonite Bakery & Cheese Shoppe.

38.2 You'll see Foodland on the right. Turn left onto Mt. Moriah Street.

43.6 You'll see the red brick Smith Chapel Church on the right. Turn left onto Old Jackson Road.

52.2 Turn left onto North Main Street at the stop sign at the T-intersection.

You are now in downtown Somerville. You'll see the Fayette County Courthouse straight ahead.

The Tennessee General Assembly established Fayette County on Sept. 29, 1824. Davy Crockett was then a state representative for the area. The county is named for Marquis de la Fayette, a French general who fought in the Yorktown campaign during the Revolutionary War. He returned to the United States in 1824 for the dedication of the Bunker Hill monument. His visit included stops in Memphis and Nashville, Tenn.

When you arrive on the street in front of the courthouse, Morris Grocery and Market is on the right. Keep to the right around the town square.

53.0 Turn right onto U.S. Highway 64. Watch for traffic.

54.2 Turn right onto Feathers Chapel just past the school.

62.1 You'll see Anderson General Merchandise on the left. Turn right onto State Route 194 (or Oakland).

62.15 Turn left onto Feathers Chapel again.

65.0 Turn left onto Ivy Road.

68.9 Turn right onto Donnelson Road.

72.8 Turn left onto Collierville-Arlington Road.

73.0 Cross Collierville-Arlington Road. Continue straight on Donnelson Road.

74.2 Turn left onto Airline Road.

75.9 Turn right onto Sumac Road.

76.8 Turn right onto Chambers Chapel at the stop sign at the T-intersection.

77.0 Turn left onto Monroe Road.

77.5 Turn right onto Cobb.

78.2 Turn right into the Belz Factory Outlet Mall parking lot, where the tour began.

For general information on lodging and attractions, contact the Memphis Convention & Visitors Bureau, 47 Union Ave., Memphis, TN 38103 (901-543-5300), Fayette County Chamber of Commerce, P.O. Box 411, Somerville, TN 38068 (901-465-8690, Hardeman County Chamber of Commerce, 500 W. Market St., Bolivar, TN 38008 (901-658-6554), or Jackson-Madison County Convention & Visitors Bureau, 314 East Main St., Jackson, TN 38305 (901-425-8333 or 800-498-4748).

Places to Stay

Boxwood Manor, 311 East Main St., Whiteville, TN 38075 (731-254-0165), is a two-story, Victorian-style home built in 1900. Innkeeper Jean Plaisance opened the house for visitors in 1998. The manor features four bedrooms, three of which access a screened porch overlooking the grounds. Whiteville is located east of this route, off State Route 100 in Hardeman County.

The Bridgewater House, 7015 Raleigh-LaGrange Road, Cordova, TN 38018 (901-384-0080), is located in a restored schoolhouse, more than 100 years old. There are two spacious guestrooms and private baths. Steve and Katherine Mistilis are the innkeepers.

Casey Jones Station Inn, 1943 Highway 45 By-Pass, Jackson, TN 38305-2499 (731-668-3636), is located at Casey Jones Village. The inn offers 53 rooms, all railroad-themed. You can even stay in an original caboose or 1890s railcar.

Highland Place Bed & Breakfast, 519 North Highland Ave., Jackson, TN 38301 (731-427-1472), offers four guestrooms/suites with private baths. After undergoing a three-month makeover, the 1911 mansion was selected as a Designer Showhouse for West Tennessee in 1995. Janice and Glenn Wall are the innkeepers.

KOA Campground (camping), 3291 Shoehorn Drive, Lakeland, TN 38002 (901-388-3053 or 800-KOA-8753, is located just off Monroe Road, just south of the ride's starting point. The campground accommodates tents and RVs. It also features cabins and a free fishing lake.

Bicycle Shops
A.J. Barnes Bicycle Emporium, 2840 Bartlett Road, Memphis, TN 38134-4502 (901-384-0889).

Bicycle City, 29 North Star Drive, Jackson, TN 38305 (731-668-0368 or 800-244-5834).

Bikes Plus Inc., 7970 Giacosa Place, Cordova, TN 38018 (901-385-8788).

Outdoors Inc., 833 Germantown Parkway, Cordova, TN 38018 (901-755-2271).

The Peddler, 1140 Germantown Parkway, Cordova, TN 38018 (901-758-9770).

BICYCLING TENNESSEE
Tour 9: Henderson-Pinson

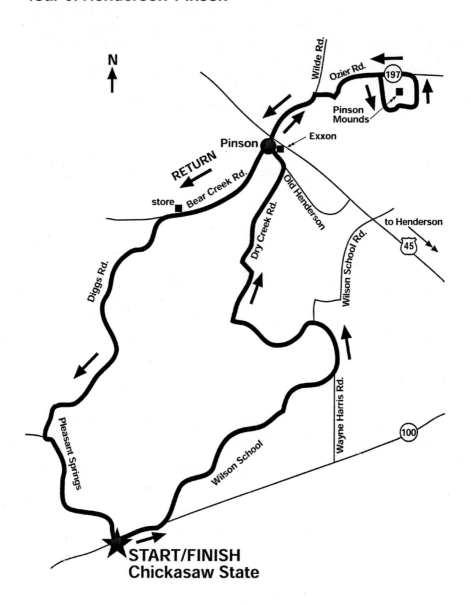

N

Wilde Rd.

Ozier Rd.

197

Pinson Mounds

Pinson

Exxon

RETURN

store

Bear Creek Rd.

Dry Creek Rd.

Old Henderson

Wilson School Rd.

to Henderson

45

Diggs Rd.

Wayne Harris Rd.

100

Pleasant Springs

Wilson School

START/FINISH
Chickasaw State

9. HENDERSON—PINSON

Easy to moderate; 28.5 miles

When Col. Thomas Henderson sent Joel Pinson and other surveyors into the swamps around the Forked Deer and Big Hatchie rivers in the 1820s, they discovered a spring and a large mound. Later, settlers discovered more mounds, hinting at an ancient fortification. R.H. Randle, president of McKenzie Male and Female College, and J.G. Cisco, a Jackson newspaper editor, investigated the mounds again in the late 1800s.

The first extensive study came from William Myers of the Smithsonian Institute in 1916, according to Robert C. Mainfort Jr., in his book *Pinson Mounds: A Middle Woodland Ceremonial Center*. Subsequent archaeological findings determined at least 15 earthworks were built on the site between 200 B.C. and 500 A.D., long before the Indian tribes we know of today inhabited the land. These prehistoric people built the largest mounds for ceremonial purposes, and the smaller mounds for burials.

Realizing its historical value, local citizens convinced the state in the early 1960s to purchase the 1,200-acre property containing most of the mounds. The Pinson Mounds State Archaeological Area is one of two such parks in Tennessee. The Central Mound Group includes the 72-foot Saul's Mound, the second highest mound in the United States. The Eastern Citadel Group includes a 900-foot remnant of an earthen embankment that encircled the area. The Western Mound Group features the 32-foot Ozier Mound, the second largest mound at the site. The Twin Mounds, built in layers of different-colored soils, hold multiple graves.

Pinson Mounds has no camping facilities, but does have picnic sites and six miles of trails, including a nature walk and boardwalk, with an overview of the Forked Deer River. Each September, Archaeofest celebrates Native American culture. The event presents award-winning drum and dance troupes and craft demonstrations. The park's museum, a mound replica, features a 4,500-square-foot exhibit space, an archaeological library and an 80-seat theater. The West Tennessee Regional Archaeology Office is also located at the park. At this writing, Pinson Mounds was one of the first state parks to charge a daily admission fee. Due to budget constraints, the state was testing admission fees at four parks. The initial fees were $3 per vehicle.

This route, a favorite among Jackson cyclists, is very rural. The terrain is relatively flat, with only a few hills. The ride begins about 20 miles south of Jackson. Take U.S. 45 south, then west on State Route 100. The entrance to Chickasaw State Rustic Park will be on your left, a few miles before reaching State Route 125.

Miles

0.0   Start ride at the entrance of Chickasaw State Rustic Park. Head east on State Route 100. Watch for traffic.

Chickasaw State Park is located in both Chester and Hardeman counties. It is situated on some of the highest terrain in West Tennessee. Visitors only use 1,280 acres of the area's 14,384 acres for recreation. The State Forestry Division and the Tennessee Wildlife Resources Agency manage the remaining forest. Hiking and mountain bike trails are open year-round. The town of Henderson is nearby.

Located along the Mobile and Ohio railroad, Henderson was a progressive Madison County community until the Civil War stalemated business in the 1860s, according to Emma Inman Williams in her book, *Historic Madison*. The town rebounded in the early

1870s with three thriving general stores, three saloons, two newspapers, a blacksmith shop, saddle shop and livery stable.

In 1879, the state legislature created a new county out of portions of Madison, Henderson, McNairy and Hardeman counties. Henderson became the seat of the new county, Chester, named for Col. Robert I. Chester, a state representative.

1.2   Turn left onto Wilson School Road.

This is a narrow, country back road. You'll ride through flat farmlands, then some rolling hills, then back to flatlands.

5.0   Wayne Harris Road is to your right. Continue straight on Wilson School Road.

The road surface improves and is clearly divided into two lanes.

6.0   Turn left onto Dry Creek Road.

This is another narrow, country back road, basically flat with one big hill. You'll enter Madison County. Road becomes Casey Road.

10.8   Turn left onto Old Henderson Road at the stop sign at the T-intersection.

You are now entering the community of Pinson. Not long after Joel Pinson discovered the mounds in the early 1800s, the town became a successful farming area, with A.S. Rogers its primary landowner. Rogers started a steam sawmill with E.R. Lancaster and a store with C.H. Hearn. Lancaster became the first postmaster. The community continued to grow with the development of the Mobile and Ohio railroad through town.

11.3   You'll see the white Pinson Methodist Church on your left. Turn right onto Bear Creek Road at the stop sign at the T-intersection. There is no street sign.

11.5   Cross U.S. Highway 45 at the stop sign. Road becomes Ozier Road (also called State Route 197).

There is an Exxon station down U.S. Highway 45 to your right.

12.6   Wilde Road is straight ahead. Bear right, continuing on Ozier Road.

14.2 Turn right into the Pinson Mounds State Archaeological Area. Follow the one-way loop around the park.

Saul's Mound, at 72 feet, is the second highest Native American mound in the United States.

15.8 Turn left onto Ozier Road at the stop sign at the T-intersection.

18.0 Cross U.S. Highway 45 at the stop sign. Road becomes Bear Creek Road.

19.9 Short Road is to your left. A convenience store is on your right.

21.6 You'll see a sign for Tamarack. Turn left onto Diggs Road. Road becomes Bear Creek Road again.

This is a narrow back road. You'll soon enter the community of Deanburg. The terrain becomes a little hilly.

25.5 You'll see the yellow-brick Pleasant Springs Methodist Church to your right and Cagle Cemetery straight ahead. Bear left onto Pleasant Springs Road. There is no street sign.

27.9 Cross State Route 100 and end ride at the entrance of Chickasaw State Park, where the tour began.

For general information on lodging and attractions, contact the Chester County Chamber of Commerce, 130 East Main St., Henderson, TN 38340 (731-989-5222), Jackson-Madison County Convention & Visitors Bureau, 314 East Main St., Jackson, TN 38305 (731-425-8333 or (800-498-4748), or Tourism Association of Southwest Tennessee, P.O. Box 450 / Henderson, TN 38340 (731-423-6937 or 800-967-2576).

Places to Stay

Boxwood Manor, 311 East Main St., Whiteville, TN 38075 (731-254-0165), is a two-story, Victorian-style home built in 1900. Innkeeper Jean Plaisance opened the house for visitors in 1998. The manor features four bedrooms, three of which access a screened porch overlooking the grounds. Whiteville is located east of this route, off State Route 100 in Hardeman County.

Chickasaw State Rustic Park (camping), 20 Cabin Lane, Henderson, TN 38340, (731-989-5141), has three campgrounds. The RV campground has 52 sites, each with water and electrical hookups. The 29-site tent campground has water available. The wrangler campground is for visitors traveling with horses. Modern bathhouses and a playground are convenient to the campsites. Chickasaw also offers 13 cottages along Lake Placid, with fireplaces and televisions.

Highland Place Bed & Breakfast, 519 North Highland Ave., Jackson, Tennessee 38301 (731-427-1472), offers four guestrooms/suites with private baths. After undergoing a three-month makeover, the 1911 mansion was selected as a Designer Showhouse for West Tennessee in 1995. Janice and Glenn Wall are the innkeepers.

Bicycle Shops
Bicycle City, 29 North Star Drive, Jackson, TN 38305 (731-668-0368 or 800-244-5834).

BICYCLING TENNESSEE
Tour 10: Pickwick Dam-Dover

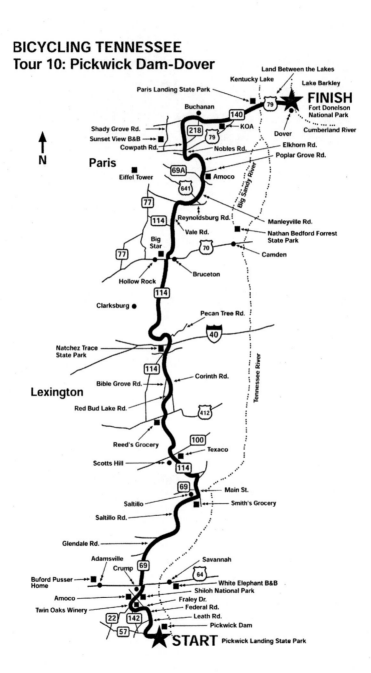

Land Between the Lakes

Kentucky Lake

Lake Barkley

Paris Landing State Park

FINISH
Fort Donelson
National Park

Buchanan

140

218

KOA

Dover

Cumberland River

Shady Grove Rd.

79

Sunset View B&B

Nobles Rd.

Elkhorn Rd.

Cowpath Rd.

Poplar Grove Rd.

N

Paris

Eiffel Tower

69A

Amoco

Big Sandy River

641

Manleyville Rd.

77

Reynoldsburg Rd.

114

Vale Rd.

Nathan Bedford Forrest
State Park

Big
Star

70

Camden

77

Hollow Rock

Bruceton

114

Clarksburg

Pecan Tree Rd.

40

Natchez Trace
State Park

114

Lexington

Bible Grove Rd.

Corinth Rd.

Tennessee River

Red Bud Lake Rd.

412

Reed's Grocery

100

Texaco

Scotts Hill

114

69

Main St.

Saltillo

Smith's Grocery

Saltillo Rd.

Glendale Rd.

Adamsville

Savannah

Crump

69

Buford Pusser
Home

64

White Elephant B&B

Amoco

Shiloh National Park

Fraley Dr.

Twin Oaks Winery

Federal Rd.

22

142

Leath Rd.

57

Pickwick Dam

START Pickwick Landing State Park

10. Pickwick Dam—Dover: A Two-Day Tour

Easy to moderate terrain, 163.1 miles

The fastest way to get from Knoxville to Nashville, Tenn., today is Interstate 40. The east-west corridor is about a three-hour drive. Of course, things have changed since 1779, when Col. John Donelson's river trip from east to middle Tennessee took four months via the Holston, Tennessee, Ohio and Cumberland rivers.

The Tennessee River has been called two rivers in one, according to Donald Davidson in his book *The Tennessee*. Once considered to be a part of the Holston River, which flows all the way from Kingsport, Tenn., on the Virginia border, the Tennessee legislature changed the Tennessee's official beginning in 1890 to the junction of the Holston and French Broad rivers just north of Knoxville. South of Knoxville, the river is fed by the Little Tennessee and Hiwassee tributaries, which oddly flow northwest against the Smoky Mountains barrier.

The Tennessee River has its own strange turns and events. "No other great American river, after pointing its course for 350 miles in one general direction, changes its mind, veers around, and flows for 200 miles in the opposite direction," Davidson writes. "No other great river of the continent, except the distant Mackenzie, flows north for as great a distance as does the Tennessee."

The river goes from Knoxville to Chattanooga, where it flows west into Alabama, through Gunthersville and Muscle Shoals. ·It starts flowing north along the Alabama-Mississippi border and enters Tennessee again at Pickwick Landing. The river then travels north across Tennessee into Kentucky before pouring into the Ohio River at Paducah. Except from the north, the river encloses Middle Tennessee.

The Tennessee provided a dangerous journey when Donelson launched his flagship Adventure on the Holston River near Fort Patrick Henry in December 1779. His mission was to lead a flotilla of 30 flatboats to French Lick via the Holston, Tennessee, Ohio and Cumberland rivers. The voyage included at least 200 pioneers and their household goods destined for the new settlement, later to be named Nashville. Authorities favored the long river journey to the backwoods of east and middle Tennessee. Only skilled hunters and Indian fighters could survive that route.

The winter months made for a slow trip through icy waters. They didn't reach the mouth of the French Broad until March 2, 1780. They passed the mouth of the Little Tennessee on March 4. More settlers from Fort Blackmore joined their journey March 5 at the mouth of the Clinch River. The snow and ice were behind them, but the temperatures remained freezing at night, and rain and wind still hindered the journey.

Once the adverse weather subsided, concern shifted toward the Chickamauga Indians. A year earlier, Col. Evan Shelby of Virginia led 600 men down the Tennessee, conquering 11 Chickamauga towns. Since then, some of the Chickamauga had reportedly returned to those towns. Donelson posted sentinels on the flatboats as a precaution.

The Adventure brigade peacefully passed the Chickamauga until they reached what is today Chattanooga. Then, the Chickamauga fired upon Donelson's group at Moccasin Bend near Lookout Mountain. They killed one passenger and captured the last boat. The rest escaped, only to battle the turbulent waters at the Suck. The Chickamauga then ambushed one boat, which got stuck on a reef. One man drowned, and an infant drowned or was killed, before the rest escaped and caught up with Donelson downstream.

In what is now Alabama, the party miraculously survived the Muscle Shoals rapids and Creek attacks. The trip north across what is now Tennessee went smoothly due to good weather, high water and no Indian attacks. Within one week, Donelson traveled 250 miles to the mouth of the Tennessee at the Ohio River, but it took a month to move the entourage up the Ohio and Cumberland rivers. The Adventure party arrived in French Lick on April 24, 1780.

Adventurers continued to explore and utilize the Tennessee River during the 19th Century. During the Civil War, Federal and Confederate armies fought to control the river, a vital artery for troops and supplies. Navigational improvements made the river an important business resource during the 1800s steamboat era through the early 1900s. Who would have dreamt it would become such a powerful source of energy.

As part of President Franklin Roosevelt's New Deal, Congress created the Tennessee Valley Authority on May 18, 1933. The agency tackled the issues of navigation, flood control, reforestation and erosion control, but it was power production that brought TVA to the forefront. Dams constructed along the Tennessee River produced vast amounts of electricity, bringing industry and jobs to the South. The electric light and modern appliances rapidly changed the quality of life in America, and TVA with reasonable electric rates helped its regional consumers buy into those conveniences.

Today, TVA claims to have the nation's third lowest production costs among the 50 largest electric utilities. Such efficiencies keep TVA reliable and competitive in the wholesale electric market.

This tour takes you across the entire state of Tennessee from south to north, bicycling just west of the Tennessee River, on the western side of the state. This is part of the state's Cycling Tennessee's Highways series. Follow the green Bike Route signs. Pickwick Dam is about 100 miles east of Memphis. To get there, drive east on Poplar Avenue out of Memphis, then continue east on State Route 57 in Collierville.

Day 1
Easy to moderate terrain; 80.1 miles

Miles

0.0   **Start ride at the entrance of Pickwick Landing State Park. Follow State Route 57 to the northwest.**

A popular riverboat stop, TVA chose Pickwick Landing to construct one of its first dams in the 1930s. Construction crews stayed in what is now Pickwick Landing State Park. In the 1970s, TVA turned the area over to the state park system, which developed the inn, cabins, marina and picnic shelters. A new 125-room inn is scheduled to open in early 2001. A $30 million, mid-rise residential condominium project on the lake is also planned.

0.1   **Turn left onto State Route 57 at the four-way stop traffic light. State Route 128 is on the right. Watch for traffic.**

4.0   **You'll see Furniture Corner on your right. Turn right onto Leath Road.**

This portion of the tour to State Route 142 consists of quiet, bumpy backroads. The first stretch takes you through farmlands. There is hardly any traffic, but the road surface is very rough in some places.

8.0   **Turn right onto Federal Road.**

10.2   **Turn left onto Fraley Drive.**

12.0   **Turn left onto Gladden Road (also called Bark Road).**

13.1   **Turn right onto State Route 142 at the stop sign. Watch for traffic.**

13.5   **State Route 142 intersects with State Route 22. Follow State Route 22 north.**

There is an Amoco station on the southwest corner, B & G Mart on the northwest corner and Ed Shaw's Restaurant on the northeast corner.

15.0   **Pass State Route 142 on the left.**

16.9   **The entrance to Shiloh National Military Park is on the right.**

After his victory at Fort Donelson, Union Gen. Ulysses S. Grant moved his 40,000 troops down the Tennessee River. He set up camp near the river at Shiloh Church, awaiting Gen. Don Carlos Buell's Army of Ohio to join him.

Confederate Gen. Albert S. Johnston led a surprise attack on Grant on the morning of April 6, 1862. The rebels pushed back the Federal troops until they reached the "Hornet's Nest" on Sunken Road. With 62 cannons, the Confederates eventually overtook the nest, capturing Gen. Benjamin Prentiss' division, but Grant developed a new line of defense near Pittsburg Landing. Growing tired, both sides fought sluggishly into the night. Johnston was killed, and Gen. P.G.T. Beauregard took command.

By the next day, Union gunboats and Buell's army joined the fight—55,000 troops strong. With 115,000 Confederates killed, wounded or missing, Beauregard withdrew from battle and marched back to Corinth, Miss., which the Union also seized within a month. In September 2000, the U.S. Congress approved incorporating a Civil War battlefield (230 acres) in Corinth, Miss., as part of the Shiloh National Military Park.

You can tour Shiloh National Military Park by bike. There are 14 historic stops along the shady loop.

20.0 Enter the community of Crump.

22.0 Turn left onto U.S. Highway 64. Watch for traffic.

A right turn takes you four miles to the town of Savannah, known as the catfish capital of Tennessee. What began as a ferry crossing and steamboat landing on the Tennessee River evolved into a bustling town in Hardin County.

The Savannah Historic District features 16 historic homes. Most date between 1869 and 1930 in the Queen Anne and Colonial Revival styles. The oldest home, built around 1830, is the Cherry Mansion. Businessman David Robinson built the home. His daughter and son-in-law, W.H. Cherry, resided there when the Union army arrived in 1862. Gen. Grant set up his headquarters in the home on March 17, 1862, until he was summoned down river to Shiloh on April 6.

The Tennessee River Museum at 507 Main Street provides a history of the river that you are paralleling on your journey. Displayed items include artifacts from the Civil War gunboats and the "City of Florence" steamboat as well as the famous Shiloh Effigy Pipe.

22.1 Turn right onto State Route 69. Watch for traffic.

If you continue straight about three miles on U.S. Highway 64, you'll enter the town of Adamsville, hometown of the legendary Buford Pusser. The late sheriff was the subject of three "Walking Tall" movies in the 1970s.

Pusser and his deputies ran aggressive raids in McNairy County, shutting down bootlegging and illegal gambling operations. He busted up 87 whiskey stills in 1965 alone, but there was a price to be paid. During his career, Pusser was shot eight times and stabbed seven times. The backlash climaxed in 1967 when he and his wife, Pauline, were ambushed driving down New Hope Road. The attack killed his wife. Pusser's jaw was shot off. He stepped down as sheriff in 1970.

On August 21, 1974, the day he announced he would portray himself in an upcoming movie, Pusser died when his Corvette mysteriously ran off U.S. Highway 64 and into an embankment.

The Buford Pusser Home and Museum is located appropriately at 342 Pusser Street. Adamsville hosts the Buford Pusser Festival each Memorial Day, which includes the presentation of the county's Law Enforcement Officer of the Year. The town also hosts the annual Adamsville Bluegrass Jamboree.

23.7 Turn right onto Glendale Road.
This portion of the tour to the town of Saltillo consists of rolling hills along the bluffs of the Tennessee River. Traffic is light, and the road surface is smooth.

26.7 Turn right at the intersection of Old Union Road. (You are still on Glendale Road.)

32.2 Turn right onto Saltillo Road.

38.6 You are now entering the town of Saltillo. Turn left onto Oak Avenue.
Weekend-getaway homes have boomed along the Tennessee. The U.S. Corps of Engineers put a stop to such a project on Swallow Bluff Island, four miles north of Saltillo. Recently sold by former Vice President Al Gore's uncle, new owners planned upscale homes and an airstrip for the island. The corps and the state's Department of Environment and Conservation were concerned about the development's effect on sediment and wildlife. Archaeologists want to protect an ancient Indian village and burial grounds, which cover two thirds of the island.

38.9 You'll see Smith's Grocery on the right. Turn left onto Main Street.

39.0 Turn right onto State Route 69.

40.1 Cross the Doe Creek Bridge and enter Decatur County.

43.7 Turn left onto State Route 202.

48.6 Turn left onto State Route 114. Watch for traffic.

A few miles east is Bath Springs. According to Lillye Younger in the Tennessee County History Series' *Decatur County*, Dr. William Hancock named the town after he discovered its sulphur water and built a health resort. Before the Civil War, the community had a successful tanning plant, which extracted acid from tree barks for use in tanning cattle hides.

55.1   Leave Decatur County. Enter Henderson County in Scotts Hill.
The town of Scotts Hill was nearly wiped off the map in 1917, according to G. Tillman Stewart in the Tennessee County History Series' *Henderson County*. A disastrous tornado ripped through the community on May 17. A fire swept through local businesses including the post office, grist mill and blacksmith shop on Oct. 16. Despite the calamities, residents rebuilt their town. It was business as usual by December.

Along State Route 114 in Scotts Hill, you'll pass Scotts Hill Market and Lancaster's Service Station on the left, and Foodland on the right just before you come upon State Route 100.

56.0   You'll see A & W Salvage Grocery on the left and Texaco Food Mart on the right. Cross State Route 100.

61.5   State Route 201 is on the right.

65.7   You'll see Reed's Grocery on the left and T & B Fisher grocery on the right. Cross U.S. Highway 412 and continue on Bible Grove Road.
The town of Lexington, the county seat of Henderson County, is a few miles to the west on U.S. Highway 412. Henderson County witnessed two Civil War battles in 1862—the Battle of Lexington and the Battle of Parker's Crossroads, according to historian Stewart.

After crossing the Tennessee River at Clifton on Oct. 11, Confederate Gen. Nathan Bedford Forrest defeated Col. Robert Ingersol's brigade in Lexington. Forrest moved north toward Kentucky, demolishing railroads supplying Union forces in Mississippi. On his way back to Clifton, Col. Dunham ambushed

Forrest's troops at Parker's Crossroads, just north of Lexington. Forrest was defeated once the Union armies of Col. Fuller and Gen. Sullivan joined the fight. Forrest and the majority of his army escaped.

You'll soon come upon a fork in the road at Bible Grove and Center Grove Church Road. Turn right.

69.6 Turn right onto Redbud Lake Road.

70.8 Turn left onto Corinth Road.

74.8 Enter Natchez Trace State Park and Forest.

Natchez Trace State Park and Forest took its name from the famous Natchez, Miss., to Nashville, Tenn., highway that existed during the 1700s and early 1800s. A western spur of the trace went through a portion of what is now this park. It is not affiliated with today's Natchez Trace, operated by the U.S. Park Service, in middle Tennessee. You can read more about the Natchez Trace in the Chapel Hill—Dickson chapter.

The park is managed jointly by the state Parks and Forestry, and Wildlife Resources divisions. It features four lakes, a swimming beach, 20-unit inn and restaurant, cabins, camping and picnic areas, hiking trails, horse riding trails, firing range and archery range.

In the spring of 1999, a fierce windstorm destroyed nearly 7,300 acres of Natchez Trace's forestland. The damage was unprecedented for a state park or state forest. Salvage was completed in the fall of 1999, but reforestation is expected to take about three years, according to Department of Agriculture officials.

75.4 Intersect with Browns Lake Road. Continue north on Corinth Road.

77.85 You'll come upon a group of red brick structures. State Route 114 intersects from the left. Follow State Route 114 north.

The Park Store is on your left. If you take a right, camping is available within a couple of miles at Cub Lake. If you continue on State

Route 114, you'll also see the Bucksnort Campground shortly on your right.

80.1   Natchez Trace State Park Headquarters and Visitors Center is on the left. End Day 1 ride.

Day 2
Easy to moderate terrain; 84.5 miles

Miles

0.0   Start ride at Natchez Trace State Park Headquarters and Visitors Center. Head north on State Route 114.

0.7   Cross over the eastbound lanes of Interstate 40. Leave Henderson County. Enter Carroll County.

0.8   Cross over the westbound lanes of Interstate 40.

If you turn right onto Pecan Tree Road, you'll come across one the oldest pecan trees in the world. The U.S. Forest Service, which estimates it was planted around 1816, helps preserve the tree using concrete fillings and steel cables. According to local lore, one of Andrew Jackson's soldiers returned home with the tree after the victorious Battle of New Orleans.

3.1   Turn left to continue on State Route 114 (or Yuma Road). Maple Lake Road is on the right.

7.4   Turn right to continue on State Route 114. State Route 424 is on the left.

11.9   Westport Road is on the left.

17.7   Buena Vista Road is on the left.

In the summertime, you'll be flanked by cornfields. You are now entering the community of Hollow Rock. According to Pauline White in a book published by Carroll County's Sesquicentennial Committee, the town is in fact named after a big hollow rock.

Hollow Rock Primitive Baptist Church was established near the rock on Old Stage Road (now U.S. Highway 70) in July 1823. A religious pilgrimage to the church soon began. Every first Sunday of May, people traveled to Hollow Rock for "Foot Washing Day." This event grew into a general, secular outing for picnics and socializing, drawing nearly 3,000 people annually, especially as more stage coach routes and railroads developed in the area. The tradition's popularity waned as nearby Bruceton grew.

22.1 **Turn right onto U.S. Highway 70.**

22.2 **Turn left onto State Route 114.**
Big Star grocery store is on your left; however, no public restrooms are available. The Iron Kettle Restaurant is also on the left.

28.7 **McKenzie-Vale Road is on the left.**

32.6 **Leave Carroll County and enter Henry County.**

34.6 **State Route 114 turns left; continue north on Vale Road.**
You'll pass through a grove of kudzu, then enter back into flat farmlands.

37.6 **You'll see the red brick Manley's Chapel Methodist Church on your right. Turn right onto Reynoldsburg Road.**

39.1 **Turn left onto Manleyville Road. You'll soon see Spring Creek Baptist Church on your left.**

40.5 **Cross U.S. Highway 641. Watch for traffic.**

44.7 **Turn left at the stop light onto State Route 69A. Watch for traffic.**

46.0 **You'll see an Amoco station on your right. Turn right onto Poplar Grove Road.**

47.5 **You'll see the white wood Poplar Grove Methodist Church on your left. Turn left onto Elkhorn Road. You'll soon cross a one-lane bridge.**

52.7 **You'll see Elkhorn Cemetery on your left. Turn left in the community of Elkhorn.**

56.1 **Turn right onto Nobles Road.**

57.8 **You'll see the Tacklebox convenience store on your right. Turn right onto U.S. Highway 79. Watch for traffic.**

Turn left onto U.S. Highway 79 to go to the town of Paris. Henry County was established in 1821. The Tennessee legislature appointed Paris as the county seat two years later.

When is was established in 1823, Paris already had five general stores and three hotels, according to W.P. Green in his book *The City of Paris and Henry County, Tennessee*. The town prospered in the 1800s, largely due to its cotton and tobacco-related industries. It continued its growth as a crossroads of the Louisville and Nashville Railroad between Clarksville and Memphis and the Nashville, Chattanooga and St. Louis Railroad between Nashville and Paducah, Ky.

Paris claims to be the catfish capital of the world. The town hosts the annual World's Biggest Fish Fry the last weekend of April. Of course, while in Paris, you must visit the Eiffel Tower. Students from Christian Brothers University in Memphis created and donated a small replica of the French landmark in 1992. It stands in Memorial Park on Volunteer Drive.

57.9 **Turn left onto State Route 218.**
You'll start to bike some rolling hills as you head toward the community of Buchanan.

59.1 **Turn left onto Cowpath Road.**

63.1 **Turn right onto State Route 140 at the stop sign at the T-intersection. Watch for traffic.**

64.4 **State Route 218 is on the right.**

68.9 **Turn left onto U.S. Highway 79 at the stop sign at the T-intersection. Watch for traffic.**
This is a five-lane highway, but there is a very broad shoulder suitable for bicycle riding. You'll soon see a Conoco station on your right. If you turn right at U.S. Highway 79 and make the next left turn, you'll find a KOA campground.

71.4 **State Route 119 is on the left.**

71.5 **Entrance to Paris Landing State Park.**

Paris Landing, named after a steamboat, was established in the 1850s. Dr. A.J. Weldon, who grew up in Henry County and practiced medicine for 20 years in Buchanan, bought the landing and 3,000 surrounding acres. Supplies arriving at the landing from the Tennessee River were transported to surrounding communities by ox cart.

The 841-acre Paris Landing State Park is on the western shore of what is now Kentucky Lake, one of the largest man-made lakes in the world. The park's marina and campgrounds are on your left. The park's hotel, restaurant, swimming pool and picnic area are on your right.

72.3 **Cross the Tennessee River/Kentucky Lake. Enter Stewart County.** You'll climb a gradual ascending bluff. Piney Campground is on the left.

77.4 **State Route 232 is on the right.**

83.1 **The road to the entrance of Land Between the Lakes is on the left.** Land Between the Lakes is the largest inland peninsula in the United States, bounded by Kentucky Lake on the Tennessee River to the west and Lake Barkley on the Cumberland River to the east. After the completion of the Barkley Dam, President John F. Kennedy created the 170,000-acre national recreation area. Control shifted from the TVA to the U.S. Forest Service in 1999.

The first campground, Rushing Creek, opened in 1964. Today, there are more than 1,000 campsites. Backcountry camping is also allowed with a permit. LBL has more than 200 miles of hiking trails, more than 80 miles of horse trails and 300 miles of undeveloped shoreline. If you are a mountain biker, LBL offers miles of old logging roads perfect for the sport. Two extensive mountain bike trails are suitable for various skill levels, and a trail expansion is in the works.

The Homeplace—1850 recreates life in the mid-19th century, featuring authentically furnished houses and barns, and demonstrations of daily chores. The Nature Station provides staff-led trips, hikes and other educational programs. The 81-seat Golden Pond Planetarium is home of the Western Kentucky Amateur Astronomers. You can also take a tour of the Elk & Bison Prairie Exhibit.

Back on the road, you'll soon be entering the outskirts of the town of Dover. After George Petty built the community's first home on the south bank of the Cumberland River, the town grew in commerce, incorporating in 1836.

84.5   Enter Fort Donelson National Battlefield. End of route.
Since the summer of 1861, the Civil War had been stalemated. The Union couldn't break the Confederate defense line from southwest Missouri to the Appalachian Mountains. Gen. Ulysses S. Grant saw the opportunity to lift the stalemate at Fort Henry and Fort Donelson. Utilizing Flag Officer Andrew H. Foote's gunboats, Grant quickly overtook Fort Henry along the Tennessee River on Feb. 6, 1862. The Union captured less than 100 Confederates; almost 2,500 rebels escaped to Fort Donelson.

On the Cumberland River, Fort Donelson had a stronger position and two powerful river batteries, but 15,000 Union troops soon surrounded it. Union gunboats fired on the fort on Valentine's Day. The river batteries' strong counterattack forced the gunboats to retreat, but Grant's daily reinforcements put the writing on the wall. When the chances arose, Confederate troops escaped with generals John Floyd and Gideon Pillow to Nashville or with Col. Nathan Bedford Forrest across Lick Creek. Remaining Gen. Simon B. Buckner asked for terms. Grant replied, "No terms except an unconditional and immediate surrender can be accepted."

The fall of Fort Henry and Fort Donelson opened up the heart of the South. Significant Union victories at Shiloh and Vicksburg soon followed.

For general information about lodging and attractions, contact, the Carroll County Chamber of Commerce, 19763 East Main St., Huntingdon, TN 38344 (731-986-4664), Decatur County Chamber of Commerce, 139 Tennessee Ave., Parsons, TN 38363 (731-847-42020), Hardin County Chamber of Commerce, 507 Main St., Savannah, TN 38372 (800-552- 3866), Henderson County Chamber of Commerce, P. O. Box 737, 149 Eastern Shores Dr., Lexington, TN 38351 (731-968-2126), Paris-Henry County Chamber of Commerce, 2508 East Wood St., P.O. Box 8, Paris, TN 38242 (731-642-3431 or 800-345-1103), Stewart County Chamber of Commerce, 323 Spring St., Dover, TN 37058 (931-232-8290), or Tourism Association of Southwest Tennessee, P.O. Box 450, Henderson, TN 38340 (731-423-6937 or 800-967-2576).

Places to Stay
Hampton Inn, P.O. Box 1612, Highway 57 S., Pickwick Dam, TN (731-689-3031), is located at the entrance to Shiloh Falls—a planned golf community. It features an outdoor pool, exercise facility and laundry services.

KOA (camping), 6290 E Antioch Rd, Buchanan, TN 38222 (731-642-6895 or 800-KOA-2815), is located off U.S. Highway 79 near Land Between the Lakes and marinas. It offers grassy, shady pull-throughs and tent sites.

Land Between the Lakes (camping), 100 Van Morgan Drive, Golden Pond, KY 42211 (502-924-2000), features three campgrounds. Hillman Ferry, nestled along the shores of Kentucky Lake between Moss Creek and Pisgah Bay, has 380 campsites opened March through November. Full hookups are available. Mountain bikes can be rented at the Outpost Supply Center. Piney Campgrounds, located on the southern tip, offers more than 300 electric sites March through November. It is a favorite for RV users, accommodating large motor homes. Camping shelters are available. You can rent a bike at the Outpost Supply Center and test your skills on the Bike Skills Court. Energy Lake, separated from Lake Barkley by the dam, is popular among camping groups March through October. Electrical hookups are available. Hiking and mountain biking trails surround the campground.

Natchez Trace State Park (camping), 24845 Natchez Trace Road, Wildersville, TN 38388 (731-968-8176 or 800-250-8616), features three campgrounds. There are 146 sites, including 30 tent sites and 116 with electrical hookups. Backcountry camping is allowed with a permit. The park also offers Pin Oak Lodge, a 20-unit facility providing single and double accommodations. Features include a recreation room, playground, tennis courts, and swimming pools.

Paris Landing State Park (camping), 16055 U.S. Highway 79 N., Buchanan, TN 38222-4109 (731-642-4311 or 800-250-8614), has 44 sites with water, electricity, picnic table and grill. Bathhouses and laundry facilities are available. The park inn offers 130 rooms—each offering a Kentucky Lake view from the western shore. It features a restaurant, tennis courts and swimming pools.

Pickwick Landing State Park (camping), P.O. Box 15, Pickwick Dam, TN 38365 (731-689-3135 or 1-800-250-8615), has 48 sites with electrical hookups. The Burton Branch Recreation Area, located on the north shore, has more than 100 tent sites. The Pickwick Resort Inn offers accommodations, lighted tennis courts, swimming pools and a playground. The state began construction on a new 125-room inn in 1999.

Riverfront Plantation Inn, 190 Crow Lane, Dover, TN 37058 (931-232-9492), is a restored Civil War-era home, operated by Fulton and Lynn Combs. Adjacent Fort Donelson, the inn offers spectacular views of the Cumberland River. The five guestrooms have private baths and screened porches.

Sunset View Bed & Breakfast, 1330 Shady Grove Road, Paris, TN 38242 (731-642-4778 or 888-642-4778), is a quiet 12-acre getaway just south-west of the route, off U.S. Highway 79. The farmhouse offers three gue-strooms and a converted Greyhound bus, which sleeps four, putting you even closer to the outdoors. Innkeepers Bill and Peggy Grooms have bicy-cles and helmets you can borrow to ride the country roads. You can also fish in the pond across the street.

White Elephant Bed & Breakfast, 304 Church St., Savannah, TN 38372 (731-925-6410), is a two-story, Victorian home on the National Register of Historic Places. There are three guestrooms. The two parlors feature high ceilings, curved bay windows and original oak fireplace mantels. Victorian-era and Civil War memorabilia adorn the home. Ken and Sharon Hansgen are the innkeepers.

Bicycle Shops
Bicycle Center of Clarksville, 1450 Madison St., Clarksville, TN 37040 (931-647-2453).

Bicycle City, 29 North Star Drive, Jackson, TN 38305 (731-668-0368 or 800-244-5834).

Bike World, 758 W Poplar Ave, Collierville, TN 38017 (901-853-5569).

BICYCLING TENNESSEE
Tour 11: Hurricane Mills-Waverly

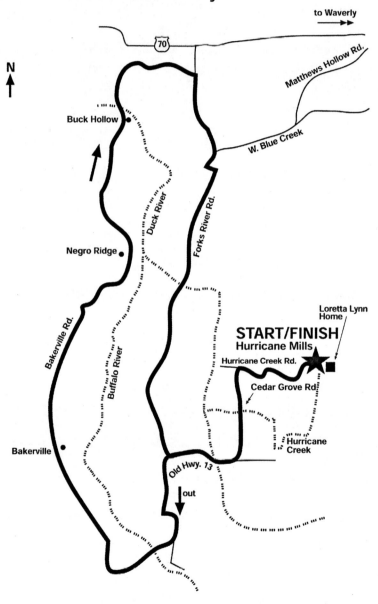

11. Hurricane Mills—Waverly

Moderate to difficult terrain, rolling hills throughout the ride with a few steep climbs; 36.3 miles

For decades, country music represented the voice of the male. During the first half of the 1900s, the few prominent female performers were limited to songs of virtuous content, and extensive touring was not a part of their itinerary. Even as more women entered the charts in the 1950s, most lyrics were squeaky clean, and their country music leaned more toward pop influences.

A coal miner's daughter from Butcher's Hollow, Ky., was one of the first artists to change that trend.

In 1961, with the encouragement and guidance of her husband, Mooney, Loretta Lynn began playing honky tonks around Custer, Wash., where they had lived and raised four children since 1951. After several appearances on singer Buck Owens' local television show in Tacoma, Norman Burleigh sent her to Los Angeles to record for his Zero label. One of the recordings, "I'm a Honky Tonk Girl" became a regional hit.

Mooney and Loretta made a promotional trip to Nashville, driving across the country, stopping at hundreds of radio stations along the way, plugging her record. In Nashville, she met Doyle and Teddy Wilburn of Sure Fire Music. When they soon called Loretta to return and record a demo, she and her family moved to Nashville. The demo, "Fool Number One," was given to singer Brenda Lee in exchange for a contract with Decca. Loretta's first major recording, "Success," was a No. 1 hit, followed by "Before I'm Over You" and "Mr. And Mrs. Used-to-Be."

Loretta became one of the most successful country music artists, remaining true to an authentic, hard country sound.

The success led to the 1966 purchase of 1,200 acres just east of the Tennessee River in western Tennessee. In fact, the Lynns bought the whole town of Hurricane Mills. They moved into a 14-room antebellum farmhouse on the property, but by no means became secluded. In fact, they opened up the Loretta Lynn Dude Ranch to fans. The campgrounds surrounding the home have been providing fun, family getaways for three decades.

A guided tour, available April through October, takes visitors through the main level of the mansion, where Mooney and Loretta lived for more than 20 years. The home tour includes the kitchen seen in Loretta's popular Crisco commercials, Mooney's jeep seen in the movie "Coal Miner's Daughter" and Loretta's Cadillac, her favorite car. Across the Hurricane Creek in Westerntown, visitors can visit a simulated underground coal mine, Butcher's Hollow Home Place—a replica of Loretta's childhood home, and Loretta's tour bus.

Mooney died recently, but Loretta still lives nearby. In fact, in addition to her numerous road dates, she performs several times a year at the ranch. In 2000, Loretta released "Still Country," her first new album since 1988, and was writing *Still Woman Enough*, a sequel to her 1976 autobiography, *Coal Miner's Daughter*.

Loretta Lynn Ranch is located about 80 miles west of Nashville. Take exit 143 off Interstate 40 and head north on State Highway 13 towards Waverly, Tenn. In about seven miles, take a left on Hurricane Mills Road. After winding a few miles through the Loretta Lynn Ranch, you'll come to Westerntown. There is extra parking in the back of the Post Office.

This bicycle route is quite hilly throughout the ride. Most of it would be qualified as rolling hills; however, there are at least two hills of significant grade. Also, there is no store directly on the route. So bring snacks and beverages, accordingly. You can stock up at Loretta Lynn's Stagecoach Hill campground store, and conveniences are available in Waverly, a few miles north of the intersection of Forks River Road and Bakerville Road on the route.

Miles

0.0 **Start ride at Hurricane Mills Post Office. Head west on Hurricane Mills Road.**

Loretta Lynn's Home is located just across the non-motorized traffic bridge over Hurricane Creek.

The Memphis Hightailers start a ride from Loretta Lynn's home in Hurricane Mills. Photo by Melanie LaRue.

2.0 **You'll see a big white house on a hill to your left. Turn left onto Cedar Grove Road.**

2.5 **Cross Hurricane Creek.**

3.7 **Turn right onto Old Highway 13 at the stop sign at the T-intersection.**

4.3 **Cross the Duck River.**

6.8 **Turn right onto Bakerville Road.**

7.4 **Cross the Buffalo River.**

8.0 **Enter Bakerville town limits.**

After an uphill, you'll enter a flat stretch, but there will be a drop off to your right. You'll also experience a few sharp curves before the next uphill.

10.8 Pass the white Bakerville Church to the right.

13.8 Dangerous intersection at Dug Hill Lane.
The road intersects with a dirt road. The terrain will flatten for awhile.

14.1 You'll begin to ascend a small mountain, one mile straight up.

17.1 You'll climb a short, steep hill, followed by a winding descent.

19.2 Cross the Duck River.
After crossing the bridge, there is a nice place to rest on the west side next to the river. The bridge is followed by another long ascent, this one more gradual.

22.1 Turn right onto Forks River Road.
If you need refreshments or want a longer ride, turn left here to continue on Bakerville Road. Within two to three miles, you'll intersect with U.S. Highway 70 in Waverly. If you turn onto Highway 70 and go east about a half mile, turn left on South Clydeton. You'll see E.W. James' Grocery up ahead.

If you want an even longer ride, turn left onto U.S. Highway 70, an official state bike route. About 10 miles west, you'll enter the town of New Johnsonville on the Tennessee River with several accommodations and conveniences. Continue west across the Hickman Lockhart Bridge. About 20 miles west of Waverly, Nathan Bedford Forrest State Park lies just north of U.S. Highway 70 on the Tennessee River.

Back on the Loretta Lynn tour, continuing south on Forks River Road, you'll encounter rolling hills, a little steeper than the rolling hills at the beginning and ending of this tour.

26.8 Cross a one-lane bridge over the Duck River.

31.0 Turn left onto State Highway 13 at the stop sign at the T-intersection.

32.1 Cross the Duck River.

32.6 Turn left onto Cedar Grove Road.

33.8 Cross Hurricane Creek.

34.3 Turn right onto Hurricane Mills Road at the stop sign at the T-intersection.

36.3 End ride at the Hurricane Mills Post Office, where the tour began.

JJ's Country Kitchen is located across the street from the Hurricane Mills Post Office. Loretta Lynn's Kitchen and Gifts, and the Buffalo River Grill are located near the Interstate 40 exit, as well as several motels.

For general information about lodging and attractions, contact the Humphreys County Chamber of Commerce, 124 E. Main St., Waverly, TN 37185 (931-296-4865).

Places to Stay

Best Western, Interstate 40 and U.S. Hwy. 13 South, Hurricane Mills, TN 37078 (931-296-4251), offers 89 rooms on 15 pastoral acres. Services include outdoor pool, whirlpool and cable television. Rooms with refrigerator and microwave are available. Small dogs are allowed.

Loretta Lynn's Family Campground (camping), General Delivery, Hurricane Mills, TN 37078 (931-296-7700), accommodates RVs and tents, including 200 pull-through sites with full hookups. Restrooms with private showers are available for campers. The park also has Boone Hill Cabins and Stagecoach Hill Log Cabins, with modern conveniences and a linen service. Activities such as campfire shows, ATV races and horseback riding are common during the peak season.

Nolan House Bed and Breakfast, 375 Highway 13 N., Waverly, TN 37185 (931-296-2511), is a National Historic Register home located 10 minutes from Loretta Lynn's Dude Ranch. An Irish immigrant built the Victorian style house in 1870. Patrick O'Lee currently operates the bed and breakfast. Each of the three guestrooms has a private bath, fireplace and entrance to the east porch. A garden offers a gazebo, croquet and horseshoes.

Bicycle Shops
Bicycle City, 29 North Star Drive, Jackson, TN 38305 (901-668-0368 or 800-244-5834).

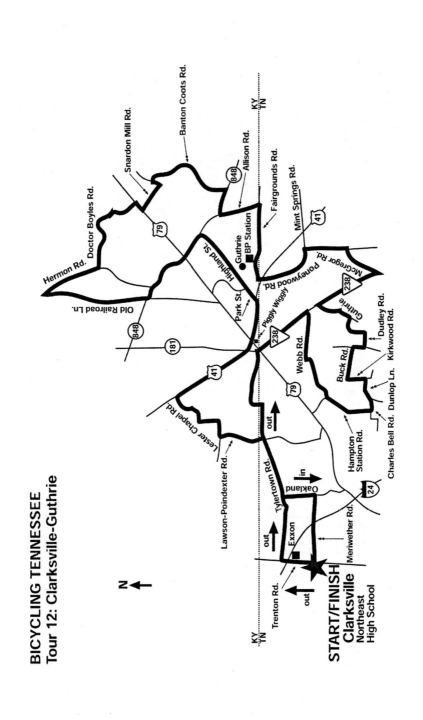

BICYCLING TENNESSEE
Tour 12: Clarksville-Guthrie

N

Doctor Boyles Rd.
Hermon Rd.
Snardon Mill Rd.
Banton Coots Rd.
Old Railroad Ln.
848
79
848
181
Park St.
Highland St.
Guthrie
BP Station
Allison Rd.
848
Fairgrounds Rd.
Mint Springs Rd.
41
Poneywood Rd.
McGregor Rd.
Piggly Wiggly
238
238
Guthrie
41
Lester Chapel Rd.
Lawson-Poindexter Rd.
Webb Rd.
79
Buck Rd.
Dudley Rd.
Kirkwood Rd.
Dunlop Ln.
Charles Bell Rd.
out
Tylertown Rd.
out
in
Oakland
Hampton
Station Rd.
24
Trenton Rd.
out
Exxon
Meriwether Rd.
START/FINISH
Clarksville
Northeast
High School

KY
TN

12. CLARKSVILLE—GUTHRIE

Easy to moderate, relatively flat throughout the ride except for a few hills in the last 12 miles; 62.1 miles

This may be the first book that discusses both cycling and tobacco. It is difficult not to think about tobacco as you crisscross the Tennessee and Kentucky border here. As the vast amount of acreage indicates, the area is a major producer of tobacco. According to the National Agricultural Statistics Service, Tennessee's Montgomery County produces more than 7.7 million pounds of tobacco annually. Across the border, Kentucky's Todd County produces more than 5.2 million pounds of tobacco.

During the 19th Century, Clarksville became a world center for dark-fired tobacco, according to Charles M. Waters in his book, *Historic Clarksville: The Bicentennial Story 1784-1984*. With 7 percent nicotine, it was called "the strongest tobacco in the world." When the Clarksville Tobacco Exchange formed in 1858, the world's leading tobacco buyers joined.

Tobacco growers faced a crisis between 1900 and 1904, when three major tobacco companies tried to control the market. According to Waters, American Tobacco, Imperial and Regi formed a Tobacco Trust that forced out independent buyers, decreasing tobacco prices to four cents a pound. In addition, the U.S. government imposed a federal tax on tobacco.

To protest these trade restraints, 5,000 growers met in Guthrie, Ky., on Sept. 24, 1904, and formed the Dark Tobacco District Planters Protective Association of Kentucky and Tennessee. The Tobacco Trust responded by boycotting the association's warehouses and offering eight to 10 cents a pound to non-members, dubbed "hillbillies" by the association.

In its third year, 25,000 growers and others assembled in Guthrie to rally support for the association. Although not officially sanctioned by the group, some members formed the Night Riders in 1906. This secret fraternal order destroyed hillbilly plant beds and barns. Confrontations occasionally turned violent, but these guerrilla tactics succeeded in increasing tobacco prices. The government soon ruled the Tobacco Trust violated the Sherman Anti-Trust Act and repealed the six-cent federal tax on tobacco. The association disbanded in 1915.

Lightning Cycles Inc. of Franklin usually hosts its Labor Day Century in this area. It's a great course for your first long, organized ride because of the flatlands. Another area ride is the Clarksville Rotary Annual Metric (CRAM). To get to the start, take Interstate 24 north of Nashville, then take the Trenton Road (Highway 48 South) exit in Clarksville. Head south on Trenton Road. Northeast High School is on the left.

Miles

0.0 **Start ride at Northeast High School. Head north on Trenton Road. You'll see an Exxon station on the right before crossing Interstate 24.**

Red Paint Hill was a happy sight for Moses Refroe, a member of John Donelson's flotilla. The flotilla is described in the Pickwick Dam—Dover chapter. Here, he and several others departed The Adventure trip in 1780, to begin a settlement where the Cumberland and Little Red rivers meet. Indian attacks, however, dissolved the settlement after several months, according to author Waters. Those that survived fled southeast to French Lick, later to become Nashville.

After the Revolutionary War, North Carolina took control of the lands that would make up Middle Tennessee. John Montgomery and Martin Armstrong developed a town around Red Paint Hill. In

1787, the North Carolina Legislature established the town as Clarksville, named after General George Rogers Clark. It would soon become the seat of Tennessee's Montgomery County.

Today, Clarksville is the state's fifth largest city. For much of the past century, the town's economy has depended on Fort Campbell, a military reservation that is primarily located in Montgomery County, but also spreads into Stewart County and Kentucky. During World War II, the U.S. Army opened the camp, housing almost 100,000 recruits in 1944. Since that war, as with most U.S. military bases, its purpose has shifted several times. It has primarily served as home for the 101st Airborne Division. The base is the world's largest army airfield.

Famous Clarksville natives include Clarence Saunders, founder of the first self-service grocery, Wilma Rudolph, who won three gold track medals in the 1960 Olympics and character actor Charles Boillin Watts.

Local points of interest include the 1858 Smith Trahern home, the L & N Train Station, the Clarksville-Montgomery County Museum and Dunbar Cave State Natural Area. At this writing, the state was seeking a new owner to take over Dunbar Cave. Annual events in Clarksville include the Old Time Fiddlers Championship, Clarksville Rodeo, Spring Jubilee and German Octoberfest.

A tornado devastated Clarksville in January 1999. Landing near the Cumberland River, the twister traveled five miles, ripping through downtown, Austin Peay State University and a residential neighborhood. The good news was no one died. In fact, only five people were hurt, with minor injuries. The bad news was it destroyed dozens of historic buildings. As of this writing, the city was still struggling to restore its downtown, particularly the historic county courthouse, which was severely damaged.

1.1   Turn right onto Tylertown Road. You'll soon cross the Kentucky state line.

7.9   Turn right onto State Route 181.

8.0   Cross U.S. 79 at the traffic light. Watch for traffic. Road crosses
      the Tennessee state line and becomes State Route 238 (also called
      Port Royal Road).

10.1 Turn right onto Webb Road.

13.0 Turn left onto Hampton Station Road at the stop sign at the Y-
      intersection.
      You are passing through the community of Hampton Station.

14.6 Turn left onto Charles Bell Road.

14.9 Turn left onto Dunlop Lane.

15.7 You'll see a church on your left. Turn left onto Kirkwood Road at
      the stop sign at the T-intersection.
      You are passing through the community of Kirkland.

16.3 Turn right onto Buck Road. Continue right on Buck Road when
      it intersects with J.H. Haley Road to the left.

17.5 Turn left onto Dudley Road.

18.6 Turn left onto Guthrie Road at the stop sign at the T-intersection.

19.9 Turn right onto Port Royal Road at the stop sign at the T-inter-
      section (no street sign).

22.1 Turn left onto McGregor Road.
      If you continue straight, you'll come to the Port Royal State
      Historical Area.

      Port Royal was one of the earliest communities and trading cen-
      ters in Tennessee. Old Indian trails and stagecoach routes crossed
      the Red River here, heading to the West. It was an encampment site
      for the Trail of Tears (see below). The state of Tennessee dedicated
      Port Royal as an historic area in 1978. Today, the 26-acre park fea-
      tures a museum, hiking trails, picnic areas and a covered, wooden
      bridge. At this writing, the state was seeking a new owner to take
      over Port Royal.

      A flood washed away the first bridge on this site in 1866.
      Another covered bridge, built in 1904, serviced the public until

1955, when a new concrete and steel bridge was built nearby. The old covered bridge deteriorated, collapsing into the Red River in 1972. The state built a replica of the covered bridge on the site in 1977. Unfortunately, heavy winds and rains disabled the structure on June 10, 1998.

24.7 **Turn left onto Poneywood Road. Continue left on Pineywoods Road after it intersects with Mint Springs Road to the right.**

26.5 **Cross U.S. 41, entering Guthrie, Ky. You'll see a BP Station straight ahead. Continue on Fairgrounds Road.**

28.8 **You'll see a two-story farmhouse on your left. Turn left onto Allison Road.**

30.2 **Turn right onto State Route 848.**

31.1 **Turn left onto Banton Coots Road.**

33.6 **Turn left onto Snardon Mill Road at the stop sign at the T-intersection.**

35.1 **Turn right onto U.S. 79 at the stop sign at the T-intersection. Watch for traffic.**

35.4 **Turn left onto Doctor Boyles Road.**

38.3 **Turn right onto Hermon Road at the stop sign at the T-intersection.**

You are passing through the community of Hermon, Ky.

40.3 **Turn left onto Old Railroad Lane.**

43.9 **Turn left onto State Route 848.**

45.7 **Cross U.S. 79 at the stop sign.**

46.3 **Turn right onto Highland Street. Highland Street eventually becomes Park Street.**

You'll soon enter the town of Guthrie. The town's most famous native was Robert Penn Warren, who won Pulitzer Prizes for both poetry and fiction. The area's tobacco war in the early 1900s inspired his 1939 novel, *Night Riders*.

Right after crossing the railroad tracks, there is a Chevron station on the right at Ewing Street.

48.8 **Continue straight on Park Street (also called U.S. Highway 41).**

50.5 **After passing the Piggly Wiggly grocery on the right, you'll cross U.S. 79 at the traffic light. Watch for traffic.**

To you, the Trail of Tears sign may refer to the hills you are finally encountering. Actually, it refers to the great injustice the United States imposed on Native Americans. The Cherokees signed 18 treaties between 1785 and 1902 that gave up tribal lands. President Martin Van Buren said, "No state can achieve proper culture, civilization and progress in safety as long as Indians are permitted to remain."

The Treaty of New Echota, signed on Dec. 29, 1835, was the most damaging for the Cherokee, according to Jeanne Williams in her book, *Trails of Tears: American Indians Driven from Their Lands.* The tribe reluctantly sold up to 8 million acres in the southeastern United States. The government demanded that the Cherokee move to western reservations that later became part of Arkansas, Oklahoma and Kansas.

Cherokee Major John Ridge led 600 Indians to the western lands shortly after the treaty was signed. More than 2,400 Indians followed in June 1838 by boat via the Tennessee, Ohio and Mississippi rivers. The bulk of Cherokees, however, waited until the last minute to leave. A drought prevented travel by the Tennessee River. The remaining Cherokees, living in detention camps, organized their own overland departure. The government provided $65 per person for the 800-mile journey.

Chief John Ross held the last council meeting near what is now Charleston, Tenn., and 13,000 Indians departed in the winter of 1838. A total of 4,000 of these Cherokees died along the Trail of Tears, mostly from exposure. The Western Cherokee welcomed the last arrivals on March 25, 1839.

53.6 **Turn left onto Lester Chapel Road (no street sign).**

55.8 **Turn left onto Lawson-Poindexter Road.**

57.3 Turn right onto Tylertown Road. You'll soon cross the Tennessee state line.

59.4 Turn left onto Oakland Road.

60.5 Turn right onto Meriwether Road.

62.1 End ride at Northeast High School on your left, where the tour began.

For general information about lodging and attractions, contact the Clarksville/Montgomery County Tourist Commission, P.O. Box 883, Clarksville, TN 37041 (931-648-0001), or Todd County Chamber of Commerce, 1209 S. Virginia St., Hopkinsville, KY 42240 (502-885-9096).

Places to Stay

Hachland Hall Bed & Breakfast, 1601 Madison St., Clarksville, TN 37043 (931-647-4084), hosts up to 25 people. The main inn's architecture is Federal. There are also three log cottages, one where President Andrew Jackson stayed as his Hermitage was being constructed near Nashville. Innkeepers are cookbook author Phila R. Hach and her husband, Adolf, an international tobacco exporter.

Holiday Inn, 3095 Wilma Rudolph Blvd., Clarksville, TN 37040 (931-648-4848), features indoor and outdoor pools, whirlpool and exercise facility. Pets are allowed.

Bicycle Shops

Bicycle Center of Clarksville, 1450 Madison St., Clarksville, TN 37040 (931-647-2453).

Van Camp's Bicycle Shop, 1352 Fort Campbell Blvd., Clarksville, TN 37042 (931-645-4858).

BICYCLING TENNESSEE
Tour 13: Chapel Hill-Burns

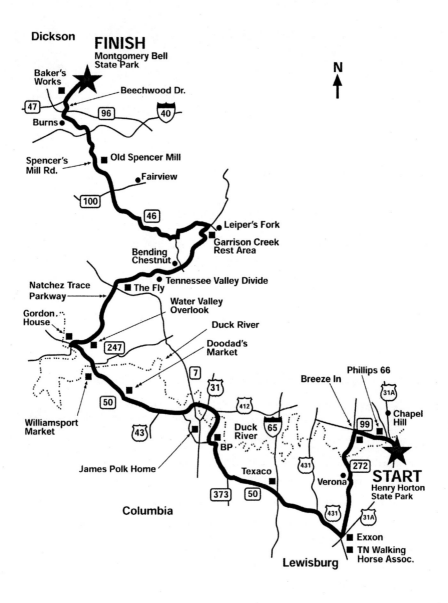

Dickson

FINISH
Montgomery Bell
State Park

Baker's
Works

Beechwood Dr.

47

96

40

Burns

Spencer's
Mill Rd.

Old Spencer Mill

Fairview

100

46

Leiper's Fork

Garrison Creek
Rest Area

Bending
Chestnut

Tennessee Valley Divide

Natchez Trace
Parkway

The Fly

Water Valley
Overlook

Gordon
House

Duck River

247

Doodad's
Market

7

Phillips 66

31

Breeze In

31A

Williamsport
Market

50

31

412

99

Chapel
Hill

43

Duck
River

65

BP

James Polk Home

Texaco

431

Verona

272

START
Henry Horton
State Park

Columbia

373

50

431

31A

Exxon

TN Walking
Horse Assoc.

Lewisburg

N

13. Chapel Hill—Burns: A Two-Day Tour

Moderate terrain; 101.0 miles

During the 18th Century, Mississippi Valley settlers shifted allegiance from the French, British and Spanish governments. In the Treaty of San Lorenzo that was signed on Oct. 16, 1795, the Spaniards ceded the land north of what is today Louisiana and east of the Mississippi River to the United States. Commerce with the rest of the nation, however, was limited. Flatboats could only transport goods downstream from the Mississippi River to Natchez, Miss. Transport north was limited to long adventures via the Gulf of Mexico and Atlantic Ocean, or dangerous, overland treks through the wilderness. A letter from Philadelphia reached Europe as fast as it reached Natchez.

Francis Baily helped carve a communications and trade route in the summer of 1797, according to William C. Davis in his book, *A Way Through the Wilderness*. Although not the first to make the trip, Baily and his 13 companions set out to explore the old Indian foot paths between Natchez and Nashville, Tenn. Their 450-mile journey took them northeast along the Path of the Choctaw Nation, the Choctaw-Chickasaw Trail and the Chickasaw Trace.

At times, Baily's men battled hunger, poison ivy and mosquitoes. The terrain varied from sandy and flat to rough and hilly. Frequently, they had to down trees to cross rivers and streams. Their encounters with the Choctaw, Chickasaw and Cherokee Indians were all friendly. Several times, the Indians pointed the expedition down the right track to their destination. The group quietly passed unnoticed near the less-friendly Creek villages. Expected to take three weeks, the journey lasted from July 4 to July 27.

After the United States established the Mississippi Territory, the government began to explore ways to provide overland communication and trade, according to Davis. Postmaster General Joseph Habersham awarded Abijah Hunt a contract in January 1800 to carry mail between Natchez and Nashville. Congress authorized building a post road in April 1800 between the two towns. Settlers and Indians developed partnerships to establish inns, ferries and trading posts along the route. A combination of federal troops and private contractors completed the road in 1809. By 1825, however, fewer travelers took this road. New routes and steam-powered transportation upstream on the Mississippi River led to its demise. Curiously, it was during this time that the road began to be called the Natchez Trace.

In the 1930s, the National Park Service began constructing today's Natchez Trace Parkway, following closely along the old trace between Natchez and Nashville. The road is closed to hauling and commercial vehicles, and provides leisurely car or bike travel year-round. History and nature exhibits, hiking trails, picnic areas, campgrounds, and bed and breakfasts dot the trace. The only visitor center is located in Tupelo, Miss.

This tour takes you over rolling hills through the heart of Tennessee, including part of the Natchez Trace Parkway. This is part of the state's Cycling Tennessee's Highways series. Follow the green Bike Route signs. Organized rides along the parkway include Race the Trace and the Columbia Cycling Club's Scenic Middle Tennessee Century. The tour starts at Henry Horton State Park, about 60 miles south of Nashville. To get there, head south on Interstate 65 from Nashville. Take State Route 99 to the east. Turn right on U.S. Highway 31A. The state park is on your left.

Day 1
Moderate terrain; 36.3 miles

Miles

0.0 **Begin ride at the entrance of Henry Horton State Park. Head north on U.S. Highway 31A.**

Henry Horton State Park is named for Tennessee's 36th governor. The park is located along the Duck River on Horton's former estate. The 1,140 acres include a resort inn and scenic golf course.

Horton was born in Alabama in 1866. He graduated from Winchester College in 1888. After teaching school for six years, he began practicing law in Tennessee, eventually serving in the state house and senate. As speaker of the senate in 1927, Horton succeeded Governor Austin Peay upon his death. Horton was elected governor in 1929.

During the Democrat's term, Tennessee abolished the state land tax, created a state aeronautics division and developed a secondary road system. After being charged with fraud, but not convicted, for his involvement with the Lea-Caldwell banks during the Depression, Horton did not seek re-election in 1933. He died in 1934.

Revolutionary War veterans from North Carolina were the first to settle in Marshall County, named for Supreme Court Justice John Marshall.

0.2 **Cross the Duck River.**

0.6 **You'll see a Phillips 66 station on the left. Turn left onto State Route 99. There is a broad shoulder. Watch for traffic.**

1.9 **Cross the railroad tracks.**

4.3 **You'll see the Breeze In Market on the left. Turn left onto State Route 272.**

6.7 **Cross the Duck River.**

10.0 Enter the community of Verona. Verona Market will be on your left.

Verona is the hometown of Buford Ellington, who alternated Tennessee's governorship with fellow Democrat, Frank Clement, for 18 years. He served from 1959 to 1963 and from 1967 to 1971. At first a segregationist, Ellington switched his position. His administration oversaw the peaceful Nashville sit-ins, some of the earliest and best-organized civil rights events during the movement. State liquor laws were also liberalized during his terms. Ellington died in 1972.

11.2 Over pass the railroad tracks.

12.1 Pass Snell Road on the right.

15.0 Turn right onto U.S. Highway 31A. Watch for traffic.

Lewisburg, the Marshall County seat, was named for explorer Meriwether Lewis. You can read more about Meriwether Lewis in the Lawrenceburg—Hohenwald chapter. Lewisburg was also the hometown of newspaperman Jim McCord.

McCord, born in Tennessee in 1879, served 13 terms as Lewisburg mayor and one term as U.S. congressman, before being elected Tennessee governor in 1945. He fought Edward H. Crump's political machine out of Memphis and implemented the state's first sales tax, earmarking it for education and teacher retirement. The tax cost him re-election for a third term, but he remained active in state government. McCord died in 1968.

15.1 Turn right onto U.S. Highway 431 (also called North Ellington Parkway) at the traffic light. Watch for traffic. Exxon and BP stations will be on your left.

If you turned left on U.S. Highway 431, the Tennessee Walking Horse Breeders' and Exhibitors' Association is about one mile on the left. The association began in Lewisburg in 1935 with 208 registered horses. Today, more than 350,000 arc registered.

The Tennessee Walking Horse is the only breed named after a state. In addition to endurance, Southern plantation owners wanted a smoother ride from their horses. The average horse's up-and-down movement meant long, uncomfortable days as the owners surveyed their land and workers.

This horse, developed primarily from Standardbreds, Morgans and Thoroughbreds, provides three, easy riding gaits. With the flat-foot walk, the horse hits the ground one hoof at a time in rhythm, nodding its head with each step. The running walk is a faster flat-foot walk. The canter is a high and rolling gait, perfected by championship horses. The gentle ride also reflects the breed's gentle personality. Roy Rogers' horse, Trigger Jr., was a Tennessee Walking Horse.

In the days leading up to Labor Day, nearby Shelbyville hosts the annual Tennessee Walking Horse National Celebration. Started in 1939, this event has turned into a 10-day festival, with up to 2,000 competing horses and more than $650,000 in prizes. The Celebration peaks with the selection of the elite world champions and the year's world grand champion.

16.1   **Over pass the railroad tracks.**

16.5   **Pass State Route 417 on your left.**

17.0   **U.S. Highway 431 intersects with State Route 50. Veer left, continuing on State Route 50. Watch for traffic.**

There is a broad shoulder for the next 15 miles but no trees near the road to protect you from the elements.

20.1   **Pass South Berlin Road on the right.**

21.6   **Enter Maury County.**

Maury County calls itself the Antebellum Homes Capital of Tennessee. Several events throughout the year offer self-guided home tours with hostesses at each site. These pilgrimages include the Spring Tour of Homes in Mt. Pleasant in May, the Majestic

Middle Tennessee Fall Tour in Columbia in September, and the Tennessee Plantation Christmas in Columbia in December.

But do not accuse Maury County of strictly living in the past. The state-of-the-art GM Saturn plant is located in Spring Hill. But to blend with the setting, the plant was designed to be hardly noticeable from the roadway. A renovated historic barn serves as its Welcome Center, and the surrounding land is still farmed. Tours are available with advance reservations. Spring Hill hosts periodic homecomings for Saturn owners, featuring free games and concerts. The manufacturer now has 400 retailers in the United States, 125 in Canada and 22 in Japan. It recently opened another plant in Wilmington, Del., and announced a $1.5 billion expansion plan for Spring Hill, to build its new SUV model and next generation S-series small coupe and sedan.

23.2 Cross Interstate 65. You'll soon see a Texaco Food Mart on your right.

The terrain begins to get a little more hilly.

28.6 Pass State Route 373 on your left.

32.3 Cross the railroad tracks.

32.5 You'll see a BP station on the right. Turn right onto Columbia East Bypass (also called Tom J. Hitch Parkway).

33.6 Cross Mapleash Avenue at the flashing yellow traffic light.

35.8 Cross the Duck River.

35.9 Turn left onto U.S. Highway 412 at the traffic light. There is a broad shoulder. Watch for traffic.

36.3 End ride on Day 1 at the intersection of U.S. Highway 412 and U.S. Highway 31.

Take U.S. Highway 31 south about two miles to enter downtown Columbia. The ancestral home of James K. Polk, our 11th president, is at 301 West 7th Street.

Polk moved with his family from North Carolina to the Tennessee frontier when he was 10. Although he had less than three years of formal schooling, he was admitted into North Carolina University as a sophomore. He graduated with honors in math and literature. He moved to Nashville to study, before opening his first law practice in Columbia.

At 27, Polk was elected to the state legislature. At 29, he was elected to the U.S. Congress, backing the policies of fellow Tennessee Democrat Andrew Jackson. He served in Congress for 14 years, including two terms as Speaker of the House, before returning home to run for governor. He served one term as Tennessee governor, but lost two re-election bids. Nevertheless, not forgetting his party loyalty, the Democrats chose Polk as their dark-horse, presidential nominee in 1844. He won the election against popular Whig Henry Clay from Kentucky.

During his presidency, Polk realized his vision for a continental nation. He negotiated the Oregon Territory south of the 49th parallel away from Great Britain. After a two-year war, Mexico ceded New Mexico and California. During his term, the United States acquired more than 800,000 square miles in the West, expanding its boundary to the Pacific Ocean. His administration also lowered tariffs and established an independent Federal Treasury.

Polk kept his campaign promise to only serve one term. He returned to Tennessee in March 1849, where he died of cholera three months later.

The ancestral home in Columbia is Polk's only surviving residence, besides the White House. His father, Samuel Polk, built the Federal-style house in 1816 while the future president was away at college. Polk moved to the residence after graduating in 1818. He stayed with his parents there until his marriage to Sarah Childress in 1824. This was his home when he began his political career, being elected to the state legislature.

The home features items from throughout Polk's life, including his presidency. It is open daily year-round.

Day 2
Moderate terrain; 64.7 miles

<u>Miles</u>

0.0 Begin ride at the intersection of U.S. Highway 412 and U.S. Highway 31. Head west on U.S. Highway 412.

In addition to the title of Miss USA 2000, Lynette Cole can also proudly claim to be Mule Day Queen. She is from Columbia, the Mule Capital of the World. The town, established in November 1817, began mule dealing in the 1840s, making it a hub for the trade. Will Rogers once said, "What the thoroughfare of Wall Street will do to you if you don't know a stock, Columbia will do to you if you don't know a mule."

In 1934, Columbia's Market Day turned into a celebration called Mule Day. The event, held each April, includes a parade, clogging contest, pancake breakfast, barbecue dinner, chuck wagon show, old time fiddlers contest, crafts fair and, of course, mule sale.

1.1 Cross the Duck River.

1.5 Under pass State Route 7.

3.1 Under pass Industrial Park Road.

4.1 Road becomes one lane as you climb a big hill.

5.3 Turn left onto the ramp to State Route 50.

5.5 Turn left onto State Route 50. Watch for traffic.

5.6 Under pass U.S. Highway 43, continuing on State Route 50.

The shoulder has eroded. Harlan Farms is on your right.

9.4 You'll see Doodad's Market on your right. Pass Williamsport Road on your right.

11.0 Enter the community of Sawdust.

12.3 Enter the community of Woodrow.

13.4 Enter the community of Williamsport. You'll soon see Williamsport Market on your left.

14.1 Cross the Duck River.

14.2 **Pass State Route 247 on the right.**

15.2 **Pass the road to Williamsport Public Lakes on your right.**

16.5 **Enter Hickman County.**

The Tennessee General Assembly established Hickman County in December 1807. It was named for Edwin Hickman, who was killed by Indians while surveying the area in April 1791, according to historian Edward Dotson. Centerville was established as the county seat in 1823. The area quickly gained notoriety for its springs and health spas.

Hickman County flourished with the ironworks, agriculture and timber industries. Prominent natives include Beth Slater Whitson who wrote "Let Me Call You Sweetheart," Sara Ophelia Colley Cannon who became famous as Minnie Pearl on the Grand Ole Opry, and Halbert Harville who became Tennessee Commissioner of Education and served in the state senate from 1965 to 1981.

17.2 **Turn right onto the ramp to Natchez Trace Parkway, just before the community of Shady Grove.**

17.4 **Turn right onto Natchez Trace Parkway.**

If you turn left on Natchez Trace Parkway, you'll find the Gordon House and Ferry Site less than ½ mile on your left. In 1802, John Gordon, former Nashville postmaster, and William Colbert, son of Chickasaw chief George Colbert, turned former military housing at the Duck River into a stand, the frontier term for wilderness inns, according to author Davis. They also bought the military flatboats and ferried travelers across the river. The Gordon House standing today was built about 1818.

*The Gordon House, built in 1818, is one of the many sites
along the Natchez Trace Parkway.*

21.2 Water Valley Overlook is on your right.

**25.1 Pass the ramp to State Route 7 on your left. The Fly Grocery is
located not far east of the Trace on State Route 7.**

29.3 Enter Williamson County.
You can read more about Williamson County in the Rockvale—
Harpeth chapter.

33.9 Tennessee Valley Divide is on your right.
When Tennessee became a state in 1796, this was the boundary
between the United States to the north and the Chickasaw Nation
to the south.

To the west of the Natchez Trace from here lies the community
of Bending Chestnut. According to Lyn Sullivan Pewitt in the book
Back Home in Williamson County, area Indians used to mark their
trails by bending chestnut saplings to the ground. One could be
found at the intersection of Bending Chestnut and Garrison roads.
Chestnut trees were predominant in the area until the 1930s, when
many succumbed to disease.

35.3 Burns Branch is on your right.

36.3 Old Trace is on your right.

The U.S. Army cleared this part of the trace in 1801 and 1802.

36.8 Garrison Creek Rest Area is on your right.

Garrison Creek was named for the nearby Army post, which stationed soldiers converting the old Indian trail into a military road.

38.2 Turn left onto the ramp to State Route 46.

38.5 Turn left onto State Route 46 at the stop sign at the T-intersection. Watch for traffic.

Leiper's Fork, also called Hillsboro, is located east of here. The town was first named Bentontown after Thomas Hart Benton's family moved to the area from North Carolina, according to Pewitt. Benton was a Tennessee state senator from 1799 to 1809. He became the most prolific lawyer in Williamson County. Benton's stature waned in 1813 when his brother, Jesse, shot future U.S. President Andrew Jackson at a Nashville hotel. Benton and Jackson remained amicable, but Benton moved from Tennessee to Missouri in 1815. The "Old Bullion" served in the U.S. Senate for 30 years.

After Benton's departure, the town name changed to Leiper's Fork. The first known landowner in the area was Hugh Leiper, who was granted 40 acres on a large fork in the Harpeth River in 1785.

State Route 46 is a two-lane, curvy highway. There is no shoulder.

45.7 Pass Pewitt Road on your right.

47.0 You'll pass a white, convenience store on your left.

51.2 Cross State Route 100. Road becomes Spencer's Mill Road.

The road narrows and becomes curvy with a few steep hills. Morning Glory Farm is on the left.

51.9 Watch out at hidden drive.

52.6 Enter Hickman County.

52.9 Enter Dickson County.

The Tennessee legislature created Dickson County in October 1803. According to Robert E. Corlew in his book, *A History of Dickson County Tennessee*, the county was named for William Dickson, a Nashville physician and U.S. congressman. His cousin, David Dickson, was the county's first court clerk.

53.2 Watch out at hidden drive.

55.3 Pass the road to the right, leading to Old Spencer Mill.

That road leads to the Old Spencer Mill. Started in 1856, the private facility today offers weekend entertainment, hayrides and frequent, living-history programs.

57.9 Martin-Gartin Cemetary is on your right.

58.1 Cross over Interstate 40.

58.7 Discovery Place is on your right.

61.4 Turn right onto State Route 96 at the stop sign at the T-intersection.

61.7 Turn left onto Beechwood Drive. Pass Girl Scout Road and the New Life Lodge on your right. You'll weave through a residential area with a few steep hills.

63.1 Turn right on State Route 47 at the stop sign at the T-intersection.

If you turn left here, you'll soon enter the towns of Dickson and Burns.

Originally called Sneedsville, Dickson was created to attract a railroad stop for the southern part of the county. The Nashville and Tuscaloosa Railroad followed, along with substantial growth, according to Corlew. Dickson was incorporated in 1873, but in 1882, incorporation was dropped after citizen disputes over taxes. The town was re-incorporated in 1899.

Dickson is the hometown of Frank Clement, who served his first term as Tennessee governor in 1953 and 1954. He was re-elected in 1954 for the governorship's first four-year term until 1959. He served again from 1963 to 1967. During his terms, the state legislature made the first constitutional changes since 1870, opened the state's Library and Archives building and allocated funds for free textbooks in all public schools. Clement died in 1969.

The town of Burns was incorporated in 1952.

64.7 You'll see Baker's Works Grocery on your right. End ride at the entrance of Montgomery Bell State Park on your left.

Now consisting of 3,782 forested acres, the land at Montgomery Bell State Park was once farmland as well as the center of Dickson County's iron industry. The park was named for one of the industry's leaders.

A hatter from Kentucky, Montgomery Bell moved to this area in the late 1700s, purchasing Robertson's furnace, according to author Corlew. Bell soon built furnaces along Jones' Creek, Turnbull Creek, Barton's Creek, Cumberland River and Piney River. Just before the War of 1812, he signed a contract with the federal government to produce cannon balls and other war materials. That timing made him the top iron ore producer in the region. His furnaces flourished over much of Middle Tennessee.

Slave labor scratched the ore from shallow deposits, hammered it into manageable sizes and washed it of dirt and debris. Workers then placed the ore into the furnaces — as hot as 3,500 degrees— where it was melted down, then cast into objects. It is said Bell didn't hesitate to use a whip to increase production. That may explain his increasing problem with runaway slaves in the mid-1800s. Bell died in 1855.

For general information on lodging and attractions, contact the Dickson County Chamber of Commerce, 119 Highway 70 East, Dickson, TN 37055 (615-446-2349); Hickman County Chamber of Commerce, 117 N. Central Ave., Centerville, TN 37033 (931-729-5774); Marshall County Chamber of Commerce, 227 Second Ave. North, Lewisburg, TN 37091 (931-359-3863); Maury County Visitors Bureau, 8 Public Square, Columbia, TN 38401 (931-381-7176 or 888-852-1860); Natchez Trace

Parkway, 2680 Natchez Trace Parkway, Tupelo, MS 38804 (662-680-4025 or 800-305-7417); or Williamson County Tourism, 109 Second Ave. South, Suite 107, Franklin, TN 37065 (800-356-3445 or 615-794-1225).

Places to Stay

Montgomery Bell State Park (camping), P.O. Box 39, Burns, TN 37029 (615-797-9052), features electrical campsites along a creek, with three bathhouses, as well as three backcountry camping areas. The park also has eight, two-bedroom cottages with a television, telephone and gas fireplace.

Montgomery Bell State Park Inn, P.O. Box 39, Burns, TN 37029 (615-797-3101 or 800-250-8613), expanded in October 1998. All rooms have a view of Lake Acorn. Amenities include a restaurant, cable television, year-round indoor pool and Jacuzzi, exercise room, exercise facility and laundry room.

Gore House Bed & Breakfast, 410 Belmont, Shelbyville, TN 37160 (931-685-0636), is a 5,000-square-foot home, located several miles east of the ride's start. Each of the three guest rooms features a private bath, television, queen-sized bed and work table. Innkeeper Sue Thelen serves breakfast in your room or in a 30-foot sun room.

Henry Horton State Park (camping), 4358 Nashville Highway, Chapel Hill, TN 37034 (931-364-7724), features 75 campsites along the Duck River, 54 with electrical hookups, tables and grills. The campground has two bathhouses. The park also has seven cabins that sleep six persons each. They feature air conditioning, fireplaces, telephones and televisions.

Henry Horton State Park Inn, 4358 Nashville Highway, Chapel Hill, TN 37034 (931-364-2222 or 800-250-8612), has 72 rooms, including four suites with kitchenettes. There is also a fitness room.

The Inn on Main Street Bed & Breakfast, 112 S. Main St., Dickson, TN 37055 (615-441-5821), is located several miles west of the ride's end. Innkeepers Brett and Misha Lashlee own this 1903 two-story home. The four guestrooms include televisions, queen- or full-sized beds, bathrooms, ceiling fans and telephones. There is a family room, dining room, study and, on each floor, a front porch.

Locust Hill, 1185 Mooresville Pike, Columbia, TN 38401 (931-388-8531 or 800-577-8264), is a restored home built in 1840. Innkeepers Bill and Beverly Beard can accommodate anyone speaking English, German and French. There are fireplaces, flower gardens and a library.

Sweetwater Inn Bed & Breakfast, 2436 Campbell's Station Road, Culleoka, TN 38451 (931-987-3077), is located between Lewisburg and Columbia. Innkeepers Tommy Young and Melissa McEwen operate this three-story mansion, decorated in the style of an 18th Century Mississippi River steamboat. Four guestrooms access an upper level porch.

Bicycle Shops

Allanti Cycling Co., 144 Franklin Road, Brentwood, TN 37027 (615-373-4700).

Bike Pedlar Cycling, 2910 West End Ave., Nashville, TN 37203 (615-329-2453).

Cumberland Transit Bicycles, 2807 West End Ave., Nashville, TN 37203 (615-321-4069).

Franklin Bicycle Co., 124 Watson Glen, Franklin, TN 37064 (615- 790-2702).

Lightning Cycles, 8735 Horton Highway, College Grove, TN 37046 (615-368-3051).

Music City Cycle Works, 1013 Hickory Ridge, Franklin, TN 37064 (615-794-6878).

Nashville Bicycle Co., 2817 West End Ave., Nashville, TN 37203 (615-321-5510).

REI, 261 Franklin Road, Brentwood, TN 37207 (615- 376-4248).

The Wheel, 11 Public Square, Columbia, TN 38401 (931-381-3225).

BICYCLING TENNESSEE
Tour 14: Lawrenceburg-Hohenwald

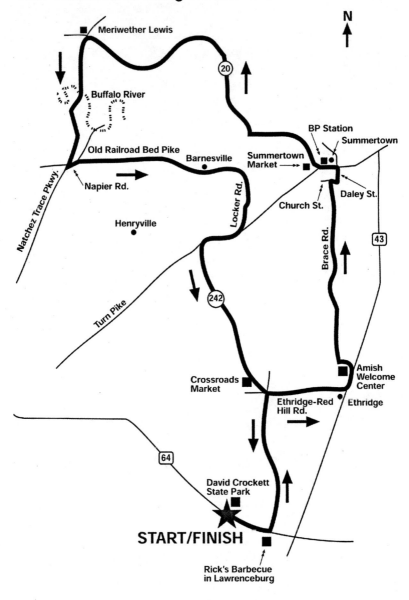

N

Meriwether Lewis

20

Buffalo River

Old Railroad Bed Pike

Napier Rd.

Natchez Trace Pkwy.

Barnesville

Summertown Market

BP Station

Summertown

Daley St.

Church St.

Locker Rd.

Henryville

Brace Rd.

43

Turn Pike

242

Crossroads Market

Amish Welcome Center

Ethridge

Ethridge-Red Hill Rd.

64

David Crockett State Park

START/FINISH

Rick's Barbecue in Lawrenceburg

14. LAWRENCEBURG—HOHENWALD

Easy to moderate terrain; 60.2 miles

David Crockett was a lifelong Tennessean. The American folk hero lived in all three regions of the state, building a reputation as a pioneer, hunter, soldier and politician, before heading to Texas and meeting his fate at the Alamo.

Crockett was born on Aug. 17, 1786 in East Tennessee, near what is today the community of Limestone. You can read more about his birthplace in the Gatlinburg—Jonesborough chapter. His father, John, had financial troubles, according to James A. Shackford in his book, *David Crockett: The Man and The Legend.* To help make ends meet, David found work in Virginia and Maryland in his early teens, returning home in the spring of 1802 at the age of 15. He married Polly Finley in August 1806.

The Crocketts leased and worked a small farm until moving west over the mountains to Middle Tennessee in 1811. While living in Lincoln and Franklin counties, Crockett established himself as a true frontiersman and hunter. He also became a soldier, serving in the Creek War. Polly died in the summer of 1815. Crockett married Elizabeth Patton, a widow whose husband was killed in the Creek War, the following summer. By this time, Crockett was a lieutenant in the militia.

He began his political career after moving further west and helping establish Lawrence County in 1817. He was elected state representative for Lawrence and Hickman counties in 1821. He began his rise as a legendary backwoods statesman, becoming known as "the gentleman from the cane," according to Shackford. The flooding of his Lawrence County gristmill led to financial problems and his move further west to Gibson County along the Obion River, about 40 miles north of what is today Jackson. He was re-elected to the state legislature in 1823, representing most of the counties established in West Tennessee at the time.

Crockett served Tennessee in Congress from 1827 to 1833. As Congressman, he adamantly favored the Tennessee Vacant Land Bill. The bill sought to sell vacant West Tennessee land to settlers at a reasonable price, with the state benefiting from the sale. Opposition continuously tabled the bill during his terms in office. Crockett narrowly lost a re-election bid for a fourth term to Adam Huntsman, a veteran who lost his leg during the Creek War. (Congress passed the land bill in 1841 after Crockett's death.)

Tired of politics, he took off with four other men in late 1835 to explore Texas. "Since you have chosen to elect a man with a timber toe to succeed me, you may all go to hell and I will go to Texas," he reportedly said before departing from Memphis. In Texas, he quickly became involved in the area's fight for independence from Mexico. He was one of 189 killed on March 6, 1836, defending the Alamo Mission in San Antonio. There is also a theory that he was captured and executed after the battle.

This tour begins about 175 miles east of Memphis. Take U.S. Highway 64 to Lawrenceburg. David Crockett State Park is on your left as you enter the town.

Miles

0.0 **Begin ride at the entrance of David Crockett State Park. Head east on U.S. Highway 64. You'll see a Texaco station on your right.**

After moving to Lawrence County in 1817, Crockett served as justice of the peace, colonel of the militia and state representative. He established a powder mill, gristmill and distillery along Shoal Creek (within today's park), until all were washed away in September

1821. When Davy Crockett's fame revived with a 1950s television show starring Fess Parker, Tennessee dedicated two parks in his honor—Davy Crockett State Historical Area in Limestone and David Crockett State Park in Lawrenceburg.

David Crockett State Park hosts David Crockett Days each August, featuring a living frontiersman demonstration set in the early 1800s. Its museum, open Memorial Day to Labor Day, depicts the life and times of Crockett. The park also hosts the David Crockett Arts and Crafts Festival each Labor Day weekend.

Although Crockett was one of the founders of Lawrenceburg in 1819, M.H. Buchanan actually mapped out the county seat, according to Viola Carpenter and Marymaud Carter in *Our Hometown Lawrenceburg: The Crossroads of Dixie*. The town and county were named for Captain James Lawrence, a War of 1812 naval hero who coined the phrase, "Don't give up the ship."

Another instrumental player in Lawrenceburg's success was George H. Nixon, who helped bring the Nashville and Florence Railroad through town. Up to 6,000 people gathered when the first locomotive came to town on Oct. 24, 1883, but passenger traffic eventually came to an end. The last passenger train, the Huckety Buck, ran through Lawrenceburg on Dec. 6, 1954. The old L & N Depot was demolished on Feb. 19, 1973.

Milestones in the 1900s included the openings of the electric and waterworks plant in December 1902, new courthouses in 1905 and 1974, and an airport in October 1962. The Bench Club, a group of "old-timers," still gathers at the town's public square to discuss affairs of the day. The square features one of only two Mexican War memorials in the United States. Officials also erected the David Crockett Monument on the square on Sept. 14, 1922. It includes his famous motto, "Be sure you are right, then go ahead."

0.7   **You'll see Rick's Barbecue on the right. Turn left onto State Route 242 (also called Buffalo Road). Watch for traffic.**

3.7 You'll see a Phillips 66 station on your right at Valley Road. Continue straight.

5.9 You'll see the Crossroads Market on the left. Turn right onto Ethridge-Red Hill Road.

In the summer, you'll weave through some cornfields here.

7.5 Ethridge-Red Hill Road becomes Main Street once you enter the town of Ethridge.

9.2 Turn left onto U.S. Highway 43 at the stop sign at the T-intersection. This is a four-lane highway, but there is a nice-size shoulder to ride in. Watch for traffic.

10.0 You'll see Amish Gallery and Amish Country Village on the left. Turn left onto Brewer Road at the Amish Welcome Center.

According to *Our Hometown Lawrenceburg*, three Amish families moved to the Ethridge area in January 1944 from southern Mississippi. They were seeking better land to farm. The following fall, more Amish families moved to the area from Wayne County, Ohio. The name comes from Jacob Ammon, a preacher from Canton of Berne, Switzerland, who broke away from the Mennonites by 1700. Many from the new sect immigrated to the United States.

The first group moving to Ethridge lived a simple life—wearing conservative, homemade clothing. They did not accept modern advances such as electricity or the automobile. A more progressive group, however, moved here in 1947 from Indiana. They were more likely to use modern conveniences. They were drawn to Tennessee for its openness to home schooling.

Ethridge now boasts 250 Amish families. Granny's Amish Welcome Center and Ten-Watt Television Station opened in 1994. Owner Sarah Evetts offers horse-drawn wagon tours, a restaurant and gift shop. The television station airs local commission meetings, ball games, gospel concerts and history programs.

10.8 Turn right onto Brace Road at the stop sign at the T-intersection.

11.5 **Turn right before the railroad tracks.**

11.6 **Turn left, crossing the railroad tracks, then a quick right (you are still on Brace Road).**

The road is a hard, gravel surface, not ideal but rideable on a road bike. A better grade resumes in three miles.

13.5 **You are entering the community of Brace. Continue straight on Brace Road.**

17.8 **Turn right onto Church Street. You are now entering Summertown.** In 1971, Stephen Gaskin and his caravan of California idealists drove into Summertown and parked their school buses and Volkswagens on a hilltop just north of here in Lewis County. The Korean War veteran, turned psychedelic English professor, created The Farm—a community spiritually committed to simple living and self-reliance. The "hippie" commune grew as large as 1,500 residents, but scaled back operations in 1982 to today's more manageable population of 200.

In the community, you'll see examples of solar building design, micro-enterprise, large-scale composting and gardening, regenerative hardwood forest management and permaculture. Permanent agriculture is the philosophy of leaving the earth in better shape than we found it. It ties in farming, landscaping and gardening with such things as plumbing, heating, architecture and money management.

The Farm began cultivating mushrooms to reduce carbon dioxide in the atmosphere and reverse global warming, but their nutritional benefits also helped open up a market. Its mail order business, Mushroompeople, supplies the mushroom trade with spawn, growing supplies, instructional literature and videos, and lore.

Like the Amish, The Farm residents do not view their simple life as a freak show. Visitations are limited, preferably for conferences and special events. For more information, call (931) 964-3574.

17.9 Turn left onto Daley Street. There is no street sign.

18.3 Turn left onto State Route 20. Watch for traffic. You'll soon see a Matheny's BP station on the right.

19.2 At the fork, you'll see the Summertown Market. Continue right on State Route 20.

22.2 You are entering Lewis County. You'll soon see an Amoco station on the right.

People began settling in Lewis County at Big Swan Creek on the Natchez Trace between 1806 and 1810, according to the series *The Goodspeed History of Tennessee*. Gordonburg was the county seat until 1843. Gen. William Carroll gave a tearful goodbye to his troops on the east bank of Little Swan Creek, about one mile north of Meriwether Lewis' grave. They were returning from the Battle of New Orleans in 1815.

29.4 You'll see a convenience store on your left.

31.4 Turn right onto the Natchez Trace Parkway entrance at the Meriwether Lewis Monument. Head south on the parkway toward Tupelo.

Meriwether Lewis and William Clark became famous after their journey from St. Louis to the Pacific Ocean, exploring the newly acquired Louisiana Territory for President Thomas Jefferson. Lewis became governor of the territory in March 1808, but administrative turmoil and personal financial troubles soon led to investigative proceedings in Washington, D.C. In September, Lewis set out for Washington to clear his name, according to William C. Davis in his book, *A Way Through the Wilderness*. The plan included sailing the Mississippi River south from St. Louis to Fort Pickering (Memphis today), and traveling overland east to the Natchez Trace, which he planned taking to Nashville.

Accounts along the way suggest Lewis was visibly distraught over his problems. Captain Gilbert Russell reportedly prevented Lewis from committing suicide at Fort Pickering, and assigned Major

James Neelly and two servants to accompany Lewis on his journey. On Oct. 8, they crossed the Tennessee River and reached the Natchez Trace. Along the trace, Neelly separated from the group to chase two runaway horses. On the evening of Oct. 10, Lewis and the servants reached Grinder's Stand without Neelly.

Owner Robert Griner (the spelling is different from the inn name) was away at the time. Lewis' deranged behavior scared Priscilla Griner and her slave, Malindy. At his request, Mrs. Griner reportedly provided Lewis with gunpowder, then retired with Malindy to a separate building. The two servants slept in the stables. During the night, they all heard gunshots. One of the servants found Lewis on the floor with one wound to the head and another to the chest. "I have done the business my good servant," he reportedly said. He died the next morning, Oct. 11.

Most all of Lewis' acquaintances presumed his fate was suicide. However, speculation began to circulate along the trace that he was murdered. Robert Griner, political enemies and the servants were all unofficially suspected, but no one was charged and convicted.

The monument here marks Lewis' gravesite. The park also features a ranger station, restrooms, picnic area and campground. Read more about the Natchez Trace in the Chapel Hill—Burns chapter. If you continue east on State Route 20, you'll soon enter the town of Hohenwald.

34.3 Cross the Buffalo River.
You'll pass Metal Ford and Napier Mine. Old Trace travelers crossed the Buffalo River at Metal Ford, including Andrew Jackson on his way to the Battle of New Orleans. Napier Mine is one of the area's largest remaining open-pit phosphate mines. The first ironworks in the Southwest were established in this area, according to author Davis. Three men founded Buffalo Iron Works at nearby McLish's Stand in 1822.

36.3 Take the Napier Road exit. Turn right onto Napier Lake Road.

36.4 Turn left onto Napier Road.

36.5 Turn right onto Old Railroad Bed Pike.
The road is bumpy, but gets better as you bike along.

41.6 You'll enter the community of Barnesville.

43.1 Turn right onto Locker Road.
The terrain becomes hillier for several miles as you wind near and around the Buffalo River.

45.1 Turn right onto Turn Pike (also called State Route 240).

46.9 Cross the Buffalo River.

47.2 Turn left onto Lawrenceburg-Henryville Road (also called State Route 242), just before entering Henryville.
Henryville was founded in 1844 near Old Town, according to *The Goodspeed History of Tennessee*. Old Town was once an Indian village on the west bank of the Buffalo River.

49.8 Cross the narrow bridge.

53.1 Veer right, heading south on Buffalo Road (still State Route 242). Watch for traffic.

53.3 You'll see Crossroads Market on your right. Continue straight on Buffalo Road.

55.5 You'll see Phillips 66 on your left at Valley Road.

58.5 You'll see Rick's Barbecue on the right. Turn right onto U.S. Highway 64. Watch for traffic.

60.2 End ride at David Crockett State Park, where the tour began.

For general information on lodging and attractions, contact the Lawrence County Chamber of Commerce, 1609 N. Locust Ave. (U.S. Hwy. 43), Lawrenceburg, TN 38464 (931-762-4911); the Lewis County Chamber of Commerce, 112 E. Main St., Hohenwald, Tennessee 38462 (931-796-4084); or the Natchez Trace Parkway, 2680 Natchez Trace Parkway, Tupelo, MS 38804 (662-680-4025 or 800-305-7417).

Places to Stay

Armstrong Bakery Bed & Breakfast, 309 Park Ave. South, Hohenwald, TN 38462 (931-796-7591), was once the town jail. The restored home is seven miles off of The Natchez Trace. It features a variety of antiques and a balcony off the two guestrooms.

Best Western Villa Inn, 2126 N. Locust Ave. (U.S. Hwy. 43), Lawrenceburg, TN 38464 (931-762-4448), has 48 rooms. Features include a pool, sauna, in-room coffee and continental breakfast in the solarium. Small pets are allowed.

David Crockett State Park (camping), 1400 W. Gaines, Lawrenceburg, TN 38464 (931-762-9408), features two campgrounds totaling 107 sites. Primitive camping is also available. A paved bicycle trail goes through the woods around the park.

Meriwether Lewis Campground (camping) offers 32 primitive sites. There are no hookups, no fees and no reservations. For more information, contact the Natchez Trace Parkway, 2680 Natchez Trace Parkway, Tupelo, MS 38804 (662-680-4025 or 800-305-7417).

Bicycle Shops

The Wheel, 11 Public Square, Columbia, TN 38401 (931-381-3225).

BICYCLING TENNESSEE
Tour 15: Springfield-Adams

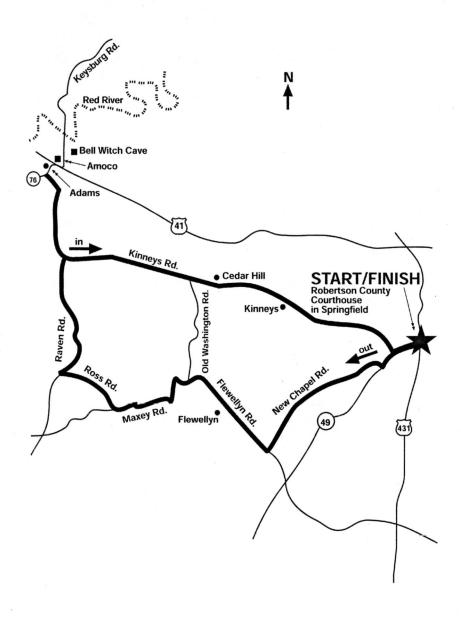

Keysburg Rd.

Red River

■ Bell Witch Cave

← Amoco

76

Adams

41

in →

Kinneys Rd.

● Cedar Hill

Kinneys ●

START/FINISH
Robertson County
Courthouse
in Springfield

Raven Rd.

Old Washington Rd.

Ross Rd.

out ←

New Chapel Rd.

Flewellyn Rd.

Maxey Rd.

Flewellyn ●

49

431

N ↑

15. SPRINGFIELD—ADAMS

Moderate to difficult, some significant bluffs before and after crossing creeks with one significant hill near Cedar Hill; 35.5 miles

Shortly after the release of the movie "The Blair Witch Project" in 1999, Chris Kirby called the sheriff one evening to report prowlers on her property. Responding to the call, the sheriff actually caught a different group of prowlers. The movie sparked a new generation's interest in the legend of the Bell Witch Cave in Adams. Chris and her husband, Walter, have owned the 101 acres that include the cave since 1993.

The Bell Witch story began in 1817, according to Yolanda G. Reid and Rick S. Gregory in their book, *Robertson County, Tennessee: Home of the World's Finest*. A spirit began to harass John Bell and his family, who had lived in Robertson County since 1804. John saw an unidentifiable animal staring at him in a cornfield. His son, Drew, saw an unidentifiable bird. His daughter, Betsy, saw a girl dressed in green, swinging from a tree limb.

Soon, the encounters turned less friendly. The spirit pulled family members' hair, pulled bed covers off them at night, constantly knocked on doors, and periodically ranted scripture or profanities. Future president Andrew Jackson experienced strange happenings when he visited the Bell home. Betsy broke up with her fiancé, Joshua Gardner, because of the witch's warnings. John Bell died in 1821, supposedly poisoned by the witch.

The stories continue through the present. The Kirbys report numerous inexplicable noises around the cave and their nearby home. They share photographs from previous visitors. Ghostly figures appear that weren't visible when the pictures were taken. Photography experts swear that there is no evidence of tampering.

Organized rides in this area include Springfield's First Presbyterian Church's Cycle for Habitat, which benefits the Robertson County Habitat for Humanity. This route, about 25 miles north of Nashville, is a very rural and scenic ride through tobacco and cattle farms. To get to the start, take Interstate 24 north of Nashville to exit 35. Head north on U.S. Highway 431. Turn left on U.S. Highway 41 (also Memorial Boulevard). Turn left on State Route 49. Robertson County Courthouse is on North Main Street to your left.

<u>Miles</u>

0.0   Start ride at Robertson County Courthouse. Head west down the hill on State Route 49.

The Tennessee General Assembly established Springfield as the Robertson County seat in 1798, shortly after statehood. The county was named for General James Robertson, who led the Nickajack Expedition against the Chickamaugans in Chattanooga. He is often called the father of Middle Tennessee. Citizens constructed the first courthouse in Springfield in the summer of 1799. Contractors Patton and McInturff built the current courthouse in 1879. William C. Smith was the architect.

Like much of Middle Tennessee, the county's first inhabitants migrated from the North Carolina territory. Early successes were found in the whiskey trade. The Internal Revenue for Tennessee reported 20 county distilleries in 1802. Early attempts to grow cotton failed, but the settlers soon discovered the land conducive to tobacco.

Residents wrestled with moral dilemmas over the whiskey distillers, but tobacco didn't seem to pose a problem. Tobacco became a prominent crop for the county. Today, the county produces more than 14.5 million pounds of tobacco annually, according to the

National Agricultural Statistics Service. Robertson is Tennessee's top county in the production of Eastern Dark tobacco, producing 8.3 million pounds in 1998. This tobacco features dark, heavy leaves. It is fire-cured, which explains the smoking barns you ride past in late fall or early winter.

You'll pass several convenience stores on the way out of Springfield.

1.2   **Turn right onto New Chapel Road.**

2.8   **After descending the bluff, you'll cross Carr Creek. Then, you'll ascend the toughest bluff of the ride.**

5.6   **Turn right onto Flewellyn Road at the stop sign. There is no street sign.**

You'll ride through the community of Flewellyn.

7.7   **After descending a bluff, Old Washington Road is to your right. Turn left onto Maxey Road at the stop sign at the T-intersection. There is no street sign.**

You'll pass through the community of Turnersville between Caleb's Creek and Miller's Creek.

11.4   **Turn right onto Ross Road. There is no street sign.**

You'll ascend a steep hill on a bumpy road, appropriately titled the Trail of Tears. This was one of the Cherokee Indian paths when the U.S. government forced their move to reservations west of the Mississippi. You can read more about the Trail of Tears in the Clarksville—Guthrie chapter.

13.1   **Turn right onto Raven Road at the stop sign at the T-intersection. Watch for traffic.**

14.4   **Cross Sulphur Fork Creek. You'll descend and ascend long, gradual hills on each side.**

16.5   **Turn left onto Kinneys Road at the stop sign at the T-intersection. Watch for traffic.**

18.3   **Enter the town of Adams.**

Named for Reuben G. Adams, the town was established along a railroad in the 1850s.

19.0   Turn right onto State Route 76 at the stop sign.

19.5   Turn right onto U.S. Highway 41 at the traffic light at the T-intersection. Watch for traffic. You'll soon see an Amoco station on your left (no public restrooms).

19.7   Turn left onto Keysburg Road.

20.4   Turn right at the Bell Witch Cave sign and follow the gravel driveway.

20.7   Turn around at the Bell Witch Cave's pavilion.

Chris Kirby and her daughter, Candy, give daily tours of the Bell Witch Cave. The business has been a profitable venture, picking up after "The Blair Witch Project" hype. Chris says psychics and psychos have visited her cave. She can now add cyclists to the list. And the helmets come in handy for the cave's low ceilings.

Bike helmets come in handy for the low ceilings at the Bell Witch Cave in Adams.

21.0   Turn left onto Keysburg Road.

21.7   Turn right onto U.S. Highway 41 at the stop sign at the T-intersection. Watch for traffic. You'll soon see an Amoco station on your right (no public restrooms).

21.9 Turn left onto State Route 76 at the traffic light.

22.4 Turn left onto Kinneys Road. Watch for traffic.

24.9 Raven Road is to your right. Continue straight on Kinneys Road.

28.4 Old Washington Road is to your right. Continue straight on Kinneys Road.

If you turn right on Old Washington Road, then turn left onto Flewellyn Road in 2.9 miles, you can workout on the bluffs you encountered at the beginning of this ride.

31.0 Enter the community of Cedar Hill.

Cedar Hill was named for the hill where John H. Bartlett built his store in 1855. The hill was covered with cedar trees.

Near Cedar Hill, the Wessyngton plantation was one of the world's largest tobacco farms in the 1800s. George A. Washington inherited the plantation from his late father, Joseph, in 1848. The property was valued at $20,000 in 1850. Within 10 years, the younger Washington built an empire. He produced a remarkable 250,000 pounds of tobacco in 1859. He also raised wheat, corn, oats, cattle, swine and sheep. Hands down, he was the county's largest slave owner. His 274 slaves—field hands and servants—did most of the work. By 1860, his property was valued at $250,000. According to authors Reid and Gregory, the characters from *Gone with the Wind* would have felt at home there.

Spectators gathered at the nearby Carr Farm in 1934, when Nashville physician Hugh Young excavated a mound. Young and his crew found the remains of ancient Indians. They were called Stone Grave Indians because they used stone slabs to build box-shaped graves, or Flat-Head Indians because the back of their skulls were flat, according to Reid and Gregory.

34.9 You'll see Korner Grocery on your right and Buy-Rite Grocery on your left. Turn left onto State Route 49 and climb the hill.

35.5 End ride at the Robertson County Courthouse at the intersection of North Main Street, where the tour began.

For general information about lodging and attractions, contact the Robertson County Chamber of Commerce, 100 Fifth Ave. West, Springfield, TN 37172 (615-384-3800).

Places to Stay
Crocker Springs Bed & Breakfast, 2382 Crocker Springs Road, Goodlettsville, TN 37072 (615-876-8502 or 800-373-4911), is an historic farmhouse built in the late 19th Century. The home features high ceilings, restored long-leaf pine floors and many antiques. In the back of the house, guests can relax in a sunroom and listen to the rippling brook that meanders through the property. Innkeepers are Jack and Bev Spangler.

Red River Valley Bed & Breakfast, P.O. Box 144, Adams, TN 37010 (615-696-2768 or 800-762-8408), offers canoeing, fishing and hunting for arrowheads along the Red River. Guests can view video reenactments of the Cherokee Trail of Tears, which camped on this farm, or visit the nearby Bell Witch Cave.

Bicycle Shops
Biker's Choice, 240 E. Main St., Hendersonville, TN 37075 (615-822-2512).

Jolly Cyclist Inc., 5514 Old Hickory Blvd., Hermitage, TN 37076 (615-885-0881).

BICYCLING TENNESSEE
Tour 16: Rockvale-Harpeth

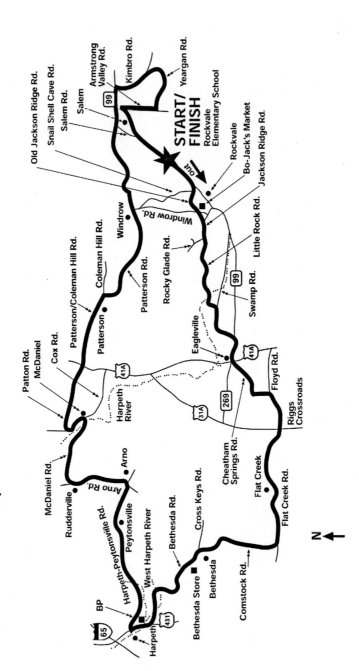

N

16. Rockvale—Harpeth

Moderate terrain, rolling hills with an occasional flat stretch, and only a couple of significant hills; 64.5 miles

Long before the white man, and even long before the Cherokee Indian, the Harpeth River Valley was inhabited by a civilization. The New World isn't as new as you think. Archeologists have found evidence of at least five major population centers along the Harpeth rivers and their tributaries, dating back as far as 700 years ago.

According to James A. Crutchfield in his book *The Harpeth River: A Biography*, it is suspected these Indians were descendents of the Mongolians who migrated from Siberia to what is now Alaska, when the Bering Strait was dry land. They have been dubbed the Temple Building Cult. Ruins of their temples and plazas can be found in mounds along the waterways.

The U.S. government bought the Harper River Valley from the Cherokee Nation on Nov. 18, 1785. When the Indians signed the Treaty of Hopewell in Hopewell, S.C., they practically gave away the most valuable land on the continent at that time. In return, they received trade goods valued at $1,300.

The valley consists of four significant rivers—the Little Harpeth, the South Harpeth, the West Harpeth and the Harpeth. Crutchfield writes that no one is sure how the rivers got their name. One theory is that the rivers were named for brothers Micajah and Wiley Harpe. Big Harpe and Little Harpe were notorious outlaws in Tennessee and Kentucky in the early 1800s. Another theory is that they were named for Harpath, a fictional character who drowns in the English classic, *The Spectator*.

171

Rutherford and Williamson counties are popular destinations for the Murfreesboro, Harpeth and Columbia bicycle clubs. The quiet roads, cattle farms and country stores offer a pleasant escape from the hustle and bustle of the city. Area rides include the Mufreesboro Bicycle Club's H.O.T. 100 and the Harpeth Bicycle Club's Harpeth River Ride.

The Murfreesboro Bicycle Club uses this route for its Two County Metric tour. The ride consists of rolling hills, with only a few significant ones. To get to the route, take State Route 99 south of Murfreesboro about 10 miles. You'll see Rockvale Elementary School on your right.

Miles

0.0　Start the ride at Rockvale Elementary School. Turn right out of the school parking lot. Head west on State Route 99 (also called Salem Pike). Watch for traffic.

1.8　Turn right onto Snail Shell Cave Road.

2.2　Turn left onto Old Jackson Ridge Road.

3.6　You'll see Bo-Jack's Market on your left. Continue straight on Windrow Road.

3.7　Turn right onto Jackson Ridge Road.

4.6　Turn right onto Rocky Glade Road.

4.7　Turn left onto Little Rock Road.

7.4　Turn right onto Swamp Road. You'll soon cross the Harpeth River.

9.3　Turn right onto State Route 99 (also called Salem Pike).

10.2　Turn left onto U.S. Highway 41A (also called State Route 16).

　　　You are riding through the town of Eagleville, originally called Manchester. One of the first settlers in the community was Absalom Scales, according to Mabel Pittard in the Tennessee County History Series' *Rutherford County*. Today, Scales' home is one of the oldest houses in the county.

　　　In the late 1800s, ghost stories began circulating around the community. Bodies began disappearing from cemeteries. After burying loved ones, families left lighted lanterns next to the graves. State officials investigated and explained Dr. C. R. Heimark's night trips to Nashville. Heimark was selling bodies to medical schools. He was fined $150 and sentenced to six months in jail. Shortly thereafter, in 1899, the Tennessee legislature made grave robbing a felony, punishable by two to five years in prison.

10.3 Turn right onto Cheatham Springs Road.

12.9 Turn right onto Floyd Road. Cross U.S. Highway 31A in the community of Riggs Crossroads.

U.S. Highway 31A once was Fishing Ford Road, the oldest thoroughfare for commerce and war in Tennessee, according to Lyn Sullivan Pewitt in *Back Home in Williamson County*. Riggs Crossroads was a weigh station for an old stage coach route between Nashville and Chapel Hill, N.C. Gideon Riggs was an early leader in the community. His descendants still gather at the Gideon Riggs Cemetery at the crossroads each Mother's Day.

14.2 Continue straight on Flat Creek Road. Use caution at the railroad crossing. You'll ride through the community of Flat Creek.

19.5 Turn right onto Comstock Road.

The Murfreesboro Bicycle Club's Two County Metric takes you through Rutherford and Franklin counties in Middle Tennessee. Photo by Vickie Spickard.

22.8 Turn left onto Bethesda Road.

You'll soon enter Bethesda, a small community of dairy and beef cattle farms. Hometown of former Tennessee Governor Henry Horton's grandfather, Bethesda was a happening place in the early 1900s. Its employers included saddle, casket, bed and chair manufacturers. Some local residents still possess the Waddey, straight-backed chairs produced there, passed down through the generations.

23.1 You'll see the Bethesda Store on your left. Continue straight on Bethesda Road.

27.2 Turn right onto U.S. Highway 431 (also called Lewisburg Pike). Watch for traffic.

Lewisburg Pike was a toll road in the 1800s. The Harpeth community is located along the pike, sandwiched between a few large hills, including Murrell Hill. John Murrell, born in Williamson County in 1804, was found guilty of riot in nearby Franklin before the age of 20, according to author Pewitt. He became one of the most notorious outlaws in the nation, primarily known as a slave stealer. Once, Murrell reportedly hid out in a cave near Triune, planning a slave rebellion. A tip off to authorities led to his capture.

27.9 You'll see a BP Station on your right. Turn right onto Harpeth-Peytonsville Road.

You'll soon enter the community of Peytonsville, formerly known as Snatchit and Little Texas. According to Pewitt, the name Snatchit came about in 1836 when a creditor snatched a $10 bill from the hand of a local debtor, Andrew Campbell. For a period after the Civil War, Peytonsville was known as Little Texas, where ex-Confederate fugitives hid in the surrounding hills. Most fugitives fled to Texas.

Peytonsville natives include the Grand Ole Opry's Sam and Kirk McGee, and Pulitzer Prize cartoonist Tom Little.

Harpeth-Peytonsville Road becomes Arno-Peytonsville Road.

34.2 Turn left onto Arno Road. You'll ride through the communities of Arno and Rudderville.

37.0 Turn right onto McDaniel Road.

39.8 You'll cross the Harpeth River. Use caution at the railroad crossing. Turn left onto Cox Road. You'll ride through the community of McDaniel.

40.4 Turn right onto Patton Road.

42.5 Turn right onto U.S. 41A (also called State Route 16).

42.6 Turn left onto Patterson/Coleman Hill Road.

46.2 Turn right onto Patterson Road.

50.0 Turn left onto Windrow Road.

54.6 Turn left onto Salem Road.

55.2 Turn left onto State Route 99 (also called Salem Highway). Watch for traffic.

55.9 Turn right onto Kimbro Road.

58.0 Turn right onto Yeargan Road.

60.2 Turn right onto Armstrong Valley.

61.8 Turn left onto State Route 99 (also called Salem Pike). Watch for traffic.

64.5 Ride ends at Rockvale Elementary School on the right, where the tour began.

For general information on lodging and attractions, contact the Rutherford County Chamber of Commerce, P.O. Box 864, Murfreesboro, TN 37133 (615-893-6565 or 800-716-7560), or Williamson County Tourism, 109 Second Avenue South, Suite 107, P.O. Box 156, Franklin, TN 37065-1056 (800-356-3445 or 615-794-1225).

Places to Stay

Flemingsburg House Bed & Breakfast, 3052 Old Murfreesboro Road, College Grove, TN 37046 (615-395-0017 or 877-443-3786), is a brick, colonial structure, built by Josiah Fleming in 1830. The community of Flemingsburg flourished until a fire in the 1850s. During the 1860s, the house and area witnessed several Civil War skirmishes. The property is now called Sweetwater Farm. There are two guest rooms and the upstairs Country Honeymoon Suite. Horseshoes, volleyball and croquet are offered for recreation. Karin and Ray Bogardus are the proprietors.

Nashville I-24 Campground (camping), 1130 Rocky Fork Road, Smyrna, TN 37167 (615-459-5818), provides 170 campsites with electric and water hookups, showers, swimming pool and grocery. It is open year-round.

Peacock Hill Country Inn, 6994 Giles Hill Road, College Grove, TN 37046 (615-368-7727), is a two-story, renovated farmhouse, that dates back before the Civil War. Ten guest rooms and suites are available. As a 700-acre working cattle and horse farm, miles of trails along Flat Creek are available for hiking, horseback riding and picnicking. You can even bring your own horses. Your hosts are Walter and Anita Ogilvie.

Bicycle Shops
Murfreesboro Bicycle Company, 710 Memorial Blvd., Murfreesboro, TN 37129 (615-896-5100).

Murfreesboro Outdoor and Bicycle, 1403 Greenland Drive, Murfreesboro, TN 37130 (615-893-7725).

Skedaddle Bicycles & Outfitters, 232 W. Northfield Blvd., Murfreesboro, TN 37129 (615-896-4950).

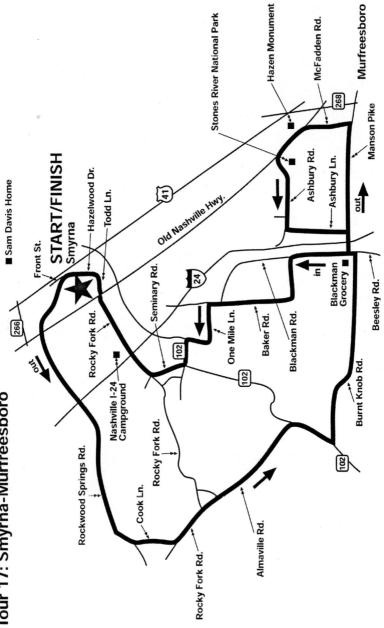

BICYCLING TENNESSEE
Tour 17: Smyrna-Murfreesboro

17. Smyrna—Murfreesboro

Easy terrain, only a few hills throughout the ride; 37.9 miles

By the winter of 1862, after the Civil War battles of Fort Donelson, Fort Henry and Shiloh, Federal troops had gained control of West Tennessee, including Nashville. At this point, the Federal strategy was to take control of the railroads that ran southward through Tennessee and Georgia. The next step was Union Gen. William S. Rosecrans' move from Nashville toward Confederate Gen. Braxton Bragg's winter headquarters in Murfreesboro.

Rosecrans' 43,000 men intended to plow through Bragg's 38,000 men, and continue their march to Chattanooga, but the assault didn't come without a high cost. The Confederates struck first on Dec. 31, 1862. The Union army fought back each attack inflicting very heavy casualties to the Confederacy. The toughest battle on this day took place in the vicinity of Round Forest. Both armies maintained their positions the next day, New Year's Day, but very little fighting occurred.

On Jan. 2, 1863, Bragg was surprised Rosecrans had not withdrawn. Rosecrans was in fact threatening the Confederates' right flank on the east side of the Stones River. Confederate forces totaling 4,500 men attacked ferociously, beating back the Union army to McFadden's Ford. But the Union quickly positioned 45 cannons 100 yards west of McFadden's Ford and put the field that the Confederates would be crossing in their sites. A total of 1,800 Confederate soldiers died or were wounded on this field; the rest withdrew.

The Stones River battles cost the lives of 13,249 Union soldiers and 10,266 Confederate soldiers. Bragg withdrew from Murfreesboro, and Rosecrans claimed victory.

The 450-acre Stones River National Battlefield is operated by the National Park Service. Much of the original 4,000-acre battlefield is now private land. Highlights of the park include the Stones River National Cemetery, established in 1865 with more than 6,000 Union graves, the Hazen Monument, believed to be the oldest Civil War monument, and Fortress Rosecrans, the largest enclosed earthen fortification built during the Civil War. The fort still stands although only 3,000 of the original 14,000 feet remains.

This route is a favorite of the Harpeth and Murfreesboro bicycle clubs; however, recent growth has brought more traffic to these rural roads. As always, practice safe biking when dealing with the few high traffic areas.

<u>Miles</u>

0.0 **Start route at the intersection of Lowery Street and Front Street in downtown Smyrna. Ride north on Front Street across the railroad tracks from Lowery Street (also Murfreesboro Road). You'll see the Smyrna Railroad Depot to your left as you cross the tracks. Front Street changes to Rockwood Springs Road.**

Smyrna, located in Rutherford County, is a fast growing community in middle Tennessee. The opening of a Nissan automobile manufacturing plant here in 1980 created 6,000 new jobs and sparked much of this growth. The manufacturer recently announced a $1 billion expansion of its engine plant in Decherd, Tenn., to better support the Smyrna plant.

The Sam Davis Home is less than two miles from the start of this route. Sam Davis Road is directly across Lowery Street (also Murfreesboro Road) from the Smyrna Railroad Depot park. A short trek east on Sam Davis Road will take you to the Confederate war hero's antebellum home.

Sam Davis was just 21 years old when the Union army captured, tried and hanged him in Pulaski, Tenn., for spying. He is remembered for his honor and loyalty to the Confederacy. When faced with choosing to die or revealing the source of papers found in his possession, he said, "If I had a thousand lives to live, I would give them all rather than betray a friend." It was later learned the papers were given to him by a Nashville woman, who seduced Union troops in that city to get information.

1.7   **Cross Nashville Highway.**

3.5   **Cross under Interstate 24.**

5.9   **Turn left onto Cook Lane. This is the first left past the Rock Springs Church of Christ.**
As you make this turn, you will see a small barn and a short silo. You will also be making two nice climbs while on Cook Lane.

7.2   **Turn left onto Rocky Fork Road at the stop sign at the T-intersection.**
Take notice of the life-sized wood carving of a lady placed next to this farm's mailbox. You will have one fairly long climb while on Rocky Fork Road.

10.8   **Turn right onto Almaville Road (also Highway 102) at the stop sign at the T-intersection. There are no street signs, but if you look across the street on Almaville Road, you will notice the mile marker 4.**

11.7   **Turn left onto Burnt Knob Road.**

15.9   **Turn left onto Beesley Road at the stop sign at the T-intersection.**
Blackman Grocery will be on your immediate left. Pizza and milkshakes are available along with the normal grocery products. It is open from 5 a.m. to 11 p.m. daily.

16.0   **Turn right immediately onto Manson Pike at the three-way intersection. Watch for traffic and several dangerous curves ahead.**

16.2   **Cross over Interstate 24.**

17.7   **Enter Murfreesboro city limits.**

19.7 **Turn left onto McFadden Road. This is the first left after passing a row of cedar trees on the left. You'll see National Park Service markers, indicating the crossing of McFadden Lane and Wilkinson Lane in 1862.**

Go around the cedar fence. This road is closed to motorized traffic.

21.3 **Turn left onto Old Nashville Highway.**

If you turn right here, within a few yards you'll see the Hazen Monument on your left (Stones River National Battlefield's Tour Stop 5). The survivors of Col. William B. Hazen's brigade erected this monument in 1863. It is the nation's oldest intact Civil War memorial.

The area surrounding the monument was the only Union position to withstand battle throughout the first day. Confederate troops attacked Round Forest at 10 a.m. but were broken up by Union artillery. An hour later, another attack only brought Confederates within 150 yards of the Union line.

Don't try this at home. This is a cannon near the Stones River National Battlefield's Hazen Monument. Photo by Vickie Spickard.

21.6 **The Stones River National Battlefield's visitor center is to your left.**

The visitor center is open daily from 8 a.m. to 5 p.m., closed only on Christmas Day. Bike parking racks, picnic tables and restrooms are available. The center features an orientation film, a display of artifacts, and official maps and guides for the park. You can bike the 1.3-mile auto loop and see Tour Stops 1-4. You may also want to check out the new greenways that are being expanded along the banks of the Stones River. These will provide even more access to this area and its colorful history.

21.9   **Turn left onto Ashbury Road. This is the second left after passing the visitor center.**

23.1   **Immediately after passing Hord Road to your right, turn left onto Ashbury Lane.**

24.4   **Cross over Interstate 24.**

25.7   **Right on Manson Pike at stop sign at the T-intersection. Watch for traffic.**

26.7   **Cross over Interstate 840.**

26.8   **Turn right onto Blackman Road at the stop sign at the T-intersection.**

Once again, you'll see Blackman Grocery straight ahead.

27.9   **Turn at the first left onto Baker Road.**

30.8   **Turn left onto One Mile Lane before arriving at Interstate 24.**

31.8   **Turn right at the four-way stop, staying on One Mile Lane.**

31.9   **Turn left onto Almaville Parkway (also Highway 102) at stop sign at the T-intersection. Watch for traffic.**

32.5   **At the Y-intersection, veer to the first right onto Seminary Road.**

33.8   **Turn right at the stop sign onto Rocky Fork Road.**

34.6   **Cross over Interstate 24.**

35.7   **Enter Smyrna city limits.**

36.2   **The Nashville I-24 Campground is on your left.**

36.3   **Turn right onto Old Nashville Highway at the stop sign at the T-intersection.**

36.4   **Turn at the first left onto Delacy Lane. There is no street sign.**

36.6 Turn right onto Todd Lane at the stop sign at the T-intersection.

37.0 Turn left onto Hazelwood Drive at the stop light at the T-intersection. Hazelwood Drive changes to Front Street. You'll see Smyrna Middle School and the Smyrna Parks Baseball Complex to your left.

37.1 At the intersection of Enon Springs Road West, continue straight on Hazelwood Drive (also Front Street).

37.9 You'll end the ride at the intersection of Front Street and Lowery Street, where the tour began.

For general information on lodging and attractions, contact the Rutherford County Chamber of Commerce, P.O. Box 864, Murfreesboro, TN 37133 (615-893-6565 or 800-716-7560).

<u>Places to Stay</u>
Clardy's Guest House, 435 East Main Street, Murfreesboro, TN 37130 (615-893-6030), features three rooms with private baths. This Victorian Romanesque house was built in 1898.

Nashville I-24 Campground (camping), 1130 Rocky Fork Road, Smyrna, TN 37167 (615-459-5818), provides 170 campsites with electric and water hookups, showers, swimming pool and grocery. It is open year-round.

Simply Southern, 2711 North Tennessee Blvd., Murfreesboro, TN 37130 (615-896-4988 or 888-723-1199), offers four rooms with private baths and a recreation room with pool table and player piano. It is located across the street from Middle Tennessee State University in the historic district.

Bicycle Shops

Murfreesboro Bicycle Company, 710 Memorial Blvd., Murfreesboro, TN 37129 (615-896-5100).

Murfreesboro Outdoor and Bicycle, 1403 Greenland Drive, Murfreesboro, TN 37130 (615-893-7725).

Skedaddle Bicycles & Outfitters, 232 W. Northfield Blvd., Murfreesboro, TN 37129 (615-896-4950).

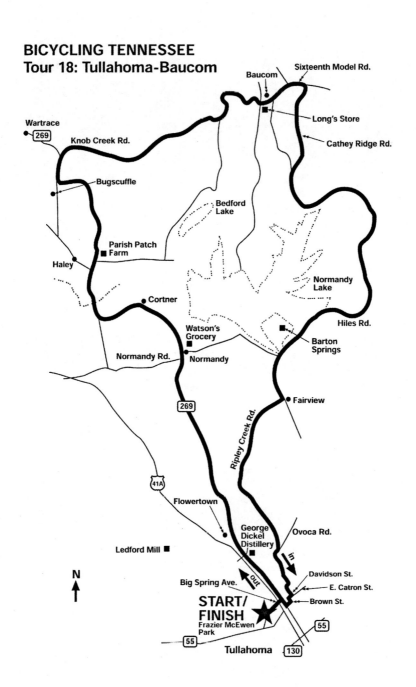

BICYCLING TENNESSEE
Tour 18: Tullahoma-Baucom

Baucom

Sixteenth Model Rd.

Long's Store

Cathey Ridge Rd.

Wartrace

269

Knob Creek Rd.

Bugscuffle

Bedford Lake

Parish Patch Farm

Haley

Normandy Lake

Cortner

Hiles Rd.

Watson's Grocery

Barton Springs

Normandy Rd.

Normandy

269

Fairview

41A

Ripley Creek Rd.

Flowertown

George Dickel Distillery

Ovoca Rd.

Ledford Mill

In

N

Big Spring Ave.

Davidson St.

E. Catron St.

START/ FINISH
Frazier McEwen Park

out

Brown St.

55

55

Tullahoma

130

18. Tullahoma—Baucom

Moderate to difficult terrain, quite a few hills with some significant; 38.2 miles

"Find out what whiskey he drinks and send all of my generals a case, if it will get the same results," Abraham Lincoln said about General Ulysses S. Grant. Wonder if Grant got an extra boost from Tennessee whiskey as he conquered the South. Southern distilleries were numerous during the Civil War era.

Whiskey is made from natural cereal grains, aged in wood casks to enhance the color and flavor. The two kinds of American whiskies are Bourbon, primarily made in Kentucky, and Tennessee whiskey. Bourbon is a sour mash whiskey. Tennessee whiskey also undergoes the sour mash process. In addition, between distillation and aging, Tennessee whiskey is slowly filtered through charcoal-packed vats for seven to 10 days. This charcoal mellowing is said to remove impurities, contributing to the spirit's smooth taste.

Today, there are only two Tennessee whiskey distillers, Jack Daniel's Old Time Distillery and George A. Dickel & Co., both located near this tour. The largest is Jack Daniel's, the country's oldest registered distillery. Daniel bought the Lynchburg business from family friend and minister, Dan Call, in 1866. Daniel was only 13 years old. Heading off a liquor tax, he registered the distillery in 1866.

"Each day we make it, we will make it the best we can," Daniel said. "Mr. Jack" became known for his formal knee-length frock coat and broad-brimmed planter's hat. In 1904, his Old No. 7 Tennessee sipping whiskey won the Gold Medal at the World's Fair in St. Louis. Daniel died of blood poisoning in 1911, stemming from an infection he received kicking his office safe in 1905. His nephew, Lem Motlow, inherited the distillery.

Since its beginning, the Jack Daniel's Distillery has used pure spring water from a nearby limestone cave. The business is open for free tours daily. Sorry, you can't have a sample taste onsite. Moore County is a dry county; however, voters approved the sale of small packaged samples in 1995.

George Dickel also took advantage of area springs when he opened his business. He registered his Tennessee whiskey distillery in Cascade Hollow in 1870. Its small facility takes one year to make the amount of whiskey that Jack Daniel's makes in two to three weeks. Dickel also applies further processing. It distills its whiskey twice. The distiller then chill mellows the whiskey before filtering it through 10 feet of crushed charcoal, made from hard sugar maple.

According to the company, "you can taste the hard work." Visit the George Dickel General Store. Free distillery tours are given on weekdays.

This tour is an option on the Highland Rimmers Bicycle Club's Elk River Century. There are several long, gradual uphills and downhills, with two major climbs down and up to Normandy Lake. To get to the start, take exit 111 on Interstate 24 between Nashville and Chattanooga. Head west on State Route 55 about 12 miles. Turn right onto U.S. 41A in Tullahoma. In about two miles, turn left onto Big Spring Road. Frazier McEwen Park will be on your right.

Miles

0.0   Start ride at Frazier McEwen Park. Head east on Big Spring Avenue.

Although Coffee County was established in 1836, Tullahoma didn't begin development until 1850, when the Nashville and Chattanooga Railroad routed through the community. The town was chartered in 1852, shortly after the development of a road between the county seat of Manchester and Tullahoma's depot.

The origin of the town name is debatable, but most believe it comes from two Choctaw Indian words, "tali" meaning rock and "houma" meaning red, according to the Historic Preservation Society of Tullahoma.

Most of the area's growth can be attributed to the military. Camp Peay, named for Tennessee Governor Austin Peay, opened in 1926 as a National Guard camp. During World War II, Camp Peay was converted and expanded into Camp Forrest, named for Confederate General Nathan Bedford Forrest. Camp Forrest was the U.S. Army's largest training facility for its infantry, artillery, engineer and signal divisions. It also served as a prisoner of war camp for German and Italian soldiers.

Tullahoma's population swelled from 4,500 to 75,000 during the war. The army closed Camp Forrest after the war, but soon selected the site for an engineering facility. In 1951, President Harry S. Truman dedicated the Arnold Engineering Development Center, named for Air Force General Henry H. "Hap" Arnold. It is still in operation today.

AEDC provides the army's most advanced and largest flight simulation test facilities. It includes more than 50 aerodynamic and propulsion wind tunnels, rocket and turbine engine test cells, space environmental chambers, arc heaters, ballistic ranges and other specialized units. The facility can simulate altitudes from sea level to over 100,000 feet and velocities from subsonic to more than Mach 20.

Places to visit in Tullahoma include the Tullahoma Fine Arts Center, the Regional Museum of Art, sporting goods manufacturer Worth Industries and the Staggerwing Museum, commemorating Walter Beech's Model 17, a milestone in aviation development in the 1930s. Each summer, the Paul Pyle Dulcimer Association hosts the Dulcimer Daze festival in Tullahoma.

0.2 **You'll see a BP station to your right. Cross North Jackson Street onto Ogee Avenue (no street sign). Watch for traffic.**

0.3 **Turn left onto North Atlantic Street (also State Route 269) at the stop sign at the T-intersection.**
Follow the railroad tracks along a shady, gradual downhill all the way to Normandy.

4.5 **Enter Bedford County.**
To get to the George Dickel General Store and Distillery, turn right on Marbury Road and follow the signs for about a half a mile.

6.5 **Enter Normandy City Limits.**
Normandy was a busy place until the railroads quit making daily stops. Nevertheless, it still greets people visiting the nearby George Dickel Distillery and Normandy Lake.

The Tennessee Wildlife Resources Agency runs the Normandy Fish Hatchery on Huffman Road, about a half a mile north of town. Breeding stock come from area lakes and rivers. The agency raises 12 species of fish here, including the endangered fresh water mussel. The hatchery offers tours. Calling ahead is recommended.

6.8 **Continue straight at the three-way stop. Watson's Grocery is across the railroad tracks to the right.**
Terrain becomes more hilly. You'll pass through the community of Cortner.

The Cortner Mill was built in this community in 1848. It was rebuilt in 1889 after a fire. Mill workers grinded, sifted and sacked Snow Drift flour, which was shipped from Cortner Station to all parts of the country. The Cortner family built the present dam in 1915. They closed the mill in 1956. Charles and Martha Parish, owners of Worth Industries, renovated it in the 1970s. Today, it operates as a restaurant on the vast Parish Patch Farm. The old sifter acts as a buffet table.

10.8 You are entering the community of Haley. You'll see Parish Patch Farm & Inn on your right.

14.0 Turn right onto Knob Creek Road.
If you continue straight, you'll soon enter the town of Wartrace.

15.8 You are entering the community of Union Ridge.

18.2 Continue to the left. Road becomes Sixteenth Model Road. You'll be entering the community of Baucom.

19.8 You'll see Long's Store straight ahead. Continue on Sixteenth Model Road to the left.

21.1 You'll see three gray silos to the right. Turn right onto Cathey Ridge Road.

24.1 After descending a steep hill, you'll see Ripley Creek (part of Normandy Lake) to your right. Get ready to ascend another steep hill. Cathey Ridge Road eventually turns into Hiles Road.

31.1 After descending a steep hill and crossing Normandy Lake, Frank Road will be to your right. Continue straight. Hiles Road becomes Ripley Creek Road.
Frank Road takes you to Barton Springs Recreational Area and Normandy Dam, operated by the Tennessee Valley Authority. Get ready to climb your last major hill. You'll ride through the community of Fairview.

35. 4 Enter Tullahoma City Limits.

36.0 Veer right, continuing on Ovoca Road.

37.1 Cross King's Lane at the traffic light. Watch for traffic.

37.4 Ovoca Road turns into Catron Street at the stop sign.

37.5 Turn left onto Davidson Street at the stop sign at the T-intersection.

37.6 Turn right onto Brown Street at the stop sign at the T-intersection.

37.8 Turn right onto N.E. Atlantic Street at the stop sign at the T-intersection.

37.9 Turn left onto Ogee Avenue.

38.0 You'll see a BP station straight ahead. Cross North Jackson Street onto Big Spring Avenue. Watch for traffic.

38.2 End ride at Frazier McEwen Park on your right, where the tour began.

For general information on lodging and attractions, contact the Bedford County Chamber of Commerce, 100 Cannon Blvd., Shelbyville, TN 37160 (931-684-3482), or Tullahoma Area Chamber of Commerce, 135 W. Lincoln St., Tullahoma, TN 37388 (931-455-5497).

<u>Places to Stay</u>
Barton Springs Recreational Area (camping), Barton Springs Road, P.O. Box 37, Normandy, TN 37360 (931-857-9222), is located right off the route. It offers 64 sites with grills, shower facilities and a swimming area on Normandy Lake.

Ledford Mill Bed & Breakfast, Route 2, Box 152B, Wartrace, TN 37183 (931-455-2546), is located just three miles north of Tullahoma off U.S. Highway 41A. The 1884 gristmill, along Shipman's Creek, is on the National Register of Historic Places. It was restored to a three-story country inn in 1996. Innkeepers Dennis and Kathleen Depert provide three guest accommodations. There is also a two-story antique shop. The waterfalls, creek, gardens and barn are only open to bed and breakfast guests after 4 p.m.

Parish Patch Farm & Inn, 1100 Cortner Road, Normandy, TN 37360 (931-857-3017 or 800-876-3017), is located just off the route. David and Claudia Hazelwood own and operate this 230-acre farm, which raises Beefalo cattle (part bison, part cow). There are 21 guestrooms and a 90-seat conference center. Past guests have included baseball greats Hank Aaron and Ted Williams.

Bicycle Shops

Skedaddle Bicycles & Outfitter, 1905 N. Jackson St., Tullahoma, TN 37388 (931-461-5664).

Woody's Bicycles, 115 Second Ave. Northwest, Winchester, TN 37398 (931-967-7020).

BICYCLING TENNESSEE
Tour 19: Jasper-Dunlap

Dunlap

Sequatchie County Park

John Burch Rd.

127

West Valley Rd.

Cookston Cave Rd.

Cartwright Grocery

Old Highway 28

Bryant's Grocery

28

Condra

283

Sequatchie River

Whitwell

283

Powell's Crossroads

Store

Valleyview Highway

Garrett's Grocery

Ketner Mill Rd.

Victoria

Ketner's Mill

28

Ketner Mill Lane

Sequatchie River

27

START/ FINISH

Marion County High School

in

R.A. Griffith Highway

N

Betsy Pack Dr.

41

out

Jasper

64

24

R & R Bait and Tackle

Tennessee-Alabama Grocery

Shellmound Rd.

Tennessee River

TVA Access Rd.

Nickajack Dam

Shellmound Loop

19. JASPER—DUNLAP

Easy to moderate; 62.0 miles

The Sequatchie Valley is sometimes called the "Grand Canyon" of Tennessee. Bordered by the Cumberland Plateau and Walden Ridge, the valley stretches 125 miles through Sequatchie and Marion counties, and continues south into Alabama, where it is called Brown's Valley. Its floor features quaint farms, hardwood forests and the picturesque Sequatchie River.

The name comes from Sequachee, a Cherokee Indian chief. The meaning of the word is debatable, but most evidence points to the phrase, "opossum, he grins," according to Henry R. Camp in his book, *Sequatchie County: A Story of a Place and its People.* The valley provided the Cherokee and early frontiersmen with an excellent hunting ground before white settlers arrived. The Griffith and Standifer families of Virginia were among the first to settle there in the early 1800s.

James Standifer served the valley as U.S. congressman from 1823 to 1825 and from 1829 to 1837, the latter as a Whig. Upon his death in 1837, another Whig, Gen. William Stone, replaced him as congressman. Stone came from a prominent family. His uncle, Thomas Stone, was a signer of the Declaration of Independence. William Stone's family first settled in the valley at the foot of the Cumberland Mountains at a place later to be called Stone's Cave. Soon, he became one of the valley's largest landowners around what is today the community of Daus. Stone served in the Creek War and the War of 1812, where he participated in the famed Battle of New Orleans.

During the early 1800s, the Sequatchie Valley resided in Bledsoe and Marion counties. Citizens in northern Marion County, however, complained about the 30- to 50-mile trip to the county seat, Jasper. Thus, the state legislature carved out Sequatchie County from southern Bledsoe County and northern Marion County in 1857.

This tour takes you through the Sequatchie Valley. You'll ride up along Walden Ridge and back along the Cumberland Plateau on the relatively flat or rolling valley floor. There is only one mountain to cross. Don't be surprised to see hang gliders overhead. The valley provides a great opportunity for their sport as well. This is part of the Chattanooga Bicycle Club's 2 for 1 Century. The first century on a Saturday takes you through the Sequatchie Valley in Tennessee. The second century on a Sunday goes into northern Georgia.

Jasper is about 20 miles west of Chattanooga, which offers several tourist attractions. You can take the world's steepest passenger railway up historic Lookout Mountain and visit Rock City, an enchanted fairyland opened by Garnet and Frieda Carter in 1932. The mountain also features Ruby Falls and the Battles for Chattanooga Electric Map and Museum. The Tennessee Aquarium in downtown Chattanooga is one of the world's largest aquariums. A 60-foot canyon and two forests feature more than 7,000 animals in natural habitats.

To get to the start of the ride, take Interstate 24 west of Chattanooga. Turn off at Kimball (Exit 152). Take U.S. 64/U.S. 72 northeast. Turn left onto U.S. Highway 41. Turn left onto Betsy Pack Drive. You'll see Marion County High School on your right.

Miles

0.0 **Start ride at Marion County High School. Head east on Betsy Pack Drive.**

Marion County makes up about 507 square miles of the Sequatchie Valley.

This area's frontier history included Hernando DeSoto's encampment on Burns Island in 1540 as well as several clashes between white explorers and Cherokee Indians along the Tennessee River. In 1780, the Cherokee attacked the Donelson Expedition near today's Memorial Bridge near Jasper. (You can read more about the Donelson Expedition in the Pickwick Dam—Dover chapter.) In 1788, the Cherokee attacked the Brown Expedition near the mouth of Battle Creek near South Pittsburg. In 1793, Ore's Expedition with 500 soldiers destroyed the Cherokee villages at Nickajack and Falling Water.

Marion County was established in November 1817. It is named for Revolutionary War hero Francis Marion. Nicknamed the "Swamp Fox of South Carolina," the sergeant fought off the British in Charleston during the war. Betsy Pack, a Cherokee woman, deeded 40 acres in 1822 that would eventually become the county seat of Jasper.

The county attracted industries using coal and iron throughout the 19th Century. English iron master James Brown and Welsh metallurgist Thomas Whitwell envisioned the area as a Southern industrial center. Old English Co. purchased 3,000 acres of land along the Tennessee River in 1873. The venture led to the formation of the South Pittsburg, Whitwell and Victoria communities. The operation merged with the Tennessee Coal and Iron Co. in 1882.

Limestone attracted industry in the early 20th Century. Richard Hardy established the Dixie Portland Cement Co. in South Pittsburg. The large cement processing facility had its own company town, Richard City. In 1910, the nation's first hydroelectric generating power plant, Hales Bar Dam, was built.

You'll pass several conveniences as you ride through Jasper.

0.6　Turn left onto U.S. Highway 41 at the traffic light. Watch for traffic.

2.6　Turn right onto Shellmound Road at the traffic light.

5.9　Turn left onto Shellmound Loop.

6.1　Turn right onto an unmarked road.

6.2　Turn left on the TVA Access Road.

If you turn right, you'll come upon Nickajack Dam. Nickajack Lake offers spectacular views of the Sequatchie Valley. This stretch along the Tennessee River is known for its annual Fall Color Cruise, when boats pass through the gorge and gather at the Shellmound Recreation Area for festivities.

8.2　You'll see Tennessee-Alabama Grocery on your left before crossing under the Interstate 24 overpass.

8.5　Cross U.S. Highway 41 at the stop sign. You'll see R & R Bait and Tackle to your right.

You'll ride through the community of Rankin Cove.

11.4　You'll see the white Ebenezer Church on your right. Turn right onto R.A. Griffith Highway (also called State Route 27). Watch for traffic.

You'll ride through the communities of Ebenezer and Mineral Springs.

12.3　After climbing the small mountain, you'll see Mom and Pop's grocery on the left. Continue straight for a nice, long downhill.

16.6　You'll see the white Oak Grove Presbyterian Church on your right. Turn left onto Ketner Mill Lane. There is no street sign.

17.7　Ketner's Mill is on your left.

This is the site of Whitwell's annual Ketner's Mill Country Fair.

Cyclists take a break at Ketner's Mill during the Chattanooga Bicycle Club's 2 for 1 Century.

18.0   Turn right onto Ketner Mill Road.

18.6   Turn left onto R.A. Griffith Highway. Watch for traffic.

22.6   You'll see a market to your right. State Route 27 continues to the right. Continue straight on State Route 283 at the stop sign.

You'll ride through the communities of Powells Crossroads and Hicks Chapel, and soon cross into Sequatchie County. This road is also called East Valley Road.

25.8   You'll see Hayes Country Store on your left.

33.7   Turn left onto U.S. Highway 127 at the stop sign. Watch for traffic.

34.9   After crossing the Sequatchie River, turn left onto John Burch Road.

You'll ride up and down a big bluff.

36.7   You'll see the Blue Plate restaurant on your right. Cross State Route 28 at the stop sign.

You are in the town of Dunlap. In the early 20th Century, the Chattanooga Iron and Coal Corp. owned 16,000 acres of coal land near Dunlap, according to author Camp. By 1920, there was Dunlap, the Sequatchie County seat, with a population of 765, and

Dunlap, the Chattanooga Iron and Coal company town, with 700 people, one-mile apart from each other.

Dunlap became known for its coke, a fixed-carbon fuel with less than 10 percent ash. The booming pig iron industry used coke as a deoxidizing agent in its production. Coke by-products included coal gas, coal tar, ammonium, sulfate and benzol. Bituminous coal was extracted from the mountains and brought to the valley floor via inclined railways. The coal was then crushed, washed and placed in beehive ovens. The heat removed volatile matter. The closed chambers retarded or prevented burning.

Beehive coking ovens got their name from their shape, according to Camp. They were built on a clay foundation topped with sand and loam—the interiors lined with coarse fire brick. During its heyday, 85 men operated 268 ovens at Dunlap. Chattanooga Iron and Coal then shipped the coke to Chattanooga, where it was heated with red iron ore in the furnace at Tannery Flats. At its peak, Tannery Flats produced 200 tons of pig iron every 24 hours.

In 1919, Southern States Iron and Coal Co. bought the Chattanooga Iron and Coal property in Sequatchie County, but an economic downturn suspended operations in 1922. The mining and coking operations never reopened. The remnants of the era can be found in Coke Oven Park, site of the Coke Oven Bluegrass Festival and Craft Show held each June.

37.2   **After passing Sequatchie County Park, turn left onto West Valley Road (also called Old Whitwell Highway) at the stop sign at the T-intersection.**

42.0   **Turn left onto Cookston Cave Road.**

42.1   **Turn right onto State Route 28. You'll see Cartwright Grocery on your right.**

42.7   **Turn right onto Old Highway 28 (also called Old Dunlap Highway). You'll soon see Bryant's Grocery on your left.**

You'll enter Marion County, riding through the communities of Condra and Red Hill.

49.5 **Turn left at the stop sign, continuing on Old Highway 28.**

You'll ride through the community of Whitwell, the original Marion County seat. Like Dunlap, the community boomed during the years of coal and coke production. After that industry subsided, the community returned to its farming roots. In addition to the Ketner's Mill Country Fair, Whitwell hosts an annual Labor Day parade.

50.3 **Turn right onto Old Highway 28, just before the stop sign at State Route 28. There is a Raceway station on State Route 28.**

50.9 **Turn right onto Valleyview Highway at the stop sign at the T-intersection**

51.4 **Ketner Mill Road is to your left. You'll see Garrett's Grocery on the right.**

You'll ride through the communities of Victoria and Sequatchie. The road becomes Betsy Pack Drive in Jasper.

62.0 **End ride at Marion County High School on your left.**

For general information on lodging and attractions, contact the Marion County Chamber of Commerce, 24 Courthouse Square Jasper, TN 37347 (423-942-5103), or Sequatchie County Executive, 307 Cherry St. East, Dunlap, TN 37327 (423-949-3479).

Places to Stay

The Club House Bed & Breakfast, 512 Mountain View Road, Dunlap, TN 37327 (423-949-4983), is located near Coke Oven Park. Stewardess Froney Rankin accommodated visiting officials and managers at the home during Dunlap's coal and coke heyday. John Smith purchased the home after the coal boom. Mike and Carol Confer bought the home from his daughter in 1994, turning it into a bed and breakfast. There are three guestrooms, with one having a private balcony.

Holiday Inn Express, 300 Battle Creek Road, Kimball/South Pittsburg, TN 37380 (423-837-1500), is located just north of Exit 152 off Interstate 24. Look for all the huge fireworks outlets (as if you can miss them). The hotel features a swimming pool and exercise facility.

Marion County Park (camping), P.O. Box 431, Jasper, TN 37347 (423-942-9146), offers 17 sites with electrical, water and sewer connections. Fishing and swimming are available.

Bicycle Shops
Bike Shop, 201 Frazier Ave., Chattanooga, TN 37405 (423-267-1000).

East Ridge Bicycles, 5910 Ringgold Road, Chattanooga, TN 37412 (423-894-9122).

Easy Chair Bikes Inc., 506 James Blvd., Signal Mountain, TN 37377 (423-886-1499).

Owen Cyclery, 1920 Northpoint Blvd., Hixson, TN 37343 (423-875-6811).

River City Bicycles Inc., 112 Tremont St., Chattanooga, TN 37405 (423-265-7176).

Suck Creek Cycle, 501 Cherokee Blvd., Chattanooga, TN 37405 (423-266-8883).

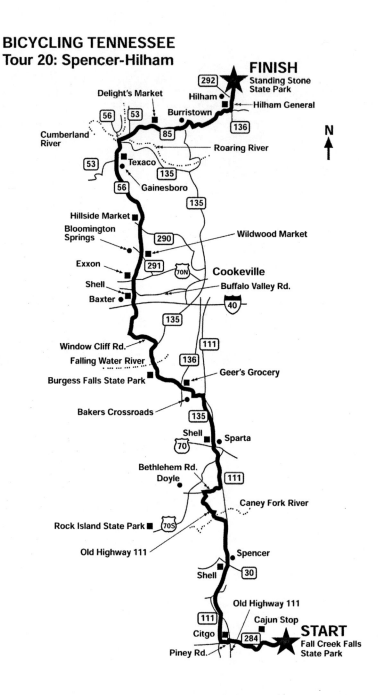

BICYCLING TENNESSEE
Tour 20: Spencer-Hilham

FINISH
Standing Stone
State Park

292
Hilham — Hilham General

Delight's Market
Burristown

56   53
85   136

Cumberland
River

Roaring River

53   Texaco
135
56   Gainesboro

135

Hillside Market
Bloomington
Springs   Wildwood Market
290

Exxon
291
70N   **Cookeville**
Shell
Baxter   Buffalo Valley Rd.

40
135

Window Cliff Rd.   111
Falling Water River   136
Burgess Falls State Park   Geer's Grocery

Bakers Crossroads
135

Shell   Sparta
70

Bethlehem Rd.
Doyle   111

Caney Fork River

Rock Island State Park   70S
Old Highway 111

Spencer
30
Shell

Old Highway 111
111   Cajun Stop
Citgo   284   **START**
                                Fall Creek Falls
Piney Rd.   State Park

N

20. SPENCER—HILHAM: A TWO-DAY TOUR

Moderate terrain; 87.2 miles

The Upper Cumberland is a unique region, neither Southern nor Appalachian in its folkways. Many of the inhabitants consider themselves the true American hillbillies, according to William Lynwood Montell in his book, *Upper Cumberland Country.*

Located in the center of the eastern United States, the region covers portions of northeast Tennessee and southeast Kentucky. For years, the region's main source of resource and commerce was the Cumberland River, which runs through its heart. According to Willis B. Boyd in *The Upper Cumberlands*, the mountains are high enough to be cool but not cold, and the valleys are low enough to be warm but not hot.

Three old Indian trails dictated movement around the Upper Cumberland in the early days. The Chickamauga Path began in what is today Georgia, entering the Upper Cumberland from the south. This trail intersected with Tollunteeskee's Trail and the Great East-West Trail. After the signing of the Third Treaty of Tellico in 1805, white settlers purchased most of the lands from the Cherokee Indians. The majority of these settlers came from Virginia and the Carolinas. The region's river bottoms provided fertile land, but the threat of floods sent many settlers to the uplands.

Employment in the 1800s primarily centered on agriculture, timber or coal. The population fluctuated greatly in the early 1900s as many residents migrated back and forth from the North for industrial jobs, particularly during the Great Depression. During this time within the region, most found economic success primarily in the urban development of Cookeville, Tenn., and Somerset, Ky. By the latter part of the century, in addition to the old reliable timber industry, the garment and tourism industries were significantly contributing to the economy.

This ride is part of the state's Highland Rim bike route. It begins along the Highland Rim in Van Buren County before soon entering the Upper Cumberland region. The route includes three beautiful state parks—Fall Creek Falls, Burgess Falls and Standing Stone. The terrain is moderate, but is particularly hilly on the second day as you near Hilham.

The beginning of this ride is about 50 miles north of Chattanooga. From Chattanooga, take U.S. Highway 27 north toward Dayton. Then take State Route 111 north. Turn right onto State Route 284 to enter Fall Creek Falls State Park.

Day 1
Moderate terrain; 54.1 miles

Miles

0.0   Start ride at the entrance of Fall Creek Falls State Park. Head west on State Route 284 (also called Archie Rhinehart Parkway).
Fall Creek Falls State Park is one of the most scenic recreational areas in the Southeast. Fall Creek Falls plunges 256 feet into a shaded pool, making it the highest waterfall east of the Rocky Mountains. Piney Falls, Cane Creek Falls and Cane Creek Cascades are smaller but just as impressive. Sparkling streams, beautiful gorges, and oak and hickory forestland also contribute to the park's 20,000-plus acres of rugged beauty.

The Environmental Education Center conducts seasonal programs including cave tours, life of a lookout, creek studies, bike tours, campfires, star watch, canoeing, scavenger hunts, softball and concerts. Annual events include backpacking trips at Fall Creek, rock climbing workshops, Fourth of July Celebration,

Mountaineer Folk Festival in September, Fall Colors Weekend in October and various educational events. Two naturalists are on duty year-round.

The park offers 50 miles of hiking trails, 25 miles of backpacking trails and 20 miles of mountain bike trails. The hiking trails are off limits to cyclists. The two mountain bike paths are not recommended for beginners. The Chinquapin Ridge Trail runs near Cane Creek at the south end of the park. Parking is available at the Newton Ford Picnic Area. Check with park officials before mountain biking here. This trail is closed to cyclists during one nine-day period, and it is open for deer hunting at the end of October and the first of November. It is recommended not to wear antlers when biking at this time. The Piney Creek Trail is a 10.5-mile out and back route, with optional side trails. Parking is available at the Piney Falls Loop.

For roadsters, a three-mile, paved bicycle path goes from the inn to the falls, crossing the main park road at the dam, near the village green. Bicycles can be rented from April to October.

The park is located on the western edge of the Cumberland Plateau in Bledsoe and Van Buren counties. This tour exits the park into Van Buren County.

Early settlers reached this area via the Caney Fork River, the Black Fox Trail, the Kentucky Road, the Wilderness Trail or the Madison Road, according to Landon Daryle Medley in his book, *The History of Van Buren County: the Early Canebreakers 1840-1940.* State legislators created the county, named for President Martin Van Buren, on Jan. 3, 1840, from portions of White and Warren counties.

As you head west, State Route 284 becomes Park Road, then Piney Road.

Fall Creek Falls is the highest waterfall east of the Rocky Mountains.

4.2   You'll see the Cajun Stop and Cajun Inn to your right.

6.2   Turn left onto Old Highway 111 at the stop sign at the T-inter-
      section.

6.4   Turn right onto Piney Road.

7.5   You'll see a Citgo station on your right. Turn right onto State
      Route 111 at the traffic light. Watch for traffic.

      There's a big shoulder that you'll want to use. There will be several
      gradual up and down climbs as you approach the town of Spencer.

14.0 Enter Spencer city limits. You'll soon see a Chevron Food Mart on
      your right.

      Spencer was founded on Jan. 7, 1850. At that time, the county seat
      boosted 164 residents, but a growing number were attracted to the
      town's Burritt College, named in honor of Elihu Burritt, a leader in
      the peace movement from Worcester, Mass. Nathan F. Trogden and

John Gillentine were instrumental in starting the college, according to Medley. The curriculum included Latin, Greek, philosophy, mathematics and Christian teachings. The college operated continuously from 1849 to 1938, except for four years during the Civil War and two semesters of financial crisis in 1889. The institution succumbed to bankruptcy in 1938, never to open again.

Spencer has prospered with the success of Fall Creek Falls State Park. Local resident James M. "Judge" Taft was influential in founding the park, courting the National Park Service and his friend, Tennessee Gov. Gordon Browning. The state bought the land in 1935 to develop for public use. Spencer also hosts an annual Mountain Music Fest.

15.7 **You'll see a Save a Lot and Shell station on your left. Pass under State Route 30.**

In a couple of miles, you'll begin a long descent down a mountain. Stay on the shoulder. You'll pass Skip's Market on the right.

19.5 **Turn left onto Old Highway 111 (also called Dr. Morgan Road) at the bottom of the mountain.**

19.6 **Turn right at the stop sign at the T-intersection. There is no street sign.**

You are riding through the community of Cummingsville. Joseph Cummings Sr., a Scottish immigrant and Revolutionary War veteran, came to what was then White County in the early 1800s, according to Medley. Cummings Spring in Spencer is named after him.

His son, Burrell Cummings, owned 175 acres in this area in 1840. The younger Cummings was a lawyer and farmer, who at different times served as a Van Buren deputy sheriff, sheriff, circuit court clerk and county judge. He also was a York Academy trustee and Burritt College board member.

20.3 **Turn left onto Cane Creek Road (also called Hodges Ferry Road). Road becomes Hodges Bridge Road.**

21.7 **Cross the Caney Fork Bridge. Enter White County.**

During the James Polk and Henry Clay presidential race in 1844, supporters for each man rallied on opposite sides of the Caney Fork River, according to the Rev. Monroe Seals in his book, *History of White County Tennessee.* One side chanted, "James K. Polk is long and tall, we'll rake him down with a hickory pole," in reference to Polk's fellow Democrat Andrew "Old Hickory" Jackson. The other side answered back with an anti-Clay chant. The verbiage became more and more cutting, and if not for the river between them, may have turned violent.

Bridgestone/Firestone Inc. recently donated 10,000 acres of land along the Caney Fork River to preserve as a wilderness. Bridgestone, which inherited the land when it bought Firestone in 1988, was unable to find an industrial buyer. The donation gives the public access to 15 miles along the river and its tributaries.

John White, a Revolutionary War veteran from Amelia County, Virginia, was the first settler in this area in 1789, according to Seals. His family and other newcomers had constant skirmishes with Native Americans. After the Treaty of Tellico in 1795, pioneers began communities later to become known as Yankeetown, Horseshoe Bend, Young's Mill and Sparta. The state legislature created the county, named for John White, on Sept. 6, 1806, out of Smith County. Rock Island, the earliest known settlement in the area, was the first county seat.

24.1 Cross Gooseneck Road (also called State Route 285). Street becomes Greenwood Road.

The community of Doyle is down the left on Gooseneck Road.

When you cross Memorial Highway, the street becomes Worley Road.

25.1 Turn right onto Bethlehem Road at the stop sign at the T-intersection.

After crossing Memorial Highway again, the street becomes Levon Sparkman Road.

27.2 Turn right onto County House Road at the stop sign at the T-intersection.

27.6 Turn left onto State Route 111.

31.1 Cross over U.S. Highway 70 South.

If you take U.S. Highway 70 South, you'll come to Rock Island State Park, a beautiful state park where the Collins River, Rocky River and Caney Fork River converge around Center Hill Lake. Camping is available.

Programs throughout the summer include interpretive hikes, canoe floats, pontoon boat tours, birdwalks, rock hops in the gorge, live animal shows, softball, volleyball and horseshoes. There are also tours of Bone Cave. The mouth of the cave sides with an old trail where immigrants entered the Calfkiller Valley. According to author Seals, bandits ambushed caravans at this location. Legend has it that a deep hole in one of the cave's chambers is full of human bones, where the bandits discarded their victims.

Annual park events include the Spring Wildflower Pilgrimage, Easter egg hunt and walleye tournament—all in April; Independence Day Celebration and Labor Day Weekend Celebration; and the Arts & Crafts Fair, Lawnchair Jam, Autumn Colors Festival and Halloween Festival—all in October.

The Highland Rim offers miles and miles of woodlands and cow pastures.

32.5 Pass under U.S. Highway 70. You'll see a Shell Food Mart and Save A Lot on the left.

You are entering the town of Sparta. According to Seals, in 1809, county authorities began looking to create a new county seat along the Calfkiller River. There is an old story that the river was given that name after an early settler's calf drowned while trying to cross it, but most historians believe it was named after an Indian chief. The new county seat became Sparta, named after an ancient Greek town on a small river.

Area places to visit include Golden Mountain Park, Virgin Falls and the Sparta Rock House, built by William Hunter for Barlow Fisk in the 1840s.

The town's most famous native is honored each year during the Lester Flatt/Martha White Hometown Memorial Bluegrass Festival, held at Foggy Mountain Music Park on Highway 70. Flatt, the voice behind the Foggy Mountain Boys, was born at Duncan's Chapel near the Putnam/Overton county line on June 19, 1914, but made Sparta his permanent home at an early age. He died on May 11, 1979, and is buried in Sparta's Oaklawn Memorial Cemetery.

The Martha White company, based in Nashville, was an early supporter of Flatt, Earl Scruggs and the Foggy Mountain Boys. The company hired the unknown band to tour the South in 1953, promoting its flour and cornmeal. They became known as the "World's Greatest Flour Peddlers." Flatt and Scruggs eventually hosted their own television show, and performed at Carnegie Hall and the Hollywood Bowl. The bluegrass legends are best remembered for performing the theme song to "The Beverly Hillbillies," a 1960s television show in which they appeared six times.

34.2   Turn onto the ramp to State Route 289.

34.5   Turn right onto State Route 289 (also called Roberts-Matthews Highway) at the stop sign.

34.6   Turn left onto State Route 135.

36.2   Turn left onto State Route 135 (also called Burgess Falls Road). You'll soon see a Citgo station on the right.

36.3   Cross over State Route 111.

37.1   Duck Pond Road is straight ahead. Turn right at the three-way stop, continuing on Burgess Falls Road. (also Cookeville Road and State Route 135).

40.4   Cross State Route 136 at the four-way stop. Geer's Grocery is on the right.

You're riding through the community of Bakers Crossroads.

43.6   The entrance to Burgess Falls State Natural Area is on the left.

The U.S. government gave this land to Tom Burgess, following his service during the Revolutionary War. On the Falling Water River here, his family ran a grist mill and later a sawmill. The city of Cookeville bought the land in the early 1920s, building a dam and powerhouse to produce electricity for its residents. Heavy rains destroyed the original structures in 1928, but a new dam and powerhouse produced electricity until 1944. By that time, the Tennessee Valley Authority's dams and powerhouses were doing the job. The 1928 dam, however, still stands in the park.

All areas of the park, including plants, animals, rocks, minerals and artifacts are now protected by the state. Recreational bicycling is only allowed in the main parking lot. There is a ¾-mile trail to the three falls. Each fall you encounter becomes more impressive than the last, with the final fall plunging into a gorge 130 feet below. The park hours are from 8 a.m. to 30 minutes before sunset. During the summer, interpretive programming is available.

At this writing, the state was considering to close Burgess Falls State Natural Area, or turn it over to another government entity or private owner.

43.7 Cross the Falling Water River Bridge. Enter Putnam County.
Putnam County was originally formed on February 1842 out of Overton, Fentress, Jackson and White counties, and named for Revolutionary War Gen. Israel Putnam, according to Walter S. McClain in his book, *A History of Putnam County Tennessee*. A proposed county seat was to be called Monticello. However, within three years, courts ruled the formation of the county unconstitutional because not enough area was left for Overton and Jackson counties. By 1854, with slight boundary changes, state legislators re-established Putnam County and named the new town of Cookeville as its county seat.

45.3 You'll see a market on your right.
46.3 Turn left onto Window Cliff Road.
This is a narrow backroad through the community of Boiling Springs. You'll go down and up a bluff at Cane Creek. You'll cross Cookeville-Boatdock Road at the stop sign. Watch out for a dangerous intersection. You'll then pass near the community of Twin Oaks.

49.3 Turn right onto Baxter Road at the stop sign at the T-intersection.
You'll ride near the community of Thomas. The terrain becomes hilly.

53.0 Pass under Interstate 40. Watch for traffic.

The road becomes State Route 56. There is big shoulder on the side. You are entering the community of Baxter.

The old Walton Road went through what is now Baxter, according to McClain. In 1797, the state legislature authorized Capt. William Walton of Smith County to construct a road from East Tennessee (at the junction of the Tennessee, Clinch, and Emory rivers) to Nashville. Putnam County had more miles of the Walton Road than any other county.

This community grew even more after the Tennessee Central Railway came to town in 1890. Originally called Mine Lick, the name was changed in 1902 to honor Jere Baxter. The town was incorporated in 1915.

54.1 **You'll see a Shell station on your left. End Day 1 ride at the intersection of State Route 56 and Buffalo Valley Road.**

Cookeville is located five miles east on Buffalo Valley Road. The city was named for Maj. Richard F. Cooke, a state senator from 1851-54 and an avid supporter of the new county. He owned a plantation near what is now Double Springs. The town especially grew when the Nashville and Knoxville Railroad routed through the town in 1890.

Points of interests include the Cookeville Depot Museum, the original 1909 depot at Broad Street and Cedar Avenue that houses railroad artifacts; Appalachian Center for Crafts, located on 600 acres overlooking Center Hill Lake; Bryan Fine Arts Center; Cane Creek Park, featuring a 56-acre lake and 100-acre park; Cookeville Drama Center; Hidden Hollow Park, an 86-acre park; and Upper Cumberland Sporting Clays, a shotgun sport park open weekends on Brotherton Mountain Road.

Day 2
Moderate terrain; 33.1 miles

<u>Miles</u>

0.0 **Start Day 2 ride at the intersection of State Route 56 and Buffalo Valley Road.**

1.2 **Cross U.S. Highway 70 North at the four-way stop. You'll soon see an Exxon Food Mart on the left.**

2.9 **State Route 291 is on the right. Wildwood Market is on the right. Continue straight.**

You're riding through the community of Bloomington Springs. Matthew Kuykendall and Ridley Draper were two of the first large landowners in this area, according to author McClain. The first house in the community was built about 1850. After the Civil War, Draper built several small cabins and established a summer resort, which eventually closed.

4.4 **Enter Jackson County.**

The state legislature established Jackson County in November 1801, according to county historian Moldon Jenkins Tayse. The original boundaries covered as many as 20 of the Tennessee counties recognized today. It is the second oldest of the 24 Jackson counties in the United States. Only Georgia's Jackson County is older. Williamsburg, named for area pioneer Sampson Williams, was the original county seat. Gainesboro was selected as the permanent county seat in 1817.

The Cumberland and Roaring rivers were sources of commerce in the early days. When the Cordell Hull Dam flooded the Cumberland River in 1963 and authorities opened a deep-water port near Gainesboro in 1981, the Cumberland River again became an important entity to Jackson County.

5.3 **State Route 290 is on the left. Continue straight.**

You'll ride through the community of Union Hill.

6.6 **State Route 290 is on the right. Continue straight. You'll soon see the Hillside Market & Deli on the left.**

7.9 **Sta Lo Market is on the right.**

11.3 Texaco station is on the left. The road widens.

You'll ride through the community of New Salem.

13.5 Enter Gainesboro city limits.

David Cox donated the land for Gainesboro, which was incorporated in 1820, according to Tayse. The town was named for Gen. Edmund Pendleton Gaines, a friend of Andrew Jackson who fought in the Battle of New Orleans.

Gainesboro is home to the Dumas Walker Tournament, a rolley-hole marbles competition held during Jackson County's Homecoming Day in August. It is named for the Moss, Tenn., rolley hole champion and title character of the Kentucky Headhunter's 1990 hit song, "Dumas Walker."

Rolley hole is a distinct cultural feature of the Upper Cumberlands, according to Montell. The game is equally popular with the young and old. In fact, the 1996 French team boasted the youngest (11) and the oldest (70) players in the World Cup Competition, held at Standing Stone State Park each September. The main ingredients to winning are a cool head, steady eye and sharp shot.

For the World Cup Competition, rolley hole is played in a 40-by-25-foot dirt yard. There are three holes lined up in the center of the yard, spaced 10 feet apart. Two teams play the game, with two players on each team. Each player gets one marble. Players move up and down the course three times—"shooting" the marble at an opponent's marble, "rolling" the marble in or within a hand's length of a hole, or "laying" in the same place. The first team with both members to make 12 holes in a specific order wins the game.

13.9 You'll see the JG Market and a Phillips 66 station on your right.

15.3 State Route 53 is on the left. Continue straight on State Route 56.

17.5 Texaco and Citgo stations are on your right. Pass State Route 56 on your left.

17.7 Pass State Route 135 on your right. Cross the Roaring River.

18.3 Turn right onto State Route 85.

The route becomes a winding, two-lane road. There is no shoulder.

21.4 Harmony Road is on your left. Continue straight on State Route 85.

22.6 Delight's Market is on your left.

You'll ride through the community of Burristown.

24.1 Strong's General Merchandise is on your right.

26.8 Greenwood Ridge Road is on your right. Continue straight on State Route 85.

You'll ride through the community of Antioch.

26.9 Enter Overton County.

The state legislature established Overton County in 1817. It was named for John Overton, a pioneer attorney in Nashville. He also co-founded Memphis with Andrew Jackson and James Winchester in 1819.

You'll ride through the community of Maxwell Chapel.

28.6 There is a market on your left.

31.0 You'll see Hilham General Store on your left. Turn left onto State Route 136.

Moses Fisk, the surveyor of the Walton Road, laid out the town of Hilham in 1805, according to McClain. Fisk was born in Grafton, Mass., in 1759. He moved to Tennessee in 1796, the year statehood was granted. He lived in Davidson, Sumner, Smith and Fentress counties before moving here. In 1806, Fisk and Sampson Williams donated 1,000 acres for the Fisk Female Academy, recognized as the first female school in the South. After burning in 1817, the school was rebuilt for males. Fisk operated the academy until it closed in 1843.

The terrain becomes very hilly as you approach Standing Stone State Park.

31.3 State Route 292 is on your left. Continue straight on State Route 136.

33.1 End ride at the entrance of Standing Stone State Park.

Standing Stone State Park, covering nearly 11,000 acres on the Cumberland Plateau, took its name from an eight-foot rock. Standing upright on a sandstone ledge, the rock was said to separate two Indian nations. When the rock fell, Indians placed a part of it upon an improvised monument. The preserved stone is located today in the town of Monterey.

Park activities include archery, basketball, horseshoes, ping pong, softball, tennis and volleyball. There is fishing on the 69-acre Standing Stone Lake. As previously mentioned, the park is host to the international Rolley Hole Marble Contest each September.

Other points of interest nearby include the birthplace of Cordell Hull, former U.S. secretary of state, and Dale Hollow Lake. Operated by the U.S. Army Corps of Engineers, the recreational Dale Hollow Lake offers fishing, hunting, camping, picnicking, boating, canoeing, hiking and horseback riding. There is also a national fish hatchery.

For general information on lodging and attractions, contact the Jackson County Chamber of Commerce, 101 E. Hull Ave., Gainesboro, TN 38562 (931-268-0971), Overton County Chamber of Commerce, 208 W. Broad St., Suite B, Livingston, TN 38570 (931-823-6421), Putnam County Chamber of Commerce, 302 S. Jefferson Ave., Cookeville, TN 38501 (931-526-2211), Van Buren County Executive, P.O. Box 217, Spencer, TN 38585 (931-946-2314), or White County Chamber of Commerce, 16 W. Bockman Way, Sparta, TN 38583 (931-836-3552).

Places to Stay

Cornucopia Bed & Breakfast, 303 Mofield St., Livingston, TN 38570 (931-823-7522), is located eight miles east of Standing Stone State Park. Built in the early 1900s, the home was owned by one of Livingston's most prominent families until 1994. It is said to have had the first bathroom in Livingston. Guests can relax on the side porch. Breakfast is served in a sky-lighted dining room. The home is just a couple of blocks from the town square, where guests can find several antique shops and eateries. Innkeepers are sisters Gay Nolfo and Margie Lewis.

Econo Lodge, 1100 S. Jefferson Ave., Cookeville, TN 38506 (931-528-1040), is located near Interstate 40 and State Route 136. Features include an outdoor pool, free movies, refrigerators in some rooms and a free continental breakfast.

Fall Creek Falls State Park Resort Inn, Route 3, Box 300, Pikeville, TN 37367 (931-881-5241 or 800-250-8610), has 144 rooms, all overlooking scenic Fall Creek Lake. Features include an outdoor pool, game room, fitness center and restaurant. Cabins can also be reserved. The park has 20 two-bedroom, furnished cabins, which can sleep up to eight people. All cabins have central heat and air and include housekeeping items, telephone, and color television.

Fall Creek Falls State Park (camping), Route 3, Box 300, Pikeville, TN 37367 (931-881-5298 or 800-250-8611), has 228 sites in three campgrounds. All sites feature tables, grills as well as water and electrical hookups. Each campground has central bathhouses and a dump station. Three backcountry campsites are available with a permit.

Happy Hollow Bed & Breakfast, 5428 Medley Amonette Road, Buffalo Valley, TN 38548 (931-858-3528 or 800-887-3155), is located a few miles west of Baxter. The Caney Fork River is visible from the home's front porch and balconies. Four guest rooms are on the second floor. Guests can relax in an outdoor hot tub. A Southern breakfast is served with fruit, home-baked breads, muffins and juice. Innkeepers are Mary JoAnn Alcorn, Emily J. Mathis and Barbara McCormack.

Historic Falcon Manor, 2645 Faulkner Springs Road, McMinnville, TN 37110 (931-668-4444), is located about 20 miles west of Spencer. The 10,000-square-foot home also offers a Victorian gift shop and weekend dinners by reservation. Innkeepers are George and Charlien McGlothin.

Standing Stone State Park (camping), 1674 Standing Stone Park Highway, Hilham, TN 38568 (931-823-6347) has 36 campsite hookups. Two bathhouses are open April through October. One features a washer and dryer. Four types of cabins are available. All have linens and cooking utensils. In the summer, cabins can only be rented by the week.

Bicycle Shops
Appalachian Cycles, 662 W. Spring St., Cookeville, TN 38501 (931-528-7848).

Cookeville Bicycles, 88 S. Willow Ave., Cookeville, TN 38501 (931-520-6161).

BICYCLING TENNESSEE
Tour 21: Jamestown-Oneida

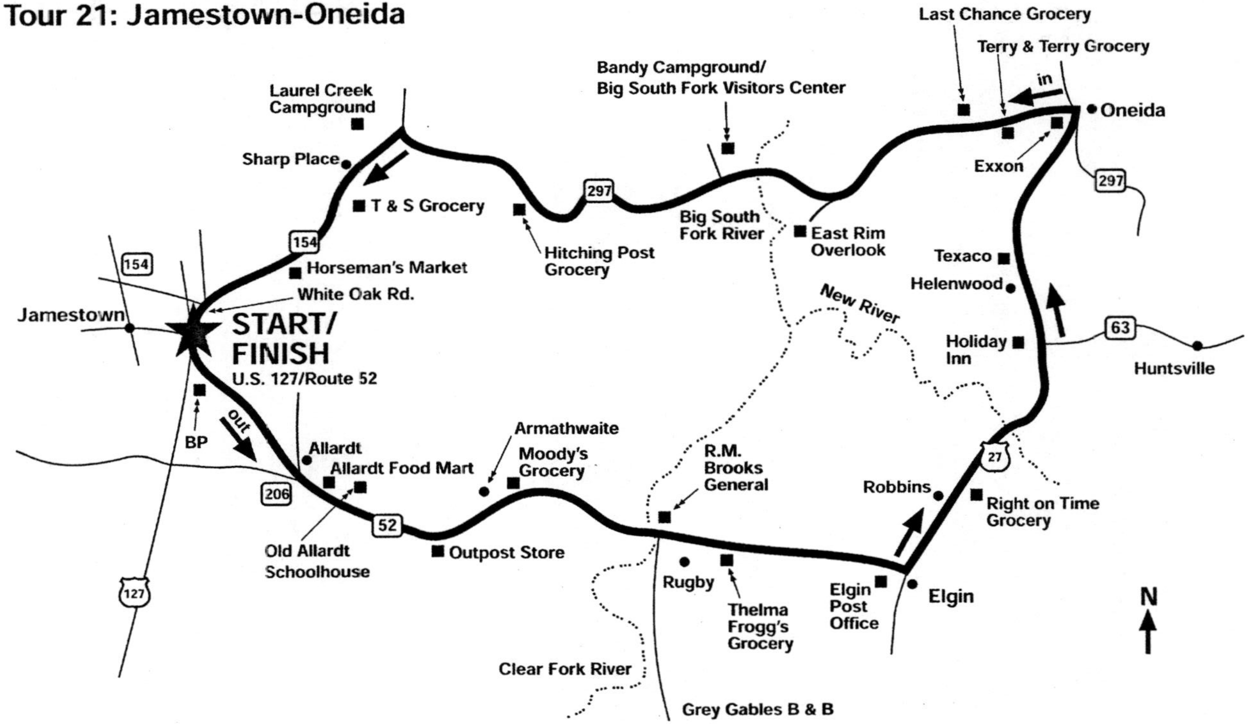

21. Jamestown—Oneida: A Two-Day Tour

Moderate to difficult terrain; 74.7 miles

Alvin C. York was born Dec. 13, 1887, near Pall Mall, TN. He worked to support his family as a hired hand on the Dixie Short Route Highway. Then he worked on Pastor R.C. Pile's farm for $20 a month plus board, according to Albert R. Hogue in his book, *History of Fentress County Tennessee.* York became an expert fox hunter, but had a weak spot for drinking whiskey and gambling. In January 1915, however, he straightened out his life, converting to Christianity and joining the Church of Christ in Christian Union. Oddly enough, this poorly educated, pacifist, country boy from the Valley of the Three Forks of the Wolf River became the most decorated soldier in World War I.

On Oct. 8, 1918, under heavy machine gun fire, the German Army stalled York's platoon's attempt to capture a railroad in the Argonne Forest of France. Commanders ordered York to lead a squad across enemy lines. Many in the squad were killed or wounded. The survivors were finally able to circle behind the German positions, where York picked off the line of German machine guns with his rifle and .45 Colt pistol. The Germans surrendered after 25 of their comrades were killed. York and seven of his men returned to the American lines with 132 German prisoners.

On his return to the states in May 1919, Americans threw him a New York ticker tape parade and a banquet in his honor at the Waldorf-Astoria. He also visited the White House. He received more than 40

Allied decorations, including the Congressional Medal of Honor and French Croix de Guerre. Despite numerous endorsement offers, York declined and returned to the Valley of the Three Forks. The state of Tennessee made him a colonel for life on the governor's staff, and provided his family rich farmland.

The Sgt. Alvin C. York State Historic Park is located in Pall Mall, about 10 miles north of this tour's start. The park features the late marksman's home and gristmill. His descendents are still involved in running the park, which is open every day year-round from 9 a.m. to 5 p.m. The state has also honored York with a 10-foot statue on the State Capitol grounds in Nashville, and several of his medals and trophies are displayed at the Tennessee State Museum in Nashville.

The home of another American dignitary is nearby. The Cordell Hull Birthplace and Museum is located in Byrdstown. The late Pickett County native was a U.S. congressman, senator, and under President Franklin D. Roosevelt, secretary of state. Hull won the Nobel Peace Prize in 1945 for his international trade agreements and his efforts to establish the United Nations.

This tour is part of the state's Cumberlands of Tennessee Heritage Trail. While scenic and historic, the route is quite challenging. There is not much shade. Log trucks are common along winding state routes 52 and 154. There are several steep climbs and descents, including a 13 percent grade descent in the Big South Fork National River and Recreation Area. I'd only recommend this tour for the experienced cyclist.

Jamestown is about 100 miles west of Knoxville. To get to the tour from Knoxville, take Interstate 40 west for about 70 miles. Get off at exit 317 at Crossville. Take U.S. Highway 127 north to Jamestown.

DAY 1
Moderate to difficult terrain, watch for logging trucks along State Route 52; 40.6 miles

<u>Miles</u>

0.0 **Start ride at the intersection of U.S. 127 and State Route 52. Head east on State Route 52. There is a BP station on the right.**
The Tennessee General Assembly created Fentress County in 1823 out of Overton County. It was named in honor of state legislator James Fentress, later to become a Confederate officer, according to Hogue. Originally called Sand Springs, then Obedstown, Jamestown was incorporated in 1837.

Mark Twain's parents lived here but left before his birth. It is said this town is the basis of Twain's setting in his book, *Gilded Age*. An old Indian trace ran through this town, taking the Cherokees from East Tennessee to the Cumberland River region.

4.3 **You'll see Burnett's Fuel Center to your left. Turn left at the stop sign, continuing on State Route 52. Allardt Food Mart is on your left.**
You are in the community of Allardt. As mining began around Wilder, Crawford and Twinton, a German-born resident of Michigan began planning a model community east of Jamestown in 1879, according to William Lynwood Montell in his book, *Upper Cumberland Country*. Bruno Gernt wanted to attract German immigrants to Allardt, named for his partner M.H. Allardt, who died while the town was being planned. Gernt promised fertile land and industrial growth. While new settlers were successful in agriculture, industrial development never materialized due to the lack of a railroad routing through the area. Many German immigrants, however, stayed and prospered in the mining and logging industries.

Allardt is home of the Great Pumpkin Festival and Weigh-Off, which includes a pumpkin cook-off, pumpkin carving, pumpkin painting, crafts, music, games and other special events. The annual festival is held the first weekend of October.

5.5　Continue straight on State Route 52.

Northrup Falls Road leading to the falls is on your right.

8.0　Continue straight on State Route 52.

The road to your left leads 4.5 miles to Peter's Bridge Access for canoeing and rafting.

9.1　Continue straight on State Route 52. You'll see the Outpost Store. Shirley Road is to your right.

10.3　Continue straight on State Route 52. Mt. Helen Road is to your left.

10.9　Enter the community of Armathwaite. You'll see Moody's Grocery.

13.9　Enter the Big South Fork National River and Recreation Area.

14.6　Cross the Clear Fork River and into Morgan County.

Morgan County was created in 1817 out of Roane County, according to Calvin Dickinson in the Tennessee County History Series' *Morgan County*. It was named for Brig. Gen. Daniel Morgan. During the Revolutionary War, Morgan served under Benedict Arnold at Quebec in 1775 and with Gen. Horatio Gates at Saratoga in 1777. In 1870, the Morgan County seat was permanently moved from Montgomery to Wartburg.

15.0　Turn left at the stop sign, continuing on State Route 52.

You'll pass through the community of Red Cliff.

15.5　R.M. Brooks General Merchandise is on your left.

R.M. Brooks General Merchandise is an old-time country store. You'll also pass the Grey Gables Bed 'n' Breakfast Inn.

15.9　Enter the town of Rugby.

Thomas Hughes founded Rugby on Oct. 5, 1880. Hughes was an English social reformer and author of *Tom Brown's School Days*, an autobiographical classic about his days at the Rugby School in England. He was seeking an experimental village for England's second sons, those that were not fortunate to inherit their family's title and estate back home, according to Doug and Dawn Brachy in their book, *Rugby: Tennessee's Victorian Village.*

American poet James Russell Lowe informed Hughes about this property in the Cumberland Plateau. The Boston Board of Aid to Land Ownership sought a buyer after a Boston firm decided not to move its workforce there. Hughes envisioned his new utopia—a hard-working, cultured society free of such evils as liquor and competitive trade. "Our aim and hope are to plant on these high-lands a community of gentlemen and ladies," he said during open-ing ceremonies.

Although the Kingstone Lisle home was built for him, Hughes only visited Rugby each fall, continuing his law practice in England. However, his mother, Margaret, lived in Rugby from 1881 until her death in 1887.

A perfect community did not materialize. Settlers experienced a severe first winter. Some second sons, called "Will Wimbles," did not exemplify a good work ethic. The British Board of Aid in London and on-site managers poorly communicated. Social and intellectual pursuits did not bring economic prosperity. Nevertheless, before his death in England in 1896, Hughes wrote, "I can't help feeling and believing that good seed was sown when Rugby was founded."

The British Board of Aid sold the property to various Americans in 1909, but local citizens have kept Rugby's history alive. Today, the non-profit Historic Rugby employs most of the town's resi-dents. The organization aims to restore the village and maintain its heritage. Many of the buildings built during the town's early years are still intact today. The three-story, restored schoolhouse is now the town's visitor center. The Thomas Hughes Free Public Library does not contain one book published after 1899. The beautiful Christ Church Episcopal welcomes members and visitors, as it has since 1887. Historic Rugby built the Harrow Road Café in 1985 on the site of two previous village restaurants, offering specialties of both the Cumberland Plateau and the United Kingdom.

Traveling on State Route 52 through Rugby, you'll pass the Harrow Road Café on your right, Christ Episcopal Church on your left and the Rugby Schoolhouse and Visitors Center on your right.

The historic Christ Episcopal Church is still an active house of worship in the community of Rugby.

18.3 You'll see Thelma Frogg's Grocery on the right.

You are now entering Scott County, created on Dec. 17, 1849, out of Campbell, Morgan and Fentress counties. It is debatable where the county got its name, according to H. Clay Smith in his book, *Dusty Bits of the Forgotten Past*. The first settlers around Brimstone Creek were from Scott County, Virginia. Julius F. Scott was a state legislator from Morgan County. Or possibly it was named for War of 1812 veteran and Mexican War hero Winfred Scott.

Scott County has prospered through mining as well as oil and natural gas production. Today, the county between the Appalachian Mountains and the Big South Fork Cumberland River Gorge makes up 536 square miles with a population of 19,788.

25.3 You'll see the Elgin Post Office on the right. Turn left onto U.S. Highway 27 at the stop sign at the T-intersection. Watch for traffic.

You are in the community of Elgin. There is a short ride to a market if you turn right onto U.S. Highway 27. Back on U.S. Highway 27 north, the road begins to wind.

27.1 Enter the town of Robbins.

27.4 You'll see the Right on Time Grocery and Deli. Broad shoulder begins.

30.7 Cross the New River.

You'll descend and ascend a steep bluff on each side of the river.

32.3 You'll see a Citgo station on your right.

33.2 You'll see a Holiday Inn Express to your left and State Route 63 to Huntsville on your right. Continue straight on U.S. Highway 27 at the traffic light.

You are in the community of Huntsville, the Scott County seat. Located in the geographical center of the county, the town was incorporated in 1965.

Huntsville is the hometown of Sen. Howard Baker, who served in the U.S. Senate from 1967 to 1985. He rose to national prominence in 1973 as vice chairman of the Senate Watergate Committee. Baker was keynote speaker at the Republican National Convention in 1976 and ran for president in 1980. For the last part of his Senate career, he served two terms as minority leader and two terms as majority leader. He was President Ronald Reagan's chief of staff in 1987 and 1988.

34.3 You'll see a Texaco station on the left.

You are entering the community of Helenwood, which made headlines in 1920 and 1955. In 1920, legend has it a man named Sexton encountered Satan at an old mine. He then created a "heathen figure" out of clay. People traveled from miles around to see the figure, paying 25 cents a look, according to author Smith. In 1955, the American Trucking Association named a local man named Pemberton as Driver of the Year for saving two women from a burning car.

Helenwood is Scott County's newest town, incorporated in August 1998.

36.9   Galloway Inn is up the road to your right.

37.4   You'll see a Subway to the left.

38.2   The shoulder narrows, and road eventually goes back to two lanes.

40.3   Dave's Exxon is on the left.

You are entering the town of Oneida, named for its resemblance to the lakes of Oneida, N.Y., according to Smith. Incorporated in 1913, it is the largest town in Scott County and located about five miles south of the Tennessee-Kentucky border. Oneida is known as the residential, commercial and industrial center of the county.

40.6   End Day 1 ride at the intersection of U.S. Highway 27 and State Route 297.

DAY 2

Moderate to difficult terrain, difficult as you enter the Big South Fork National River and Recreation Area; 34.1 miles

Miles

0.0   Begin Day 2 ride at the intersection of U.S. Highway 27 and State Route 297. Head east on State Route 297 (also called Alson Industrial Lane). Road turns into West Third Avenue.

0.8   Continue on State Route 297 at the stop sign at the T-intersection. You will soon pass a Marathon station on your right.

5.0   Turn left at the stop sign, continuing on State Route 297. You'll see Terry & Terry Grocery on your left.

6.9   You'll see the Last Chance Grocery & Deli on your right.

9.0   After climbing a steep hill, you'll enter the Big South Fork National River and Recreation Area.

Only a few hundred thousand people visit Big South Fork National River and Recreation Area each year, compared to the 8 million that visit the Great Smoky Mountains. It's a secret that folks like Sen. Baker would like to keep.

As he explains in his book with John Netherton, *Big South Fork Country*, the Tennessee Electric Power Co., the U.S. Corps of Engineers and the Tennessee Valley Authority all proposed dams along the river at various times during the 20th Century. When those plans didn't materialize, it was Baker, under the advice of Bailey Guard, minority counsel of the Senate Environment and Public Works Committee, who suggested turning the area into a 100,000-acre national park. With congressional support in 1974, Big South Fork became the only park developed by the Corps of Engineers, which handed it over to the Interior Department upon completion.

For millions of years, the region was virtually undisturbed by man, except for long hunters like Daniel Boone and a few coal mining operations after the Europeans discovered the New World. Rocky soil sent most pioneers to better farmlands along the Cumberland and Tennessee rivers. Today, the Big South Fork, one of only three national rivers, is a sportsman's paradise. Canoeists and rafters enjoy riding the rapids, ranging from the easy Class I to expert Class V. Fishermen enjoy catching up to eight types of bass, 11 types of shiners and other fishes.

The Big South Fork National River and Recreation Area is open year-round. Summer activities include photography workshops and astronomy programs. There is a Storytelling and Craft Festival each September. The Cumberland Color Caper and Cultural Heritage Day are held each October. Swimming is available at Bandy Creek Pool during the summer. Horseback riding and mountain biking are permitted in certain areas. During hunting seasons, it is recommended you wear orange while biking or hiking the backcountry.

Nearby, the Blue Heron Mining Community in Kentucky features an outdoor museum exhibiting the life and times of the coal miner. The Big South Fork Scenic Railway runs between Blue Heron and Sterns, Ky.

10.6 **Road to the left leads to the East Rim Overlook.**

12.1 **Back on State Route 297, the road becomes winding and steep.**
There is a 13 percent grade downhill. I recommend you walk your bike down.

13.8 **Cross the Big South Fork River.**
You'll pass the Leatherwood Trail and begin a steep climb back up a bluff.

13.9 **Bandy Campground and Visitors Information is located two miles down the road to your right.**
The visitor's center is open year-round, except Christmas. It provides visitor information, backcountry permits and book sales.

15.5 **Enter Fentress County and Central Time Zone.**
You'll soon enter Scott State Forest, one of 13 forests managed by the state's Department of Agriculture. Tennessee has 13 million acres of forest, which supports the $15 billion, 60,000-job forest products industry. The state protects forestlands from fire and insects, and advises loggers and landowners on integrating environmental protection into their harvesting operations. It also provides planting and marketing recommendations.

17.9 **Leave Big South Fork National River and Recreation Area.**

18.8 **You'll see the Hitching Post Grocery on your left.**

19.7 **Old West Town is on your right.**

20.9 **Laurel Creek Rustic Retreat is down the road to your right.**

24.4 **Turn left onto State Route 154 at the stop sign at the T-intersection.**
You are passing through the community of Sharp Place. If you turned right at this intersection, Wildwood Bed and Breakfast, and Pickett State Park are located down the road.

Pickett State Park and Forest consists of 17,372 acres and features unusual rock formations, natural bridges, several caves and remnants of an ancient Indian settlement. Its botanical variety is said to be the most diverse in Tennessee, outside the Great Smoky Mountains.

Fishing is allowed year-round at the 15-acre Arch Lake. Rowboats and canoes can be rented. No personal boats are allowed. Activities include horseback riding, swimming and hiking. Nine trails are available to explore, ranging from ½-mile to 2 ½ miles. Overnight camping is allowed on some trails. The Old Timers Day Music Festival is held each September.

Back on State Route 154, the road is winding with no shoulder. Watch for logging trucks.

25.9 Laurel Creek Campground is down the road to the right.
The road continues to be winding.

27.5 T & S Grocery is on your left.

29.9 Horseman's Market is on the right.
You'll ride a significant downhill.

32.4 Turn left onto White Oak Road.
The road becomes bumpy and narrow.

33.4 Turn left onto U.S. Highway 127 at the stop sign. Watch for traffic.
A big shoulder becomes available.

33.9 Veer right onto the ramp to State Route 52.

34.1 End ride at the intersection of U.S. Highway 127 and State Route 52, where the tour began.

For general information on lodging and attractions, contact the Fentress County Chamber of Commerce, P.O. Box 1294, Jamestown, TN 38556 (931-879-9948), Morgan County Resource Council, P.O. Box 325, Wartburg, TN 37887 (423-346-3000), or Scott County Chamber of Commerce, P.O. Box 4442, Oneida, TN 37841 (800-645-6905).

Places to Stay

Big South Fork National River and Recreation Area (camping), 4564 Leatherwood Road, Oneida, TN 37841 (800-365-2267 or 931-879-4869), has three campgrounds. Reservations are recommended. Bandy Creek Campground has 100 sites with water and electricity, 50 tent sites and two group camps. Restrooms, showers and swimming pool are available. Blue Heron Campground has 49 sites with water and electricity. Restrooms and showers are available. Alum Ford has eight primitive sites, portable toilets and no drinking water. Backcountry camping is also available with permit.

Delia's Guest House, 1277 Bertram Road, Jamestown, TN 38556 (931-879-2511), is owned and operated by sisters Wilda Gernt and Wanda Conway. Located three miles south of Jamestown, the house features three guest bedrooms, two baths, a living room, kitchen, dining room and laundry. A continental breakfast is provided.

Grey Gables Bed 'n' Breakfast Inn, P.O. Box 52, Rugby, TN 37733 (423-628-5252), is located along the route in Rugby. Eight bedrooms are decorated with country and Victorian antiques. Bill and Linda Brooks Jones are the innkeepers.

Newbury House B & B, P.O. Box 8, Rugby, TN 37733 (423-628-2441), served as Rugby's first boarding house. Built in 1880, the home underwent restoration in the spring of 1985. Five upstairs bedrooms reflect the Victorian era. An additional two-room suite features a fireplace. Breakfast is served at the Harrow Road Café.

The Old Allardt Schoolhouse, 1860 Michigan Ave., Allardt, TN 38504 (931-879-8056), was built around 1910. It features two bedrooms and two baths. There is a complete kitchen, fireplace and front and back porches. Charles and Lowanda Gernt are the innkeepers.

Pickett State Park (camping), 4605 Pickett Park Highway, Jamestown, TN 38556 (931-879-5821), features 40 campsites with tables and grills. Twenty sites have water and electrical hookups. A modern bathhouse is available. The park also offers five chalets, five rustic stone cottages and five wooden cottages, including appliances, utensils and linens.

Bicycle Shops
Appalachian Cycles, 662 W. Spring St., Cookeville, TN 38501 (931-528-7848).

Cookeville Bicycles, 88 S. Willow Ave., Cookeville, TN 38501 (931-520-6161).

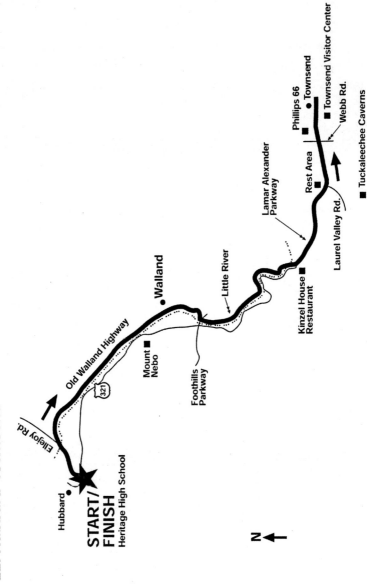

BICYCLING TENNESSEE
Tour 22: Hubbard-Townsend

Ellejoy Rd.

Hubbard

START/ FINISH
Heritage High School

Old Walland Highway

321

Mount Nebo

Walland

Foothills Parkway

Little River

Lamar Alexander Parkway

Kinzel House Restaurant

Rest Area

Laurel Valley Rd.

Phillips 66

Townsend

Townsend Visitor Center

Webb Rd.

Tuckaleechee Caverns

N

22. HUBBARD—TOWNSEND

Easy to moderate; 24.2 miles

The Joshua Jobe family was one of the first pioneer families to settle in Cades Cove, a beautiful serene area, now a part of the Great Smoky Mountains National Park. Apparently, no one had settled permanently in the cove before the Jobes in 1821, not even the Cherokee Indians.

The early settlers, most from Virginia, North Carolina and upper East Tennessee, discovered rich and fertile land and a plentiful supply of deer and bear, writes Carson Brewer in the *Cades Cove Tour* guide. Corn was the major crop, but residents soon developed mills to grind their wheat into flour. They produced fruits, rye and barley. They also grew some tobacco and cotton, and raised cattle and hogs. Aside from agriculture, they made their living as blacksmiths, storekeepers and distillers. The distillers' products included corn whiskey, apple brandy and peach brandy. The most successful wild crop was chestnuts until a fungus killed most the chestnut trees in the early 20th Century.

The Cades Cove population grew to 685 by 1850, fluctuating throughout the latter part of the 19th Century, reaching 708 in 1900. Residents founded several Protestant churches, which became the cove's spiritual and social centers. They held baptisms in area streams.

Tennessee and North Carolina began buying land in Cades Cove in 1927, quickly relinquishing it to the federal government for a new park. Cades Cove residents at the time of the park's creation in 1934 were allowed to stay until their death; however, most decided to leave the area sooner rather than later. Very few resisted. The last schoolhouse closed in 1944. The post office closed by 1947.

Today, Cades Cove is one of the most popular destinations in the Great Smoky Mountains. More than 70 historic buildings reflect Cades Cove's pioneer days, including early settler John Oliver's log home, Primitive Baptist Church, Methodist Church and Cable Mill. Outdoor enthusiasts enjoy the park's trails, streams and easy access to wildlife viewing, including the cove's deer population, numbering around 1,000.

Road cycling is discouraged in the Great Smoky Mountains National Park, especially during the peak tourist seasons of summer and late fall. Cades Cove, however, is the exception to the rule. The Cades Cove Bike Shop rents bikes April through October. Also, from Memorial Day to Labor Day, on Wednesdays and Saturdays, the 11-mile, one-way loop is closed to motorized traffic from sunrise to 10 a.m. Only bicyclists and pedestrians are allowed.

Caves Cove is located only seven miles east of Townsend, the area known as the Peaceful Side of the Smokies. This bicycle tour incorporates what is called the Little River Run and the Townsend Bicycle Trail. It is a relatively flat, shady ride along the Little River, and back. There are only a few hills. Yellow bike signs along U.S. Highway 321 caution motorists of your presence.

To get to the route's start, go east on U.S. Highway 321 from Maryville about seven miles. Turn left onto Old Walland Highway. You'll soon see Heritage High School on your right.

Miles

0.0   Begin ride at Heritage High School. Head east on Old Walland Highway.
You'll start in the community of Hubbard.

The first big wave of settlers moved to this area in 1785. They came from Virginia and North Carolina, mostly of Scottish—or Irish-descent. The Tennessee legislature created Blount County out of a portion of Knox County in 1795, making it the 10th oldest county in the state.

The county was named for William Blount. When Congress approved the succession of North Carolina's western lands, Blount became governor of the territory south of the Ohio River. Operating from Sullivan County, Blount encouraged immigration into the territory, according to Oliver Taylor in his book, *Historic Sullivan*. The area's population blossomed from 6,000 in 1791 to 77,000 in 1795.

Blount was president of a constitutional convention, convening in Knoxville on Jan. 11, 1796, to form a new state. John Sevier was elected as the first governor of Tennessee. Blount and William Cocke were elected the state's first U.S. senators. Blount died on March 21, 1800, and is buried in Knoxville.

The lumber trade was the first major industry in Blount County. Various industries now account for business in the area. There are more than 100 manufacturing plants in the county. The largest employer is Aluminum Company of America (Alcoa), which has operated in Blount County since 1912.

0.3 **Road intersects with Ellejoy Road. Turn right, continuing on Old Walland Highway.**
You'll pass the Mill House Restaurant, Swimming Hole Bridge and Misty Hollow Cabins.

*Old Walland Highway is a popular bike route for area cyclists.
Photo by Susan Schulman.*

3.9   Continue left on Old Walland Highway.
You'll ride through the community of Walland. You'll pass
Creekside Log Cabins.

5.1   Pass under the Foothills Parkway.
Although conceived in the 1920s and approved by Congress as a
scenic highway on Feb. 22, 1944, the Foothills Parkway has been in
development a long time. Construction began at Walland on Feb.
9, 1960, but construction kinks, rock slides and landowner con-
cerns have slowed its completion. Currently, only 23.1 miles of the
parkway are open to traffic. In addition, the 14.9-mile section
between here and Wears Valley is partially finished.

Citizens established the Foothills Parkway Association in 1990.
Based in Sevierville, the association supports the parkway's completion. Once the 72-mile Foothills Parkway is complete, it will offer
spectacular overviews from the northwest boundary of the Great
Smoky Mountains National Park, of which the route parallels.

6.5   There is an overlook on the right.
You'll pass Hawks Cove Cabin Rentals and Environmental Camp.

9.2 **Cross the Little River. You'll see The Kinzel House Restaurant straight ahead. Turn left onto U.S. 321 (also called Lamar Alexander Parkway). There is a small shoulder. Watch for traffic.**
Lamar Alexander was born in Blount County in 1940. He attended Vanderbilt and New York University Law School. He began his life in politics managing several campaigns and serving as an assistant to Sen. Howard Baker.

In 1978, Alexander walked 1,022 miles across the state during his campaign for Tennessee governor. He served as governor from 1979 to 1987. The son of two teachers made education his top priority. His Better School Program and a career ladder pay plan for teachers received national interest.

After serving two terms as Tennessee governor, Alexander served as president of the University of Tennessee and as U.S. Secretary of Education. He returned to the national spotlight during his two campaigns for the Republican nomination for president. Both campaigns were unsuccessful.

You'll ride through the community of Kinzel Springs, and pass a rest/picnic area on the left. At the time of this writing, the state was proposing to widen U.S. 321 from this point to the national park, to better accommodate tourist traffic.

10.8 **Enter Townsend City Limits.**
Townsend offers several craft communities and malls. Local artists sell handmade crafts. Tourists can also learn how to make various crafts at the Earthtide School of Folk Art. For fishing enthusiasts, Little River Outfitter offers fly-fishing demonstrations and workshops.

The Little River Railroad Museum in Townsend is open April through October. The non-profit museum, operated by volunteers, explains the history of the Little River Railroad and Lumber Co. Donations are accepted.

The Townsend area offers numerous bed and breakfast accommodations, and eateries. I recommend Smokin' Joe's on Lamar Alexander Parkway. The pork barbecue is the best that I have tasted outside of Memphis, and the blackberry cobbler is out of this world.

10.9 Pass Laurel Valley Road to right.
Laurel Valley Road to the right leads to Tuckaleechee Caverns in two miles. Bill Vananda and Harry Myers turned their childhood playground into a tourist attraction. Billed as the "greatest sight under the Smokies," the caverns feature intriguing rock formations and passageways. It is open for tours March 15 to November 15.

11.0 Bike path begins to the right.

11.5 You'll see a Phillips 66 station to your left. Cross Webb Road.

12.1 Turn around at the Townsend Visitor Center.
This is the site of the Townsend Heritage Festival and Old Timers Day held in the fall. The event features cake walks, bake sales, story telling, bluegrass jamming and clogging. Visiting musicians are welcomed to join in the fun.

Inside the center, you'll find tons of literature on attractions and activities in and around the Smoky Mountains. If you can't find it here, you can't find it anywhere.

12.7 You'll see a Phillips 66 station to your right. Cross Webb Road.

13.2 Bike path ends. Head west on U.S. 321 (also called Lamar Alexander Parkway). There is a small shoulder. Watch for traffic.

13.3 Pass Laurel Valley road to the left.

13.4 Leave Townsend City Limits.
You'll pass the rest/picnic area on the right.

15.0 You'll see The Kinzel House Restaurant on the left. Turn right and cross the Little River. Turn left onto Old Walland Highway.

17.7 Pass overlook to your left.

19.1 Pass under the Foothills Parkway.

20.3 Continue right on Old Walland Highway.

23.9 Road intersects with Ellejoy Road. Turn left, continuing on Old Walland Highway.

24.2 End ride at Heritage High School to your left, where the tour began.

For general information on lodging and attractions, contact the Townsend Visitors Center, 7906 E. Lamar Alexander Parkway, Townsend, TN 37882 (800-525-6834 or 865-448-6134).

Places to Stay

Abode and Beyond Bed & Breakfast, 275 Little Mountain Way, Townsend, TN 37882 (888-862-2633 or 865-448-9097), is a wooden home that has two guestrooms. The suite features a king-sized bed and gas stove. Both rooms have a television and VCR, and access to a private bath and kitchenette. Continental breakfast is served. The innkeepers also provide entertainment. David "Buffalo Bill" Nelson recites cowboy poetry. Jean Nelson plays folk instruments.

Richmont Inn, 220 Winterberry Lane, Townsend, TN 37882 (865-448-6751), offers scenic views of Laurel Valley and Rich Mountain. The living and dining areas are furnished with 18th century English antiques and French paintings. Guestrooms feature fireplaces, king-sized beds, private baths and balconies. The innkeepers are Jim and Susan Hind Sr., and Jim and Hilda Hind Jr.

Tuckaleechee Campground (camping), 7259 E. Lamar Alexander Parkway, Townsend TN 37882 (865-448-9608), is open year round. There are 50 full hook-up sites for recreational vehicles. There are also 100 tent sites—nine with water, electric and cable television hook-ups. Seventeen primitive sites are available. Other campground features include river sites, laundry facilities, bathhouse with showers, firewood and tube rentals.

Bicycle Shops

Chain Reaction, 2408 E. Lamar Alexander Parkway, Maryville, TN 37804 (865-681-4183).

Farragut Freewheeler, 11531 Kingston Pike, Concord Farragut, TN 37922 (865-671-2453).

Mountain View Bicycles, 1632 W Broadway Ave., Maryville, TN 37801 (865-977-4200).

BICYCLING TENNESSEE
Tour 23: Gatlinburg-Jonesborough

N ←

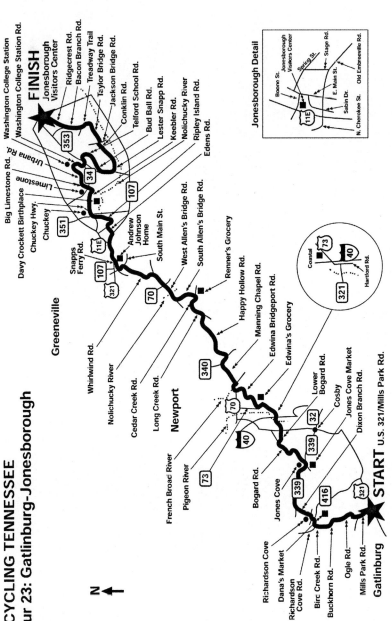

23. GATLINBURG—JONESBOROUGH: A TWO-DAY TOUR

Moderate to difficult terrain; 112.2 miles

The world recently celebrated the passing of 2,000 years, but of course, the earth is much older. The rock core underlying this region alone is billions of years old, according to Connie Toops in her book, *Great Smoky Mountains*.

Waters flooded this range around 800 million years ago. Only the ancient peaks rose above the sea. The flood moved particles from the peaks to the ocean. Sand, gravel and mud trapped sea creatures in deep deposits. These sedimentary deposits formed limestone, sandstone and shale. The collision of the North American and African continental plates 300 million years ago crushed the sedimentary rocks, forcing them to rise above the base core, forming today's Great Smoky Mountains, the widest stretch among the Appalachian Mountain range.

One person's lifetime is miniscule, compared to the time nature takes to change the world. Rome wasn't built in a day. Neither was the Great Smoky Mountains. Nature meticulously created the region's crags and coves during ages of mountain building, erosion and fluctuating climates.

Today, the Great Smoky Mountains is the most popular national park in the United States. A record 9.6 million people visited the park in 1998, ahead of the Grand Canyon, which reported about 5 million visitors that same year. The Great Smoky Mountains offers naturalist activities, 800 miles of trails (including part of the famous 2,160-mile Appalachian

Trail), camping, horseback riding and fishing. Wild animal spottings, including bear and deer, are numerous. Points of interest include Clingmans Dome, the highest point in Tennessee, and Newfound Gap, where you can stand on the Tennessee-North Carolina border.

This route takes you along the foothills of the Great Smoky Mountains National Park and the Cherokee National Forest. It is one of Cycling Tennessee's Highways' mountain routes. While there are no mountain assaults, the terrain gets quite hilly in places. A recent Bicycle Ride Across Tennessee (BRAT) in the eastern part of the state was called "Welcome to Triple Crank, Tennessee."

This tour starts about 40 miles from Knoxville. To get to the start from Knoxville, take Interstate 40 east. Get off at Exit 407 and head south on State Route 66 toward Sevierville. State Route 66 becomes U.S. Highway 441. In Gatlinburg, turn left onto U.S. Highway 321. Go about one mile to the intersection with Mills Park Road.

DAY 1
Moderate to difficult terrain; 65.1 miles

Miles

0.0   **Start ride near the entrance of Mills Park, at the intersection of U.S. Highway 321 and Mills Park Road. Head north on Mills Park Road.**

Isaac Thomas, a Virginia trader, was one of the first settlers in this area around 1780. He did business with the Cherokee Indians. He settled along the Pigeon River's west bank, opposite Sevierville. The state legislature created Sevier County out of Jefferson County in 1794. It is named in honor of John Sevier, governor of the State of Franklin and first governor of Tennessee. You can read more about Sevier in the Johnson City—Blountville chapter. The county seat of Sevierville was founded on March 31, 1795, but did not incorporate until 1901.

The towns of Gatlinburg, Pigeon Forge and Sevierville offer a wide range of accommodations and family entertainment.

Gatlinburg offers more than 400 shops and 100 restaurants. Attractions include Camp Thunder Fun Center, Christus Gardens, Earthquake—The Ride, Gatlinburg Aerial Tramway, Gatlinburg Fun Mountain, Guinness World of Records Museum, Ripley's Believe or Not Museum, Motion Ride Movie Theater, Smoky Mountain Winery and Star Cars Museum, to name just a few. Annual events include Winterfest, Gatlinburg Gospel Jubilee, Mountains of Chocolate, Smoky Mountain Trout Tournament, Smoky Mountain Music Festival, Gatlinburg Scottish Festival (in Mills Park) and Gatlinburg Craftmen's Fair.

Pigeon Forge attractions include Dollywood, Dixie Stampede, Louise Mandrell Theater and Ogle's Water Park. Sevierville attractions include Floyd Garrett's Muscle Car Museum and Lee Greenwood Theater.

0.6 **Turn right onto Ogle Road at the stop sign at the T-intersection. There is no street sign.**
This is a smooth but winding back road.

1.8 **You'll see Heritage Hollow Cabins on the right. Turn left onto Buckhorn Road at the stop sign.**
You'll pass Mountain Arts.

2.6 **Bear right onto Bird Creek Road at the stop sign. Watch for traffic.**

3.6 **You'll see Bird Creek Market on the right.**
You'll pass the Cornerstone Inn, Teakou Resort, Saved Heart's Retreat, and several other resorts and inns as you go down a steep hill.

At 6,642 feet, Clingmans Dome in the Smoky Mountains is the highest point in Tennessee.

7.0 You'll see Dana's Market and Grill on the right.

7.1 **Turn right onto Pittman Center Road (also called State Route 416).**
You'll pass Caton's Chapel.

7.7 **Enter the community of Richardson Cove.**

8.3 **J & J Grocery is on the right.**

8.6 **Turn left onto Richardson Cove Road. You'll see a Baptist church on your right.**

8.9 **Turn left onto Dixon Branch Road.**
You'll do a steep climb, then a downhill. You'll pass Twin Creeks Farm and Bear Mountain.

11.3 **Turn right onto State Route 339 at the stop sign at the T-intersection. Watch for traffic.**
You'll pass through East Fork and Crockettsville. The road becomes winding. You'll pass Arnold Estates and Smoky Mountain Retreat.

17.7 **You'll see the Goodie Shop and Baxter's Grocery on the right.**

18.0 **You'll see Jones Cove Market on the left.**
You'll ride through the community of Jones Cove.

19.1 **Turn left onto Bogard Road.**

20.5 Enter Cocke County.

The state legislature created Cocke County out of Jefferson County in 1797. It is named for William Cocke, a veteran of the Revolutionary War and the War of 1812, and a legislator at various times for Virginia, North Carolina and the former State of Franklin.

The state of Tennessee recently purchased 6,800 acres in Cocke County from International Paper. More than 2,000 of those acres will create the first new state forest in more than 50 years. The rest of the acreage will be added to Cherokee National Forest.

24.2 You'll see Jenkins Chapel on the right. Turn right onto Lower Bogard Road.

26.5 Turn right onto State Route 32 at the stop sign at the T-intersection.

26.6 Turn left onto U.S. Highway 321 (also called Wilton Springs Road). Watch for traffic. You'll see Wilton Hardware and Market.

28.9 Turn left onto Hartford Road at the stop sign at the T-intersection, continuing on U.S. Highway 321.

29.1 You'll see a Coastal station on your left. Pass under Interstate 40. The road becomes State Route 73.

32.1 You'll see Edwina's Grocery. Turn right onto Edwina Bridgeport Road.

You'll pass through the community of Edwina. This is a narrow back road, a little rough in spots.

36.8 Turn right onto U.S. Highway 70 at the stop sign at the T-intersection. Watch for traffic. Hungry Boy Restaurant is on the right.

You'll pass through the community of Bridgeport. Newport, a little ways down U.S. Highway 70 to the west, is the Cocke County seat. The Pigeon River runs through downtown Newport, where the streets are narrow and managed by single traffic signals. You can visit the Cocke County Museum there.

38.0 Cross the French Broad River Bridge.

38.3 Turn left onto Manning Chapel Road.

You're in for a steep climb and downhill on a winding road.

41.7 **At the fork in the road, turn right onto State Route 340 (also called Baltimore Road) at the stop sign.**
You'll ride through the community of Baltimore.

42.6 **You'll see a log house on the left. Turn left onto Happy Hollow Road.**
This is a narrow, winding back road with a thick forest canopy. The pavement is a little rough at first but improves.

45.5 **Peanut Road is on the right. Turn left onto Long Creek Road.**
You'll ride through the community of Long Creek.

49.0 **Enter Greene County.**
State legislators created Greene County out of Washington County in 1783. The county is named in honor of Nathaniel Greene. The Revolutionary War soldier succeeded Horatio Gates as commander of the Army of the South, which forced the British out of Georgia and the Carolinas.

50.7 **Bear right onto Cedar Creek Road.**
You'll ride through the Cedar Creek community along the edge of Meadow Creek Mountain. Cherokee National Forest is now in view. You can read about Cherokee National Forest in the Jonesborough—Elizabethton chapter.

52.5 **Nolichucky Road is on the left. Turn right, continuing on Cedar Creek Road.**

53.5 **You'll see Renner's Grocery straight ahead. Turn left onto South Allen's Bridge Road.**
This is a narrow back road. Slow down at the elephant crossing.

56.2 **Turn right onto West Allen's Bridge Road at the stop sign at the T-intersection. Cross the Nolichucky River on Allen's Bridge. You'll encounter big bluffs.**

59.3 **You'll see Country Cabin Crafts on the right. Cross State Route 70. Watch for traffic.**

61.0 You'll pass Links Hill Country Club and the University of Tennessee Tobacco Experiment Station. Turn left onto Whirlwind Road.

You'll pass numerous tobacco fields on this tour. Greene County produced 10.8 million pounds of tobacco in 1999, according to the National Agricultural Statistics Service. In other counties along this route, Cocke produced 2.2 million pounds of tobacco, Sevier, 780,000 pounds, and Washington, 6.1 million pounds.

65.1 Turn left onto South Main Street in Greeneville at the stop sign at the T-intersection. End Day 1 ride.

Before 1998, Andrew Johnson was the only U.S. president to be impeached. It was just one of the many highlights in his long political career.

Johnson came to Tennessee from North Carolina as a runaway teenager in the 1820s. He soon opened a tailor shop in Greeneville and married Eliza McCardle. His road to political power didn't miss a step—Greeneville alderman, Greeneville mayor, Tennessee state legislator, Tennessee state senator, U.S. representative, Tennessee governor and U.S. senator.

When the Civil War broke out, President Lincoln appointed Johnson as military governor of Tennessee. Although Tennessee had seceded from the North, Johnson was a staunch unionist. In 1864, Lincoln selected him as his second-term running mate. Johnson assumed the presidency upon Lincoln's assassination on April 15, 1865. Preferring leniency on the South, he fought strong congressional opposition, vetoing 29 pieces of Reconstruction legislation.

Congress overrode his veto of the Tenure of Office Act. It required congressional approval before the president could remove appointed officials. Johnson viewed the act as unconstitutional and challenged it, removing Secretary of War Edward Stanton. Instead of being resolved in the courts, Congress impeached him. He was acquitted in 1868 by one vote. Years later, in 1926, the U.S. Supreme Court ruled the Tenure of Office Act unconstitutional.

Johnson returned to Greeneville in 1869. After several attempts to re-enter politics, he was once again elected U.S. senator in 1875, the only president to serve as senator after the presidency. He died of a stroke six months later.

The Andrew Johnson National Historic Site consists of four locations—the visitor center and tailor shop, early Johnson home, the Andrew Johnson homestead and the Andrew Johnson National Cemetery. It is open year-round except Thanksgiving, Christmas and New Year's Day.

Other places to visit in Greeneville include the Nathaniel Greene Museum, Doak House Museum and Dickson-Williams Mansion.

DAY 2
Moderate to difficult terrain; 47.1 miles

<u>Miles</u>

0.0 **Begin Day 2 ride at the intersection of Whirlwind Road and South Main Street in Greeneville, heading north on South Main Street.**

On the tour, you may pass numerous yard signs posting the Ten Commandments. There is a movement in East Tennessee to allow the public display of this biblical doctrine. Several county commissions have passed ordinances permitting the Ten Commandments posting in such places as courthouses and public schools. Proponents say the Ten Commandments signify the nation's Christian foundation and promote moral principles. Opponents say it violates the separation of church and state, and freedom of religion. Religion and faith are matters of the heart and soul, not the government, they say.

0.9   Turn right onto U.S. Highway 321 (also called Spencer Street). Watch for traffic.

1.7   Turn right onto State Route 107 (also called Tusculum Boulevard). You'll see the Jack Rabbit Shell station on the left. Continue on State Route 107.

2.5   Turn left onto Snapps Ferry Road.

3.3   Turn right onto the ramp to U.S. Highway 11 East.

3.4   Turn right onto U.S. Highway 11 East. Watch for traffic.
> You'll have a big shoulder to ride on for a little while. You'll pass a Holiday Inn and other conveniences.

4.9   Turn right onto State Route 107 (also called Erwin Highway). Pioneer Market is on the right.
> You'll enter the town of Tusculum.

6.4   Turn left onto Edens Road.
> This is a narrow back road.

7.5   Turn right onto Ripley Island Road at the stop sign at the T-intersection. There is no street sign. You'll pass under a railroad bridge and by a golf course on the left.

10.8   Turn right onto Chuckey Highway at the stop sign at the T-intersection.

12.3   You'll see the Voice of Calvary Thrift Shop on the left and the House of Hidden Treasures on the right. Turn right onto State Route 351.
> You'll pass through the community of Chuckey.

12.5   You'll see Johnson Hardware straight ahead and an old depot on the left. Turn left onto Charles Johnson Road.

14.3   Davy Crockett Road intersects at your left. Continue right on Davy Crockett Road.
> You'll pass Davy Crockett Birthplace Park. The legendary frontiersman was born on the banks of the Nolichucky River near the mouth of Limestone Creek. The Davy Crockett Birthplace Association presented three acres of this property to the state in

1973. Purchasing more land, the state added a campground and hiking trail by 1976. The park includes a Davy Crockett musuem, a replica of what his boyhood cabin may have looked like, and a monument erected by the Ruritan Club in the 1960s. The park hosts the annual Buffalo Run Cruise-In each summer and the Davy Crockett Celebration each August. You can read more about Davy Crockett in the Lawrenceburg—Hohenwald chapter.

The Nolichucky River originates in the Appalachian Mountains. Bass, crappie, bluegill, redeye and catfish can be caught here. There is no boat ramp, but small boats can access the river from the park.

15.1   **Enter Washington County.**
You can read about Washington County in the Johnson City—Blountville chapter.

15.4   **Turn left onto Keebler Road.**

16.8   **Turn left onto Big Limestone Road. The bicycle route sign is missing.**
You'll pass through the community of Limestone.

17.4   **You'll see a cemetery on the left. Turn right onto Urbana Road.**

20.4   **Turn right onto Washington College Station Road at the stop sign at the T-intersection.**

21.4   **Veer right onto Newt Good Road.**
You'll enter Washington College, Tenn., and pass Washington College Academy on your left. Founded in 1780 by Samuel Doak, the academy is now a co-ed boarding and day college-prep school, affiliated with the Presbyterian Church. The rural campus sits on 155 acres.

21.9   **You'll see a school ahead. Turn left onto Old State Route 34.**

22.8   **Road intersects with State Route 353. Continue north on State Route 353.**

23.3   **At the fork in the road, turn right onto Telford School Road.**

23.6   **Turn right onto Bill West Road.**

25.2 **Cross Washington College Road at stop sign. Street becomes Jarrett Road.**

You'll experience some steep hills.

26.4 **Turn right onto Bud Ball Road.**

27.1 **Turn left onto State Route 353 (also Bailey Bridge Road) at the stop sign.**

27.4 **Turn right onto Lester Snapp Road.**

This is a winding, narrow back road through tobacco and cornfields. There is one steep hill to climb.

Tobacco is a major crop of Greene, Cocke, Sevier and Washington counties.

28.7 **Turn right onto Frank Stanton Road at the stop sign at the T-intersection.**

You'll come upon a steep hill and ride along the Nolichucky River.

31.8 **Continue straight on State Route 353.**

32.0 **State Route 353 turns right. The street becomes Conklin Road.**

Watch out for upcoming dangerous curves.

35.6 **Turn right onto Jackson Bridge Road at the stop sign at the T-intersection.**

35.7 You'll see Conklin Puritan Club on the left. Turn left onto Taylor Bridge Road.

You'll pass through the community of Conklin.

39.2 After a steep downhill, turn left onto Treadway Trail Road.

You'll experience some more steep hills.

40.2 Treadway Trail Road turns left. Continue straight on Bacon Branch Road.

42.1 Turn right onto Ridgecrest Road.

44.8 Cross State Route 81 at the stop sign. Watch for traffic. Road becomes Forestview Drive.

45.5 Turn right onto Old Embreeville Road at the stop sign at the T-intersection.

45.7 At Mountain View Estates, turn left onto Stage Road.

46.4 Turn left onto Spring Street.

46.9 Turn left onto East Main Street.

47.0 Turn right onto Boone Street.

47.1 End ride at the Jonesborough Visitors Center.

You can read about Jonesborough in the Jonesborough—Elizabethton chapter.

For general information on lodging and attractions, contact the Gatlinburg Visitors and Convention Bureau, P.O. Box 527, Gatlinburg, TN 37738 (800-568-4748 or 865-430-4148, Greene County Partnership, 115 Academy St., Greeneville, TN 37743 (423-638-4111), Historic Jonesborough Department of Tourism, 117 Boone St., Jonesborough, TN 37659 (423-753-1011 or 800-400-4221), or Newport/Cocke County Tourism Council, 360 E. Main St., #141 Court House Annex, Newport TN 37821 (423-625-9675).

Places to Stay

Blair-Moore House Bed & Breakfast, 201 W. Main St., Jonesborough, TN 37659 (888-453-0044 or 423-753-0044), is located in the Jonesborough Historic District. The home, built in 1832, features two rooms and a suite, all with private baths and private porches. There is a full gourmet breakfast and complimentary refreshments. Innkeepers are Jack and Tami Moore.

The Colonel's Lady Inn, 1120 Tanrac Trail, Gatlinburg, TN 37738 (865-436-5432 or 800-515-5432), is located near the tour's start. Operated by the Quadrozzi family, all rooms feature king- or queen-sized beds, private bathrooms, indoor jetted tubs or outdoor hot tubs, and cable TV. Some rooms have a fireplace and kitchen.

Cornerstone Inn Bed & Breakfast, 3966 Regal Way, Gatlinburg, TN 37738 (865-430-5064), is just off the route, near the Great Smoky Arts & Crafts Community. The three guestrooms are named after Arnold McDowell paintings. They feature the artwork of McDowell and Jim Gray. The innkeepers are Kay and Don Cooper.

Davy Crockett Birthplace Park (camping), 1245 Davy Crockett Park Road, Limestone, TN 37681 (423-257-2167), has 73 sites available on a first-come, first-serve basis. All sites have water and electricity hookups; 54 have sewer hookups. A pool and bathhouse are available.

First Tennessee Park (camping), 1521 Persimmon Ridge Road, Jonesborough, TN 37659 (423-753-1555).

Hawley House Bed & Breakfast, 114 E. Woodrow Ave., Jonesborough, TN 37659 (800-753-8869 or 423-753-8869), is the oldest house in the state's oldest town. The 1793 home features a wrap-around porch and private baths. Innkeepers are R.I.C. and Marcy Hawley.

Hilltop House, 6 Sanford Circle, Greeneville, TN 37743 (423-639-8202), is a 1920 circa manor house with mountain views. The three, non-smoking rooms feature cable television. Two rooms feature sitting areas and verandas.

LeConte RV Resort and Campground (camping), 1739 Parkway E., Gatlinburg, TN 37738 (865-436-5437), is located near the start of the tour. It features an outdoor pool and hot tub, laundry facility and game room.

Nolichuckey Bluffs Bed & Breakfast, 400 Kinser Park Lane, Greeneville, TN 37743 (800-842-4690 or 423-787-7947), features three rooms with private baths and mountain views. One room has a Jacuzzi. Patricia and Brooke Sadler are the innkeepers.

Bicycle Shops
Bike Zoo, 4445 Kingston Pike, Knoxville, TN 37919 (865-558-8455).

Cedar Bluff Cycles, 9282 Kingston Pike, Knoxville, TN 37922 (865-692-1010).

Extreme Sports, 7116 Maynardville Pike # B, Knoxville, TN 37918 (865-922-1907).

Greenlee Bicycle Shop, 1402 N. Broadway St., Knoxville, TN 37917 (865-522-8228).

Harper's Schwinn, 118 Northshore Dr. SW, Knoxville, TN 37919 (865-588-5744).

Interwheel Sports Inc., 2321 Sutherland Ave., Knoxville, TN 37919 (865-524-0000).

River Sports Outfitters Inc., 2918 Sutherland Ave., Knoxville, TN 37919 (865-523-0066).

Shifting Gears, 636 Middle Creek Road, St. 2, Sevierville, TN 37862 (865-908-1999).

West Hills Bicycle Center, 5113 Kingston Pike, Knoxville, TN 37919 (865-584-2288).

BICYCLING TENNESSEE
Tour 24: Johnson City-Blountville

Blountville

126   37

Appalachian Caverns   Patterson Hill Rd.

Cave Hill Rd.   ● Galloway Mill

Big Hollow Rd.→   out   ←← Old Beaver
Creek Rd.

Buffalo Rd.   ● Buffalo

S. Fork Holston River

Enterprise Rd.

Rocky Springs Rd.

Warren Rd.

11E

N

Amoco

Allison Rd. →

Marathon →   ● Piney Flats

Rocky Mount   ←← Piney Flats Rd.

in   Austin Springs Rd.

Hyder Hill Rd.

Watauga River

Harper Lane   out

River Market   ● Watauga

Riverview Rd.   ←← Watauga Rd.

11E

Unaka Ave.   Woodlyn Rd.

11E   181

Watauga Ave.

out

State of Franklin St.

Johnson City

Lamont St.
Winter St.   ←— Second St.

11E   State of Franklin St.

Veterans Administration   ★ START/FINISH
East Tennessee State University

24. JOHNSON CITY—BLOUNTVILLE

Easy to moderate terrain; mostly flat until Piney Flats when you'll encounter some rolling hills; 46.2 miles

Before there was the state of Tennessee, there was the state of Franklin. After the Revolutionary War, the U.S. Congress recommended states cede their outlying western lands to help reduce debt incurred by the war. In April 1784, North Carolina quickly surrendered the land that would later become Tennessee, but reserved control until Congress approved the measure.

This angered residents in the established western counties of Sullivan, Washington and Greene counties, who believed North Carolina was not providing them with much support in the first place, according to Oliver Taylor in his book, *Historic Sullivan*. At a convention in Jonesborough the following August, delegates from these counties voted to permanently cede from North Carolina and form their own state, named for Benjamin Franklin. They elected John Sevier as governor in March 1785.

North Carolina would not recognize the new state, causing frictions between the North Carolina loyalists and the Franks. John Tipton led the opposition to the Franks. A mini civil war developed when North Carolina seized Sevier's slaves while he was away Indian fighting. On his return, Sevier and 150 men surrounded Tipton's home, demanding his surrender. Tipton summoned 180 loyalist troops, whose threat caused Sevier to retreat. Tipton later captured Sevier, who escaped during his trial in Morgantown, N.C. Thus ended the state of Franklin.

This is the Tri-Cities Road Club's ride to and from the Appalachian Caverns. It begins in Johnson City, which along with Kingsport and Bristol make up this tri-city area. To get to the start, take Interstate 81 from Knoxville. Turn off at exit 57-A and take Interstate 181 into Johnson City. Turn off at exit 31 onto University Parkway and follow the signs to the campus.

<u>Miles</u>

0.0 **Start ride in East Tennessee State University parking lot behind the Citgo station. Cross State of Franklin Street, entering the Veterans Administration campus.**

Washington County has the distinction of being one of the first pioneer settlements west of the Alleghanies. According to the Washington County Historical Association, Europeans settled in this area in the 1760s, forming the Watauga Association in 1772. The area name was changed in 1775 to the Washington District, which North Carolina incorporated in 1777. After the state of Franklin failed, the area soon became a part of Tennessee, which split off Washington County to include the counties of Sullivan, Greene and Carter.

Gen. John T. Wilder helped develop the county seat of Johnson City in the late 1800s, according to *Johnson City: The Way We Were*. The city continued to grow with the completion of the Carolina, Clinchfield & Ohio Railroad in 1915. Today, it is Washington County's largest city, with more than 50,000 residents. Local attractions include Hands On! Regional Museum and Tipton-Haynes Historic Site, an 18th Century home built by John Tipton, a member of the 1776 Constitutional Convention. Events include Springfest and the Spring Doin's Festival in May, and the Pepsi 4th of July Fireworks Extravaganza.

East Tennessee State University, where the tour begins, was founded in 1911 as East Tennessee Normal School. Today, the school has an enrollment of about 12,000. Special programs include the nation's most comprehensive study of bluegrass and country music, and the only master's degree in storytelling, which you can read about in the Jonesborough—Elizabethton chapter. The Mountain Home VA Medical Center is primarily affiliated with ETSU's James H. Quillen College of Medicine. The 915-bed facility handles general medicine and surgery, alcohol treatment, psychiatry and nursing home care.

0.1   **Veer right onto Lake Drive East at the stop sign.**

0.4   **Turn right onto Dogwood Avenue at the stop sign.**

0.5   **Veer left onto Second Street at the stop sign.**

0.7   **Turn right onto Lamont Street at the stop sign (no street sign).**

1.5   **You'll see the First Church of God. Turn left onto West Watauga Avenue at the stop sign. Watch for traffic.**

2.1   **West Watauga Avenue becomes East Watauga Avenue at North Roan Street. Continue straight on East Watauga at the traffic light.**

2.4   **Pass under Interstate 181.**

3.9   **Turn right onto Steel Street.**

4.0   **Turn left onto East Fairview Avenue at the stop sign.**

4.1   **Turn right onto Smith Street.**

4.3   **Cross the railroad tracks and turn left onto Woodlyn Road, traveling along the tracks.**

5.9   **Woodlyn Road intersects with Dalewood Road at the stop sign. Veer left and cross the tracks, continuing on Woodlyn Road.**

7.0   **Turn left onto Watuagua Road.**
       You'll pass through the community of Ahra.

7.4   **You'll see P & J Auto Sales to your right. Turn right onto Riverview Road, following along the Watauga River. You'll soon see the River Market on the left.**

8.6 **Veer right onto Herb Hodge Road. You'll cross the Watauga River near the community of Watauga Flats. Road becomes Hyder Hill Road at the Sullivan County line. You'll pass by Riverstone Park.**

The state carved Sullivan County out of Washington County in 1779. It was named after Gen. John Sullivan, an officer in the Continental Army. Residents, such as Moses Looney, held county courts in their homes until 1795. Being in the vicinity of a main overland route and at the head of the Tennessee River system, the county population doubled between 1790 and 1795. Today, more than 140,000 people reside in Sullivan County.

11.6 **Turn right onto Austin Springs Road (also called Old Highway 11E).**

13.6 **Turn left onto Piney Flats Road.**

You'll pass through the community of Piney Flats.

14.4 **You'll see a Marathon station to your left and Amoco station to your right. Cross U.S. Highway 11E at the traffic light. Watch for traffic. Road becomes Allison Road.**

The Rocky Mount Historic Site is just south of here on U.S. Highway 11E. You can read about Rocky Mount in the Jonesborough—Elizabethton chapter.

15.9 **Veer right onto Warren Road.**

The rolling hills begin on this road.

17.3 **Turn right onto Enterprise Road at the stop sign. Cross the Rainbow Bridge. Road becomes Beaver Creek Road.**

21.0 **Turn left onto Buffalo Road. You'll see Buffalo Puritan Club on your right. Cross the Sam M. Feathers Bridge.**

You are crossing the upper branch of the Holston River in the community of Buffalo. The north and south forks of the Holston River join in Kingsport and travel 140 miles before turning into the Tennessee River. The river is named for Stephen Holston, the first person to travel its currents, according to Southern History, Folklore and Culture web site. In the early days of settlement,

Sullivan County resident William King built a shipping port on the river to export salt downstream. The most famous journey that began on the Holston was John Donelson's trip to French Lick in 1780. You can read about that adventure in the Pickwick Dam—Dover chapter.

22.0   Turn right onto Big Hollow Road.

22.5   You'll see a white house on the left. Turn right onto Cave Hill Road. Road narrows.

22.9   Appalachian Caverns is on your left. Turn right onto Patterson Hill Road.

The Linville brothers lived in this cave in the county's early days, according to author Taylor. They spent long periods away hunting. Upon a return from one hunting trip, the brothers encountered a band of hostile Indians. One brother was wounded. The other brother carried him back to the cave, where he subsequently died and was buried. Over the years, the cave has served as an Indian shelter, moonshine hideaway and teenage hangout.

Today, the caverns are opened year-round for tours, featuring elaborate lighting and almost one mile of dry walkways. A one-hour guided tour takes visitors through its corridors and rooms, with ceilings reaching as high as 135 feet. Formations range from helixes to large columns. Minerals such as manganese, iron, calcium and copper present a multi-colorful tour. Casual dress and comfortable shoes are recommended (cycling shoes, especially with cleats, may not be stable enough). The temperature is around 52 degrees year-round.

The Appalachian Caverns Foundation also offers a "wild trip," which lasts more than three hours, to undeveloped parts of the cave.

You are a few miles south of Blountville, the second oldest town in Tennessee. According to Taylor, James Brigham deeded 30 acres of his land in 1792 to form the Sullivan County seat. The largest initial investors were John Tipton, Elkanah Dulaney and William Deery. The present courthouse, built in 1853, survived a fire set by Federal forces in 1863. It was remodeled in 1920, with additions made in 1958.

A view inside the legendary Appalachian Caverns in Blountville.
Photo by Susan Schulman.

24.0   You'll see Galloway Milling Co. to your left. Turn right onto Old Beaver Creek Road at the stop sign. Road narrows.
You'll pass through the community of Galloway Mill.

24.4   Turn right, continuing on Beaver Creek Road. Cross the Rainbow Bridge. Road becomes Enterprise Road.

26.3   Continue straight on Enterprise Road.

28.5   Turn left onto Warren Road.

30.0   Veer left onto Allison Road at the stop sign.

31.5   You'll see a Marathon station to your right and Amoco station to your left. Cross U.S. 11E at the traffic light. Watch for traffic. Road becomes Piney Flats Road.

32.3   Turn right onto Austin Springs Road at the stop sign.

35.8   Turn left onto Harper Lane. You'll cross the Watauga River near the community of Watauga Flats. You'll enter Washington County.

36.0 Turn left onto Riverview Road at the stop sign. You'll soon see the River Market on the right.

38.7 You'll see P & J Auto Sales to your left. Turn left onto Watauga Road at the stop sign.

39.1 Turn right onto Woodlyn Road.

40.2 Woodlyn Road intersects with Dalewood Road at the stop sign. Cross the tracks and veer right, continuing on Woodlyn Road.

41.8 Cross the railroad tracks and turn right onto Smith Street.

42.3 Turn left on East Unaka Avenue at the stop sign. Watch for traffic.

43.7 Pass under Interstate 181.

44.1 Road becomes West Unaka Avenue at the traffic light. Continue straight.

44.5 Road becomes Winter Street. Continue straight.

44.8 Turn right on Lamont Street.

45.4 Turn left onto Second Street, entering the Veterans Administration campus.

45.6 Veer right onto Dogwood Avenue at the stop sign.

45.8 Veer left onto Lake Drive East.

46.1 Veer left at the stop sign. No street sign.

46.2 Cross the State of Franklin Street. End ride in East Tennessee State University parking lot behind the Citgo station, where the tour began.

For general information on lodging and attractions, contact the Johnson City Chamber of Commerce, 603 E. Market St., Johnson City, TN 37601 (423-461-8000), or the Sullivan County Executive, 3411 Highway 126, Blountville, TN 37617 (423-323-6417).

Places to Stay

The Jam N Jelly Inn Bed & Breakfast, 1310 Indian Ridge Road, Johnson City, TN 37604 (423- 929-0039), has six guestrooms furnished with antiques and antique reproductions. The main floor common area features a large, stone fireplace. The second floor common area features a large-screened television. A hot tub is available on the back porch. Innkeepers are Bud and Carol Kidner.

Rocky Top Best Holiday Trav-L-Park (camping), 496 Pearl Lane, Blountville, TN 37617 (423-323-2535 or 800-452-6456).

SmithHaven Bed & Breakfast, 2357 Feathers Chapel Road, Blountville, TN 37617 (423-323-0174 or 800-606-4833), is an 1851 colonial farmhouse featuring three guestrooms and a wrap-around veranda. It is less than two miles from the Bristol Motor Speedway. John L. VanArsdall is the innkeeper.

Bicycle Shops
Norris Schwinn Bicycle, 1412 Knob Creek Road, Johnson City, TN 37604 (423-928-8900).

Piney Flats Bicycles, 5585 Highway 11 E., Piney Flats, TN 37686 (423-538-9005).

Two Wheel Transit, 1402 W Market St., Johnson City, TN 37604 (423-926-3993).

BICYCLING TENNESSEE
Tour 25: Jonesborough-Elizabethton

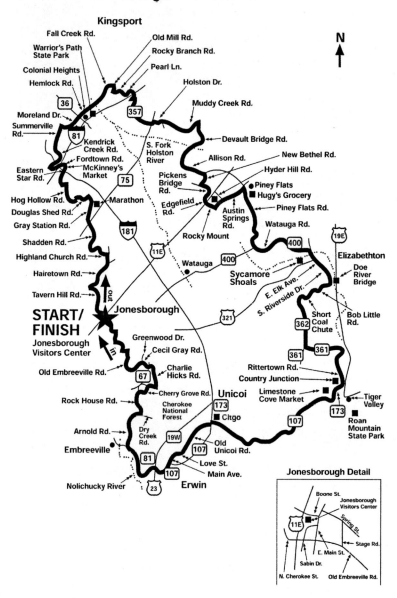

Kingsport

N

Fall Creek Rd.
Old Mill Rd.
Warrior's Path State Park
Rocky Branch Rd.
Colonial Heights
Pearl Ln.
Hemlock Rd.
Holston Dr.

36
357
Muddy Creek Rd.

Moreland Dr.
Summerville Rd.
81
Devault Bridge Rd.
Kendrick Creek Rd.
S. Fork Holston River
New Bethel Rd.
Allison Rd.
Fordtown Rd.
Hyder Hill Rd.
Eastern Star Rd.
McKinney's Market
75
Pickens Bridge Rd.
Piney Flats
Hugy's Grocery
Hog Hollow Rd.
Marathon
Edgefield Rd.
Piney Flats Rd.
Douglas Shed Rd.
181
Austin Springs Rd.
Gray Station Rd.
Watauga Rd.
Shadden Rd.
Rocky Mount
400
19E
Highland Church Rd.
11E
Watauga
400
Elizabethton
Hairetown Rd.
Sycamore Shoals
Doe River Bridge
Tavern Hill Rd.
out
E. Elk Ave.
S. Riverside Dr.
START/ FINISH
Jonesborough
321
362
Short Coal Chute
Bob Little Rd.
Jonesborough Visitors Center
Greenwood Dr.
Cecil Gray Rd.
361
361
in
Old Embreeville Rd.
67
Charlie Hicks Rd.
Rittertown Rd.
Country Junction
Tiger Valley
Cherry Grove Rd.
Unicoi
Limestone Cove Market
Rock House Rd.
Cherokee National Forest
173
Cltgo
173
Arnold Rd.
Dry Creek Rd.
19W
107
107
Roan Mountain State Park
Embreeville
81
Old Unicoi Rd.
Love St.
Nolichucky River
23
107
Main Ave.
Erwin

Jonesborough Detail

Boone St.
Jonesborough Visitors Center
Spring St.
11E
Stage Rd.
E. Main St.
Sabin Dr.
N. Cherokee St.
Old Embreeville Rd.

25. JONESBOROUGH—ELIZABETHTON: A TWO-DAY TOUR

Moderate to difficult terrain; 104.0 miles

As Jerry Clower's story about coon hunting in Mississippi flowed over the airwaves from Nashville's Grand Ole Opry to Jimmy Neil Smith's carload of students in East Tennessee, the high school journalism teacher had an idea. That idea led to the first National Storytelling Festival in 1973. He also founded the National Association for the Preservation and Perpetuation of Storytelling, now the National Storytelling Association. These events created a renaissance of storytelling across America, which continues today.

The Storytelling Foundation International hosts the National Storytelling Festival in Jonesborough on the first weekend of each October. *People Magazine* once stated, "When autumn comes to Tennessee, televisions go dark and old-time storytellers revive a nearly lost art." The three-day event features more than 100 hours of entertainment and performances by the nation's leading storytellers.

The renewed interest in storytelling also led to an interesting chain of events at East Tennessee State University in nearby Johnson City. In the 1970s, Dr. Flora Joy introduced storytelling to the school's Language Arts/Reading Methods courses. When ETSU offered a course called "Basic Storytelling" in the mid-1980s, more than 40 students enrolled. "Advanced Storytelling" soon followed.

Today, in conjunction with the National Storytelling Association, ETSU offers the nation's only storytelling degree, under its master's degree program in reading. Storyteller Tommy Oaks was the first graduate in 1989. Since then, more than 120 students have graduated from the program.

This tour is a part of the state's Cycling Tennessee's Highways' mountains series. While there are no mountain assaults, the terrain gets quite hilly in places. The journey takes you around the state's tri-cities area of Johnson City, Kingsport and Bristol, and winds through the Appalachian Mountains. Jonesborough is about 90 miles northeast of Knoxville. To get to the start of the ride from Knoxville, take Interstate 40 east, then Interstate 81 north. Take exit 23 and head east on U.S. Highway 11 East, through Greeneville to Jonesborough. Turn right onto Boone Street. The Jonesborough Visitors Center is on the right.

DAY 1
Moderate to difficult terrain; 55.3 miles

Miles

0.0 **Start ride at the Jonesborough Visitors Center. Head south on Boone Street.**

Jonesborough is the oldest town in Tennessee. Established in 1779 as the county seat of Washington County, North Carolina, it was named for Willie Jones, a North Carolina representative who supported the state's move westward. Of course, the town became part of Tennessee when it became the 16th state in 1796.

The town underwent much restoration and preservation in the 1970s, becoming the first entire Tennessee town listed on the National Register of Historic Places. Jonesborough offers several quaint antique shops and eateries. You can relax, have a sandwich, play checkers and shop, all in one place. Sites to visit include the Dillworth Diner, The Cranberry Thistle, Wetlands Water Park, The Parson's Table, The Salt House, Sheppard Springs Music Barn

& Playhouse and Old Town Hall. At this writing, the new National Storytelling Center was under construction on West Main Street. Its offices and gift shop are located at the restored historic Chester Inn, where several U.S. presidents have stayed. A map for a self-guided walking tour is available at the Visitors Center, or Times & Tales Tours can guide you through all the sites, complete with a little storytelling.

The Jonesborough-Washington County Museum tells the history of the town and county. Historical interpretive programs are available. The museum moved the historic Oak Hill School from Knob Hill to Jonesborough in August 1996. The small schoolhouse hosts the museum's heritage education program.

Annual events include the Herb Fest, Jonesborough Garden Tour & Tea, Celtic Festival, Jonesborough Days, Quiltfest, Labor Day Concert in the Park, National Storytelling Festival, Old Town Hoe Down, Halloween Haunts & Happenings, Tellabration, Christmas Craft Show, Christmas Stories, and Holiday Tour of Homes and Churches.

The first 18 miles of this tour feature rolling hills with a rural and suburban mix.

0.1 **You'll see an Exxon station to your right. Turn right onto Sabin Drive.**

0.2 **Turn right onto North Cherokee Street.**

0.3 **Cross U.S. Highway 11 East. Watch for traffic. There is a BP station to your right.**

1.0 **Street becomes Tavern Hill Road.**

1.8 **Cross Boone's Creek.**
You are riding through the community of Walters.

3.1 **Turn right onto Hairetown Road at the stop sign.**

5.3 **At the fork in the road, turn left onto Highland Church Road at the stop sign.**

5.7 **Turn left onto Shadden Road.**

9.3 After crossing State Route 75, you'll see a Marathon station on your right. Turn right onto Gray Station Road at the stop sign.

10.6 Turn left onto Douglas Shed Road.

11.7 Turn left onto Ford Creek Road.

11.9 Turn right onto Hog Hollow Road.
You'll ride under a canopy of trees for a bit.

13.7 Turn right onto Eastern Star Road at the stop sign at the T-intersection. Watch for traffic. You'll soon cross Interstate 181 and see McKinney's Market on your left at Mitchell Road.
You'll enter Sullivan County. The county was founded in the home of Moses Looney on Feb. 7, 1780, 16 years before Tennessee statehood, according to Oliver Taylor in his book, *Historic Sullivan*. It was named in honor of Gen. John Sullivan. North Carolina appointed Isaac Shelby as the county's colonel-commandant.

Isaac Shelby's father, a Wales native, moved to Sapling Grove (now Bristol, Tenn.) in 1771 and built a fort named Shelby's Station. The elder Evan Shelby led several battles against the Chickamauga Indians. Isaac Shelby was a herder and surveyor in Sapling Grove before joining the military. After successful Revolutionary War campaigns in North Carolina, Shelby and his Sullivan County mountain men joined John Sevier's troops in 1779, storming King's Mountain in South Carolina. The battle forced Lord Cornwallis' retreat. Thomas Jefferson said the battle "turned the tide of the revolution."

Shelby later became Kentucky's first governor in 1792.

15.1 Turn left onto Fordtown Road at the stop sign.
You'll ride under a canopy of trees on a winding road.

16.1 Turn right onto Kendrick Creek Road at the stop sign at the T-intersection. You'll pass under 181.
You'll ascend and descend a hill.

17.3 After crossing Interstate 181 again, turn left onto Summerville Road.

You'll ascend and descend a hill.

19.4 **Turn right onto Moreland Drive at the stop sign. Watch for traffic. There is a good-sized shoulder to ride on.**

You'll enter Kingsport city limits. In most cases, eastern Tennessee cities were incorporated long before their western counterparts. Kingsport was a relatively late bloomer, but nevertheless its beginning well researched. Three men—a financier, a promoter and a designer—professionally developed the industrial town, incorporated in 1917, according to Margaret Ripley Wolfe in her book, *Kingsport Tennessee: A Planned American City.*

Up until the 1900s, mountain barriers and insufficient transportation hindered development of this area along the Holston River. The completion of the Carolina, Clinchfield and Ohio Railroad through Southern Appalachia lifted this isolation in 1915. The railroad's chief promoter, George L. Carter, was also instrumental in luring the first investments along the line.

John B. Dennis, son of a prominent northeastern banker, followed suit, envisioning the town of Kingsport as an industrial center. In December 1915, Dennis hired regional native, J. Fred Johnson, to passionately promote the community. As president of the new Kingsport Improvement Company, Johnson invoked the "Kingsport spirit" and recruited business to town, including big hitters such as Corning Glass Works, Borden Mills and Tennessee Eastman. He sought industrial citizens who didn't pander to cheap land, tax concessions and reduced utility rates. Professionals—doctors, lawyers and such—followed. Dennis and Johnson, however, were careful not to turn the fast growth into haphazard development. They hired John Nolen as the town's professional planner.

A 1905 Harvard graduate with a background in landscape architecture, Nolen became interested in the budding business of New Town planning verses City Beautiful projects. Nolen's firm, based in Cambridge, Mass., presented its first general map of Kingsport in 1919. It featured refinement of the city's "church circle" and business district. New planned developments included the railroad station, the city's first professionally planned residential area, row houses along Shelby Street, and Armstrong Village, a model African-American community. Nolen's associate, Earle S. Draper, worked closely with Johnson on the plan. New York-based architect Clinton MacKenzie implemented most of the city's early professional designs.

Not all of Nolen's designs were implemented, including Armstrong Village, but the planning set the stage for prosperity in the town's first decade. Kingsport became a vital part of the tri-city area it shares with Bristol and Johnson City.

Points of interests in Kingsport include the Netherland Inn Historic House Museum, Exchange Place and Bays Mountain Park & Planetarium.

20.4 **You'll see Food City on the left and a Texaco station on the right. Turn right onto State Route 36 (also called Fort Henry Drive) at the traffic light. Watch for traffic.**

20.8 **You'll see Coastal and Exxon stations on your left. Turn left onto Colonial Heights Drive. Watch for traffic.**

22.3 **After crossing the railroad tracks, turn right onto Hemlock Road at the stop sign at the T-intersection. You'll cross Patrick Henry Lake on the Holston River over the Ralph Helton Bridge.**

22.4 **You'll see the entrance to Warrior's Path State Park straight ahead. Turn left onto Fall Creek Road.**

Warrior's Path State Park is in the vicinity of an ancient Cherokee trading path. The Tennessee Valley Authority opened the 950-acre park to the public in 1952. The TVA operates the park's Patrick Henry Reservoir on the Holston River. Activities include fishing, golfing, horseback riding and hiking. There is a paved walking/biking path around Duck Island, a disc golf course and olympic-sized swimming pool, opened Memorial Day to Labor Day. At this writing, several mountain bike trails were under construction.

Programs feature nature walks, campfire talks and wildlife demonstrations. Events include the Spring Festival, Folklife Festival, Environmental Education Workshop and Adopt A Tree.

24.8 **Turn right onto Old Mill Road.**

25.6 **Turn left onto Childress Ferry Road at the stop sign at the T-intersection.**

Access to a mountain bike trail is located down the road to the right.

25.8 **Turn right onto Rocky Branch Road. Enter Kingsport city limits again.**

26.5 **Turn left onto Pearl Lane.**

If you continue straight, there is a KOA campground.

27.3 **Turn right onto Browder Road at the stop sign at the T-intersection. Watch for traffic. A Phillips 66 station is on your right.**

There is a big shoulder to ride on. You pass several businesses including a Red Carpet Inn, Sleep Inn, La Quinta and Exxon station.

27.8 **Cross Interstate 81; route becomes State Route 357. Watch for traffic.**

30.1 **Before the airport exit, turn right onto the ramp to State Route 75.**

30.3 **Turn left onto State Route 75. Watch for traffic. There is a shoulder to ride on.**

Village Market is on your left.

30.7 **You'll see Northeast State on your right. Turn right onto Holston Drive.**

31.4 **Turn right onto Muddy Creek Road at the four-way stop.**

You are riding through the Holston community. You'll ascend and descend a hill.

33.4 **Veer right onto Devault Bridge Road.**

You'll cross Boone Lake on the Holston River. You'll cross two narrow bridges, and the terrain becomes hilly.

37.3 **Veer left. Route becomes Haw Ridge Road. Sister's Place Deli & Store is on the left.**

You'll ride a winding downhill.

37.7 **Rocky Springs Road is to your left. Route becomes Allison Road.**

You are riding through the community of Rocky Springs.

39.7 **Turn right onto New Bethel Road.**

40.2 **Continue riding on New Bethel Road.**

40.8 **Turn left on Pickens Bridge Road at the stop sign at the T-intersection.**

The road becomes winding.

41.5 **Turn right onto Edgefield Road.**

42.8 **Cross U.S. Highway 11 East at the stop sign. Watch for traffic.**

43.1 **Turn left onto Austin Springs Road at the stop sign at the T-intersection. Route becomes Main Street.**

43.5 **Hyder Hill Road is to your left. Continue straight on Austin Springs Road.**

Hyder Hill takes you to the Rocky Mount Historic Site. This is the oldest, original territorial capital in the United States. William Cobb built Rocky Mount in 1770. William Blount served as governor of the Southwest Territory from here. The Southwest Territory covered U.S. land south of the Ohio River and west of North Carolina.

Today, the Rocky Mount Historic Site is a living museum. Costumed workers offer visitors first-person interpretations of 18th Century life as they go about their daily tasks of farming, cooking, weaving and candle making, throughout the seasons.

45.6 **Turn right onto Piney Flats Road (also West 4th Street) at the four-way stop. Watch for traffic. Hugy's Grocery is on the left.**

You will enter the community of Piney Flats.

47.4 **Enter Carter County.**

European settlers began arriving in the Carter County area in 1769. At that time, it was called the Watauga Settlement, the first of four permanent settlements west of the Appalachian Mountains. The settlement was located on the Watauga River, central to Sycamore Shoals. Upon statehood, Tennessee established Carter County in 1796. It was named after Landon Carter, the son of settler John Carter.

49.4 Turn left onto State Route 400.
You are riding through the community of Watauga.

52.5 You'll see a Phillips station on your left before a big downhill.

54.0 You'll see Pierce's Grocery on your left. Turn right onto State Route 400 at the stop sign at the T-intersection. Cross the Watauga River into Elizabethton city limits. A Marathon station is on your right.

54.7 You'll see a McDonald's restaurant on your right. Cross U.S. Highway 321 at the traffic light.

54.9 You'll see Paty Building Materials on the right. Turn left onto East Elk Avenue at the traffic light.

55.3 End Day 1 ride at the intersection of East Elk Avenue and South Riverside Drive.
Elizabethton was originally known as Sycamore Shoals. Early settlers founded the Watauga Association here in 1772. It offered the first majority rule system in American government. Five people were elected to the court, which combined executive, legislative and judicial duties. The area soon became a frontier hub connecting settlements throughout the Carolinas and Southwest Territory.

On March 17, 1775, the Transylvania Purchase took place at Sycamore Shoals. The Transylvania Co. bought more than 20 million acres from the Cherokee, the largest real estate transaction in U.S. history. For 2,000 pounds of sterling and 8,000 pounds worth of goods, the Cherokees sold the entire Cumberland River watershed and lands extending to the Kentucky River. Dragging Canoe was the only chief to oppose the sale.

Chief Dragging Canoe, aided by the English, returned to Sycamore Shoals to take back the land in the summer of 1776. Settlers took refuge at nearby Fort Watauga, commanded by Lt. Col. John Carter, Capt. James Robertson and Lt. John Sevier, among others. Old Abram of Chilhowee led an attack on the fort, but after two weeks, the pioneers prevailed.

The Overmountain Men assembled at Sycamore Shoals on Sept. 25, 1780. Their search over the mountains for British Major Patrick Ferguson and his Tory militia led to the Revolutionary War's Battle of King's Mountain in South Carolina. Colonels John Sevier and Issac Shelby led an attack on Oct. 7, 1780, killing Ferguson and defeating his troops in a little more than an hour. Some believe that was the first in a series of crucial defeats that led to the end of the Revolutionary War.

Today, the state operates the Sycamore Shoals Historic Area in Elizabethton. The Visitors Center features historic displays and a theater. A reconstruction of Fort Watauga stands near the Sycamore Shoals river crossing, about 1,500 yards southwest of the original site. Annual events include Muster at Fort Watauga, Native American Festival, The Wataugans Outdoor Drama, Fort Watauga Knap-In, Overmountain Victory Trail Celebration, Overmountain Victory Trail March, Thanksgiving Garrison at Fort Watauga, Christmas Garrison at Fort Watauga, Christmas Craft Show and Winterfest Christmas Tree Exhibit.

DAY 2
Moderate to difficult terrain; 48.7 miles

Miles

0.0   Begin Day 2 ride at the intersection of East Elk Avenue and South Riverside Drive. Head south on South Riverside Drive. Route becomes a one-way street.

Elizabethton became the Carter County seat in 1799. It was named after Laudon Carter's wife, Elizabeth Maclin Carter. The John and Landon Carter Mansion in Elizabethton is the oldest frame house in Tennessee. It was built between 1775 and 1780. The home is open for tours from May 15 to August 15. Costumed interpreters also provide candlelight tours during Christmas at the Carter Mansion.

As you head south on South Riverside Drive, you'll pass the Doe River Covered Bridge on your left. This white clapboard bridge spans 134 feet across the river. Built in 1882, it is the oldest operational covered bridge in the state. The surrounding park is the site of the Covered Bridge Celebration, a four-day music festival held each June.

0.5   **Turn right onto Oak Street (also called Johnson Avenue). Stop 1 Market is on your right.**

0.6   **Turn left onto State Line Road.**

1.9   **You'll see Loveless Cabinet Shop. Turn right onto Bob Little Road.**

2.3   **Turn right, continuing on Bob Little Road.**
      This winding road features rolling hills.

4.1   **Turn right onto Short Coal Chute Road at the stop sign at the T-intersection.**
      You'll enter the community of Big Spring.

4.2   **You'll see Big Spring Church of Christ straight ahead. At the fork, turn left onto State Route 362 (also called Gap Creek Road) at the stop sign.**
      The road becomes winding. You'll soon ride through the community of Gap Creek.

7.9   **Continue straight onto State Route 361.**
      You'll ride along the north side of Stone Mountain.

10.1 **You'll see Harmony Freewill Baptist Church on your left. Turn right onto Rittertown Road.**

You'll cross a one-lane bridge on this winding road.

11.4 Turn right onto U.S. Highway 19 East. Watch for traffic. Periodically, there is a shoulder to ride on.

A cyclist charges a hill on U.S. Highway 19, not far from Roan Mountain State Park.

12.7 Turn right onto State Route 173. You'll soon see Country Junction store on the right.

You'll pass through Tiger Valley. If you continue straight on U.S. 19, you'll come to Roan Mountain State Park, an outdoorsman's paradise consisting of 2,006 acres with high mountain peaks serving as the backdrop. One peak, The Roan, has an elevation of 6,285 feet. The Kingsport Bicycle Association's annual "Roan Groan" ride takes you to the top. The park's trails take you along the Doe River or lead to the highlands grassy balds. This is the longest stretch of grassy balds in the world. They cover 10 miles, from Carver's Gap on The Roan to Big Hump Mountain. Trout fishing is available on the Doe River.

The Dave Miller Homestead on Strawberry Mountain is open from Memorial Day to Labor Day. Dave and Louise Miller settled here in 1870. Miller and his son, Nathaniel, purchased the property from Gen. John Wilder in 1904. Upon Nathaniel's death in 1924, his son Frank inherited the farm. Frank served as the homestead's interpreter from 1983 to 1995.

Roan Mountain State Park programs include guided hikes and tours, Owl Prowl, Tour to the Highlands of the Roan, In Search of the Lost Peg Leg Mines, Reading the Forest, Frog Frolics, Life After Dark, Morning Bird Walks, Tiny Flying Wonders and Folklore of the Appalachians.

Annual events include the Easter Egg Hunt and Bonnet Contest, Roan Mountain Spring Naturalists Rally, Rhododendron Festival, Nature Discovery Week, Roan Mountain's Price is Right, Roan Mountain's Independence Day Activities, Highland of Roan Nature Excursions, Roan Mountain Butterfly Count, Young Naturalists Workshops, Campers Night-Lights Contest, Summer Concert Series and Roan Mountain Fall Naturalists Rally.

Back on State Route 173, the road becomes winding. You'll pass through the community of Piney Grove.

17.0 Enter Unicoi County.

The General Assembly created Unicoi County out of half of Washington County and half of Carter County on March 23, 1875. The name originates from an Indian word meaning white, fog-like or fog-draped, according to historians Hilda Britt Padgett and Betty Washburn Stevens.

The county grew rapidly with the construction of the Charleston, Cincinnati and Chicago railroad in 1886, the Ohio River and Charleston railroad in 1893, the South and Western Railway in 1902 and the Carolina, Clinchfield and Ohio railroad in 1908. The Clinchfield has been called "America's Most Unusual Railroad," crossing four mountain ranges and five major watersheds. There are 80 bridges and 55 tunnels along its 277-mile route. The major employer was the railroad until Southern Potteries opened in 1916. The maker of hand-painted dinnerware hired as many as 1,000 workers in the 1940s. The plant closed in 1957, but the economy quickly rebounded with the opening of the Davidson Chemical Co., which supplied fuel for nuclear-powered Navy ships.

And now for something completely different. On Sept. 12, 1916, at a circus performing in Kingsport, an elephant named Mary killed her trainer. Authorities wanted to execute the elephant, but had inadequate guns for the job. Subsequently, they took Mary to a railroad yard in Unicoi County and hanged her by a chain from a crane, usually used to clear train wrecks.

19.2 Turn right onto State Route 107 at the stop sign at the T-intersection. Limestone Cove Market is on your right. Watch for traffic.
You'll ride through the community of Limestone Cove. You'll pass the Limestone Cove Recreational Area (camping) and North Indian Creek Campground.

24.0 You'll see Little Bear's Market-Produce.

24.7 Turn right onto State Route 173 at the stop sign at the T-intersection. A Citgo station is on your right.

24.8 You'll see Jerry's Restaurant and the Unicoi Baptist Church on your left. Turn left onto Tennessee Street. Then cross the railroad tracks.
You'll enter Unicoi city limits. This area went by the names of Greasy Cove, Head of the Big Lane in Greasy Cove, Swingleville, Limonite and Unicoi City, before finally incorporating as Unicoi in 1994.

Farmhouse Gallery & Gardens serves as the local attraction. You can take a tour of wildlife artist Johnny Lynch's studio and gallery, take walk through the gardens and along the stream, or relax in a rocking chair on the porch of a 150-year-old log cabin. The gallery and gardens handles weddings, catered events, picnics and bus tours by reservation. The town hosts the Unicoi Strawberry Festival each spring.

25.0 Turn left onto Old Unicoi Road at the four-way stop. Unicoi Water Utility is on your right. Follow route along the railroad tracks.

28.3 You'll see Harmon Memorial Church. Turn left onto Jackson Avenue (also Zane Whitson Jr. Drive). You'll see an Amoco station.

29.3 Cross State Route 107 (also Main Street). Road becomes North Elm Avenue.

You'll enter Erwin city limits. Erwin is the Unicoi County seat. The area went by the names of Unaka, Longmire and Vanderbilt, before changing to Erwin on Dec. 5, 1879. According to Padgett and Stevens, the town was named in honor of David J.N. Ervin, who donated 15 acres for the town. Post office authorities mistakenly recorded the name Erwin, and it has never been corrected.

The Erwin National Fish Hatchery was established in 1897. The original superintendent's home, built in 1903, is now the county's Heritage Museum. Nine rooms are open to the public. The relocated, one-room Greasy Cove Schoolhouse is on the grounds. There is also an amphitheater, where the Heritage Players perform several historical plays each year. The museum is opened May through October and three weeks in December.

30.6 Turn right onto Love Street at the traffic light. Do not follow the blue bicycle route sign.

30.7 Turn right onto Main Avenue at the stop sign at the T-intersection.

31.0 Turn left onto State Route 107 at the traffic light. Joe's market is on the right.

31.4 Pass under U.S. Highway 23. Route becomes State Route 81, traveling along the Nolichucky River.

You'll ride up and down steep inclines.

33.4 Enter Washington County.

You can read about Washington County in the Johnson City—Blountville chapter.

35.2 Riverside Market in on the right.

35.5 You'll see Embreeville First Freewill Baptist Church on the right. Turn right onto Arnold Road.

You'll ride through the community of Embreeville. You'll ride under a canopy of trees along the river, then up a long gradual hill.

37.4 Turn right onto Dry Creek Road.

38.0 Turn left onto Rock House Road. There is no street sign.

If you continue straight, you'll enter the Cherokee National Forest. This 630,000-acre forest runs from Chattanooga to Bristol along the North Carolina border, divided by the Great Smoky Mountains National Park. There are 650 miles of trails, including 150 miles along the Appalachian Trail. Nationally designated trails include the Overmountain Victory Trail, John Muir National Recreation Trail and Warrior's Passage Trail. White-water rafting is available. The Ocoee River in the state's southeast corner hosted the 1996 Olympic Canoe and Kayak Slalom Competition. The park also offers fishing, camping and horseback riding.

Both the northern and southern section of Cherokee National Forest offer hundreds of miles of forest roads, bike trails and multiuse trails, making it an ideal destination for road and mountain cyclists.

Back on Rock House Road, you are in for a steady climb.

39.2 Turn right onto Cherry Grove Road at the four-way stop.

You'll ride up and down some steep hills, under a canopy of trees on a narrow back road.

40.7 Turn right onto Charlie Hicks Road at the stop sign at the T-intersection.

You'll continue to encounter some steep hills under a canopy of trees. Then you'll ride a fast hill down the mountain.

42.3 Turn right onto State Route 67 (also called Cherokee Road). The bike route sign is missing. Watch for traffic.
You are riding through the community of Little Cherokee.

42.8 Turn left onto Cecil Gray Road.
This winding road features rolling hills, some steep.

43.7 Turn left onto Greenwood Drive at the stop sign at the T-intersection.
You'll ride through the community of Greenwood.

44.8 Continue straight on Old Embreeville Road. Do not turn left on Greenwood Drive or Bill Jones Road.
You'll ride through the community of Woodlawn.

47.3 At Mountain View Estates, turn left onto Stage Road.

48.0 Turn left onto Spring Street.

48.5 Turn left onto East Main Street.

48.6 Turn right onto Boone Street.

48.7 End Day 2 ride at Jonesborough Visitors Center, where the tour began.

For general information on lodging and attractions, contact the Elizabethton-Carter County Chamber of Commerce Tourism Council, P.O. Box 190, Elizabethton, TN 37644 (423-547-3852 or 888-547-3852), Historic Jonesborough Department of Tourism, 117 Boone St., Jonesborough, TN 37659 (423-753-1011 or 800-400-4221), Sullivan County Executive, 3411 Highway 126, Blountville, TN 37617 (423-323-6417), or Unicoi County Chamber of Commerce, 100 S. Main Ave., P.O. Box 713, Erwin, TN 37650 (423-743-3000).

Places to Stay
Comfort Inn, 1515 U.S. Highway 19 E. Bypass, Elizabethton, TN 37643 (423-542-4466), offers an outdoor pool, exercise room, cable television and a free continental breakfast. Some rooms have refrigerators.

Doe River Inn, 217 Academy Street, Elizabethton, TN 37643 (423-543-1444), is a Victorian home built along the banks of the Doe River in 1894. There are two guestrooms and a large living area with a fireplace, formal dining room and sun room. Innkeepers Frank and Mary Shepard serve a gourmet breakfast each morning.

Hawley House Bed and Breakfast, 114 E. Woodrow Ave., Jonesborough, TN 37659 (800-753-8869 or 423-753-8869), is the oldest house in the state's oldest town. The 1793 home features a wrap-around porch and private baths. Innkeepers are R.I.C. and Marcy Hawley.

May-Ledbetter House Bed & Breakfast, 130 W. Main Street, Jonesborough, TN 37659 (423-753-7568), has wrap-around porches overlooking historic Jonesborough's Main Street. The inn, built in 1904, features hand-sewn quilts and wall hangings. Innkeepers Doug and Donna provide a full country breakfast. Garden dining is available, overlooking a fish pond and perennial gardens.

Roan Mountain State Park (camping), 1015 State Highway 143, Roan Mountain, TN 37687 (423-772-0190 or 800-250-8620), has 107 campsites with grills and picnic tables, available on a first-come, first-serve basis. There are six bathhouses with hot showers. Also, 30 rustic cabins are available for rental. Each cabin, equipped with appliances, linens and cooking utensils, accommodates six people.

Warrior's Path State Park (camping), P.O. Box 5026, Hemlock Road, Kingsport, TN 37663 (423-239-8531), offers 135 campsites with tables and grills, available on a first-come, first-serve basis. Of those, 94 have water and electrical hookups. Modern bathhouses are on-site.

Bicycle Shops
Boyd's Bicycle Shop, 10 7th St., Bristol, TN 37620 (423-764-4932).

Larry's Cycle Shop, 718 E. Center St., Kingsport, TN 37660 (423-247-2751).

Rock 'n' Road Bicycles, 4260 Fort Henry Dr. # 8, Kingsport, TN 37663 (423-239-6649).

APPENDIX

Tourism Information
Tennessee Association of RV Parks and Campgrounds
P.O. Box 39
Townsend, TN 37882

Tennessee Bed and Breakfast Innkeepers Association
5431 Mountain View Road, Suite 150
Antioch, TN 37013
(800) 820-8144

Tennessee Department of Tourism
320 Sixth Ave. North, 5th Floor, Rachel Jackson Bldg.
Nashville, TN 37243
(615) 741-2159 or (800) GO2-TENN

Cycling Contacts
Bicycle Federation of Tennessee
P.O. Box 2823
Murfreesboro, TN 37133
(615) 893-3357

Bicycle Ride Across Tennessee (BRAT)
c/o Tennessee State Parks

Seventh Floor, L & C Tower, 401 Church Street
Nashville, TN 37243
(615) 532-0001 or (888) TN-PARKS

Cycling Tennessee's Highways
c/o Tennessee Department of Transportation
Attn: Bicycle Coordinator
505 Deaderick St., Suite 900, James K. Polk Bldg.
Nashville, TN 37243
(615) 741-5310

Mississippi River Trail
c/o Lower Mississippi Delta Development Center
7777 Walnut Grove Road, Box 27
Memphis, TN 38120
(901) 624-3600

Natchez Trace Parkway
c/o National Park Service
2680 Natchez Trace Parkway
Tupelo, MS 38801
(601) 680-4025 or (800) 305-7417

Smoky Mountain Bicycle Tours
P.O. Box 4056
Maryville, TN 37802
(800) 746-7791

Road Cycling Clubs
Allanti Cycling Club
330 Franklin Road
Brentwood, TN 37027

Blood, Sweat and Gears Bicycle Club
315 N. Park Street
McKenzie, TN 38201

Chattanooga Bicycle Club
P.O. Box 11495
Chattanooga, TN 37401

Columbia Cycling Club
1116 W. 7th St., PMB #127
Columbia, TN 38401

Harpeth Bicycle Club
P.O. Box 680802
Franklin, TN 37068

Highland Rimmers Bicycle Club
P.O. Box 1752
Tullahoma, TN 37388

Kingsport Bicycle Association
P.O. Box 958
Kingsport, TN 37662

Memphis Hightailers
P.O. Box 111195
Memphis, TN 38111

Murfreesboro Bicycle Club
PO Box 766
Murfreesboro, TN 37133

Smoky Mountain Wheelmen
P.O. Box 31497
Knoxville, TN 37930

Tennessee Cycle Club
P.O. Box 1401
Clarksville, TN 37041

Tri-Cities Road Club
1923 Paty Drive
Johnson City, TN 37604

0-595-21811-3